WEDDING PHOTOGRAPHY SUCCESS

Smart Business Techniques for Maximum Profits

Contracts, engagements, ceremony, postproduction, album sales & more!

Russell R. Caron

Amherst Media, Inc. ■ Buffalo, NY

About the Author

Russell owns and operates Russell Caron Wedding Photography, based in Maine, with his wife, Liz. Russ photographed his first wedding over 30 years ago, and Liz and Russ have been shooting as a husband-and-wife team approaching ten seasons. They're full-time, year-round photographers, and their wedding photography takes them all across Maine and New England, and to destination locations. Russ holds a Master Photographer degree, is a Certified Drone Photographer, and is a Certified Professional Photographer, all by the Professional Photographers of America. He is also an FAA-Certified Unmanned Aerial System (drone) Pilot.

Published by:
Amherst Media, Inc.
PO BOX 538
Buffalo, NY 14213
www.AmherstMedia.com

Publisher: Craig Alesse
Associate Publisher: Katie Kiss
Senior Editor/Production Manager: Barbara A. Lynch-Johnt
Senior Contributing Editor: Michelle Perkins
Editor: Beth Alesse
Acquisitions Editor: Harvey Goldstein
Editorial Assistance from: Carey A. Miller, Roy Bakos, Jen Sexton-Riley, Rebecca Rudell
Business Manager: Sarah Loder
Marketing Associate: Tonya Flickinger

ISBN-13: 978-1-68203-430-9
Library of Congress Control Number: 2019957429
Printed in the United States of America
10 9 8 7 6 5 4 3 2 1

AUTHOR A BOOK WITH AMHERST MEDIA

Contents

Introduction

After deciding to make wedding photography my sole, full-time venture, I managed to get some (okay, maybe several) things right, though I made my fair share of mistakes along the way. My goal in writing this book is to help current and aspiring wedding photographers, whether working full time or part time, to avoid the many, often costly mistakes I made, as well as to achieve better success sooner, with fewer frustrations, and save money along the way. This guide will walk you through the entire wedding photography process, from beginning to end, that my wife Liz and I use. It will cover business as well as technical aspects. All throughout, I'll share the many essential strategies that have worked for our business success.

It takes a fair amount of business savvy to run a successful wedding photography business that stands on its own and lets the owner live a decent life. After all, unlike the gas station, hair salon, spa, coffee shop, grocery store, and others that not only thrive, but depend upon, repeat customers, this one is different—so much so that if all goes according to plan, your wedding photography customers should never need your services again! So, you want these clients to refer

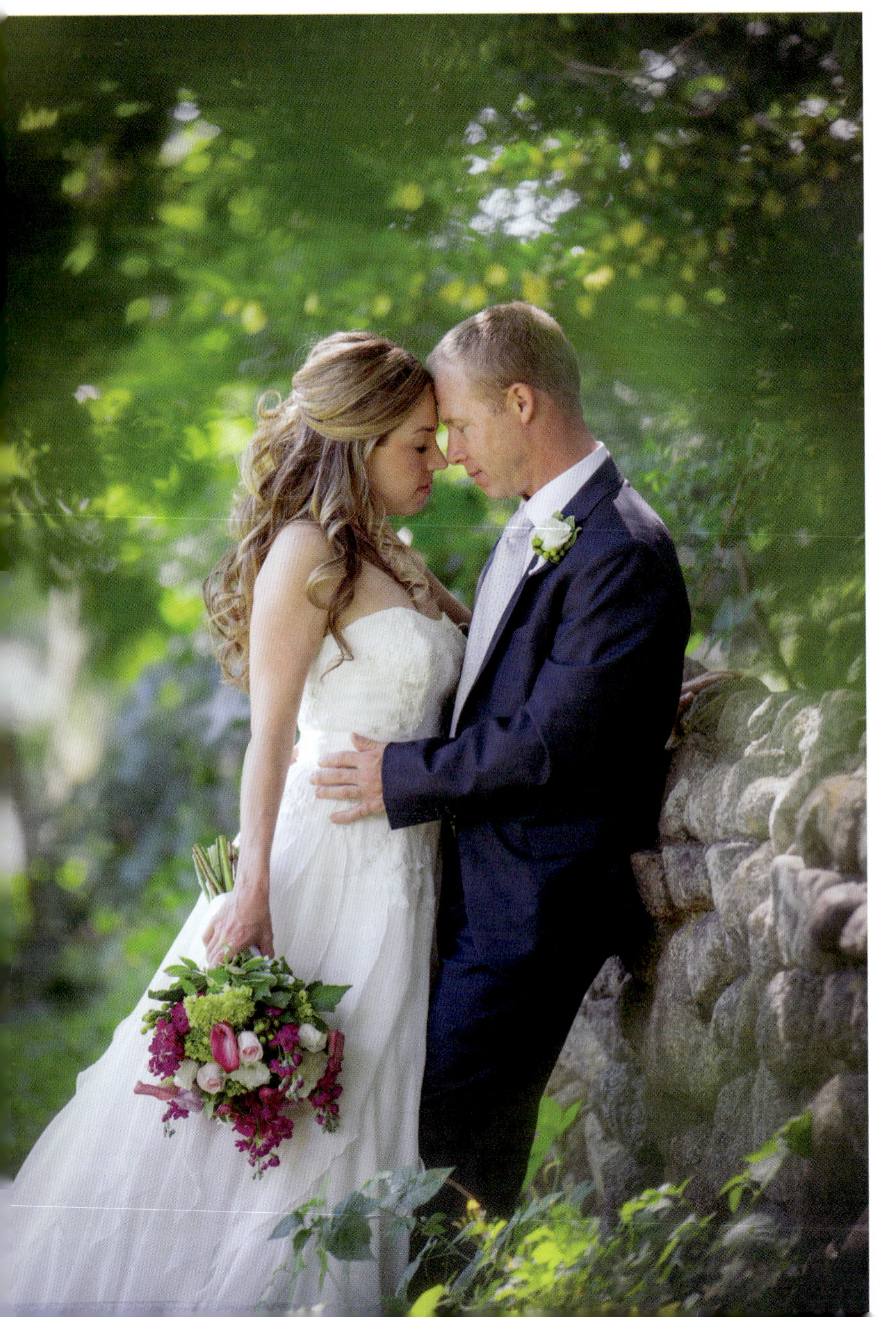

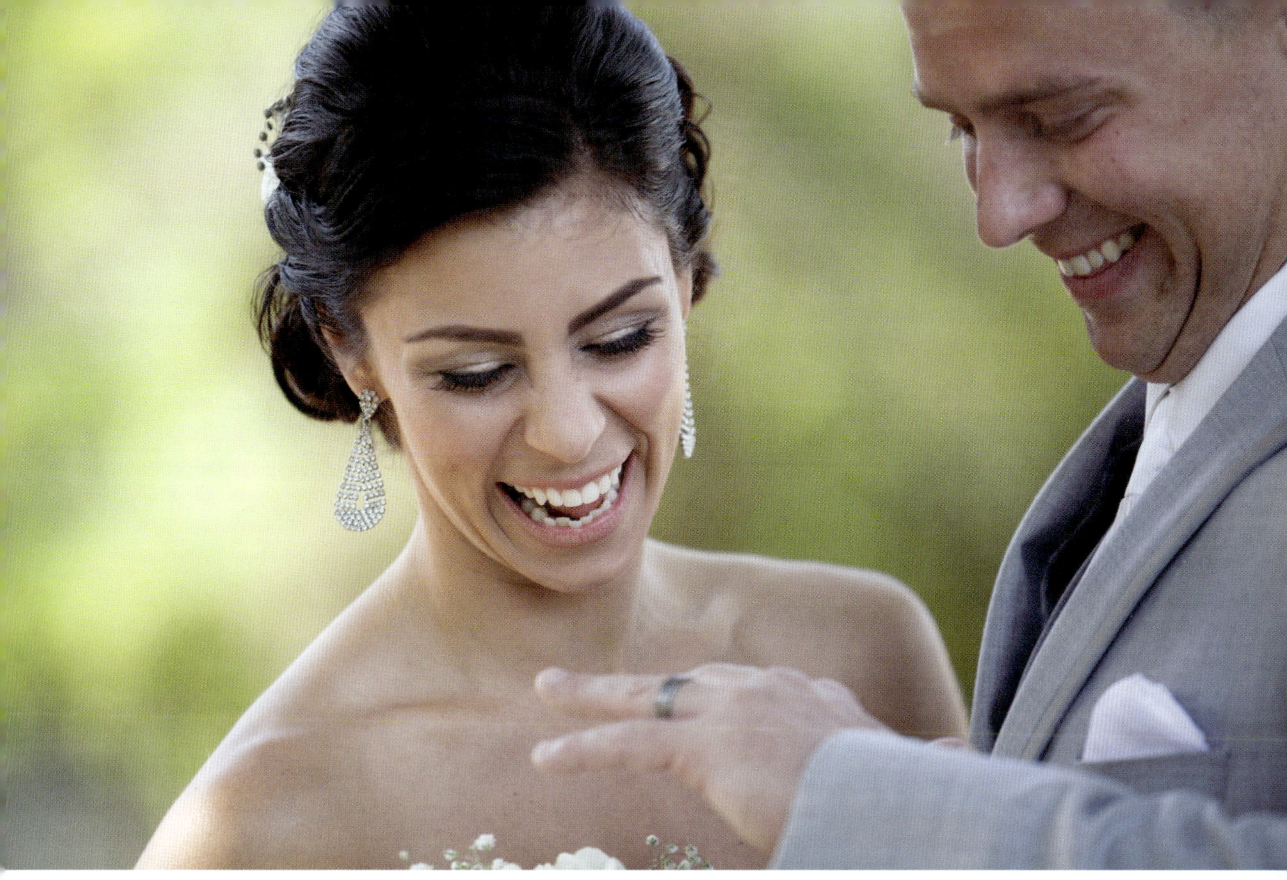

you to their friends, or have parents come back to you when other family members are getting married. In this book, we will walk you through just how to do these things.

Of course, there are often many ways to do things. What you'll read here reflects what we've found to work best for us. There are other approaches to the same end, but every key concept and idea presented here bears consideration, as it's worked very well toward our success.

While we don't profess to know all the answers every time, we've photographed enough weddings over the years that rarely, if ever, does anything present itself to us before, during, or after a wedding day that we don't immediately know how to handle.

Everything we're going to offer here, when applied as best you can, will help you stand out from the crowd. Standing out is a simple way to describe differentiation. Differentiation is one of the most often-cited traits we've heard in the wedding photography workshops we've attended. It makes sense: if you're just like everyone else, why would someone single you out

We want you to be able to make a sound living doing what you love to do.

and buy services from you, unless that reason was low price? Well, low price is something we very much want to help you avoid. We want you to be able to make a sound living doing what you love to do.

Whether you're doing this full time as the only wage earner in your household, full time with a partner or spouse, full time with a partner or spouse who works in a different career, or if you're a part-time wedding photographer, every aspect we're going to cover can help you win. This book is for you, so long as you're willing to work hard.

Prerequisites and Assumptions

This book contains helpful information for newcomers and seasoned pros. Let's start with this basic premise: you love weddings. If you don't, you need to reconsider heading down the wedding photography career path.

This book contains helpful information for newcomers and seasoned pros.

We also assume that you have a fundamental working knowledge of photography terms and techniques and possess decent-quality camera bodies with high-quality, fast lenses, and backups for everything. If you don't (yet) meet these criteria, the book will still be useful as you work toward that goal, and will provide insight into the things you'll identify as areas in which to focus for optimal growth and learning.

We also assume your photography business has a functional website with a contact form, and that you maintain fresh and steady content on social media outlets such as Instagram, Facebook, and Pinterest.

This is a good time to point out that, for clarity and consistency, we're going to base our scenarios in this book on the wedding being between a bride and a groom, though everything we say will work just the same for two grooms or two brides.

Let's get started! First, we'll take a look at how much time photographing a wedding actually involves. The answer may surprise you.

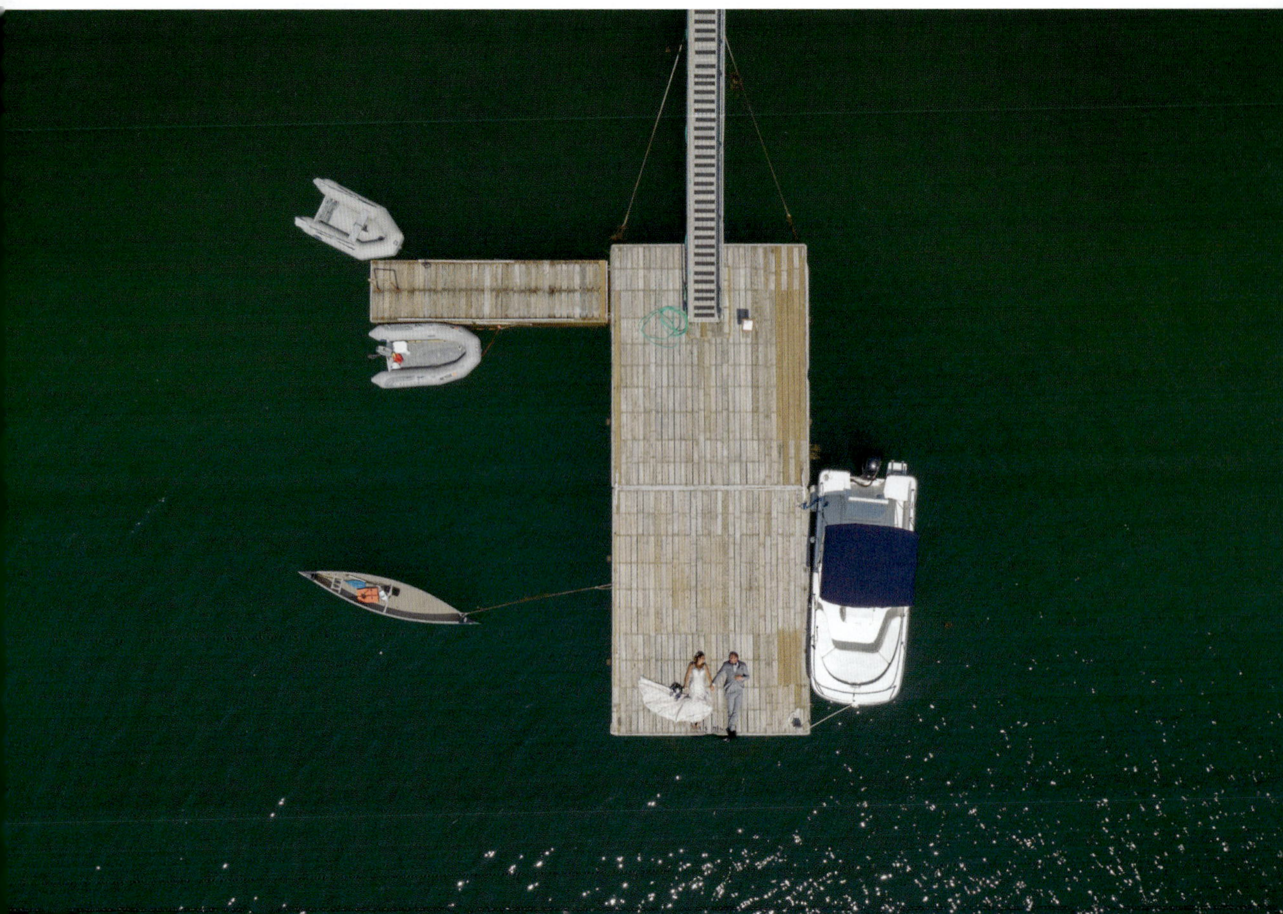

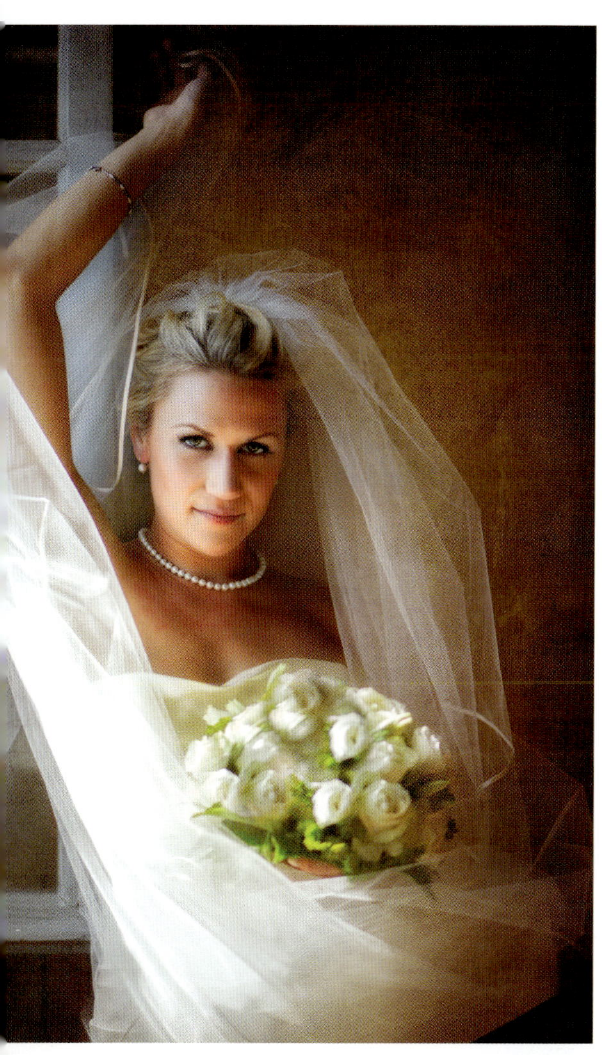

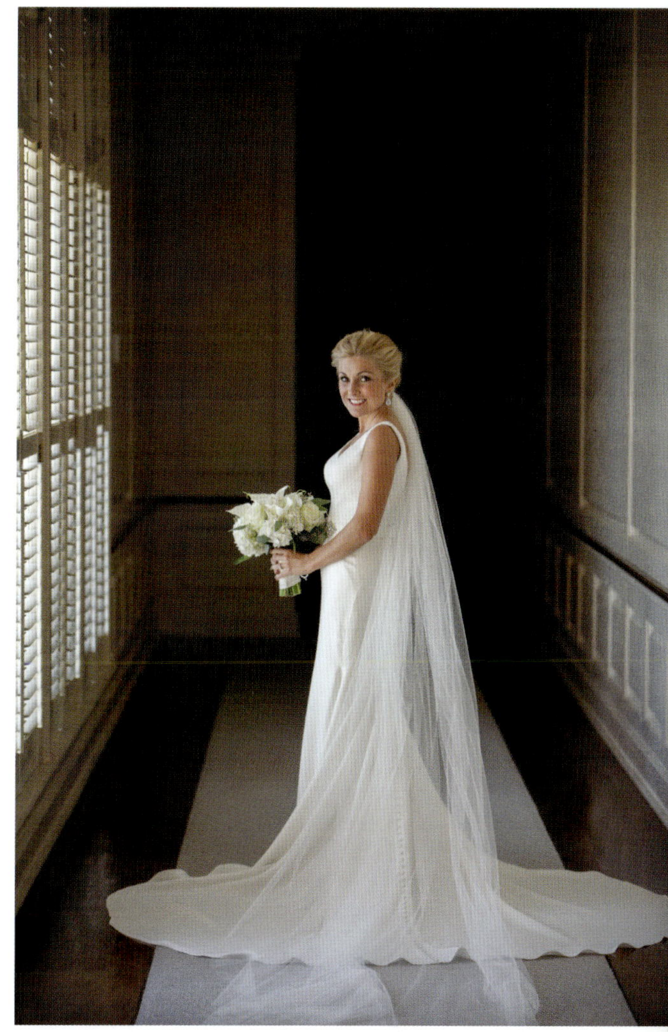

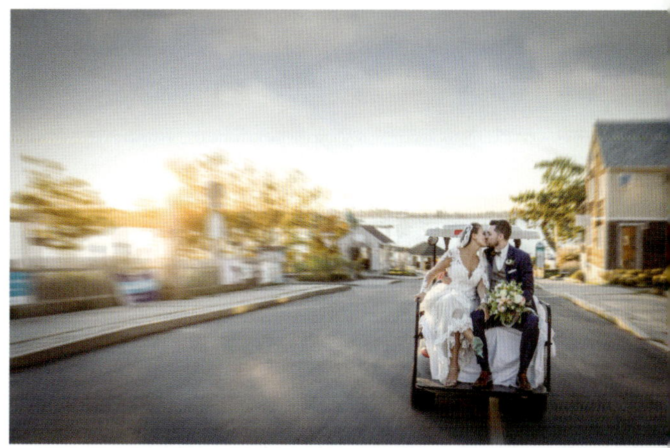

Part 1
Everything Before the Wedding

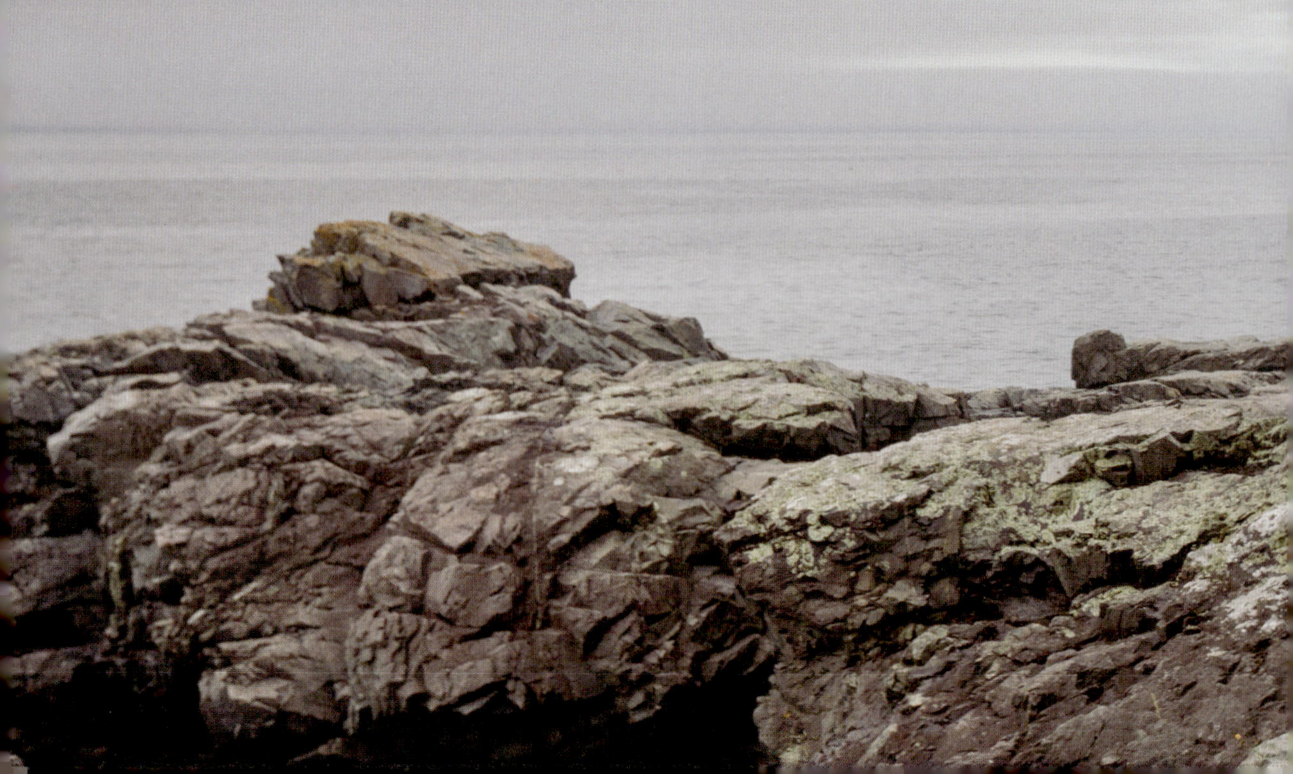

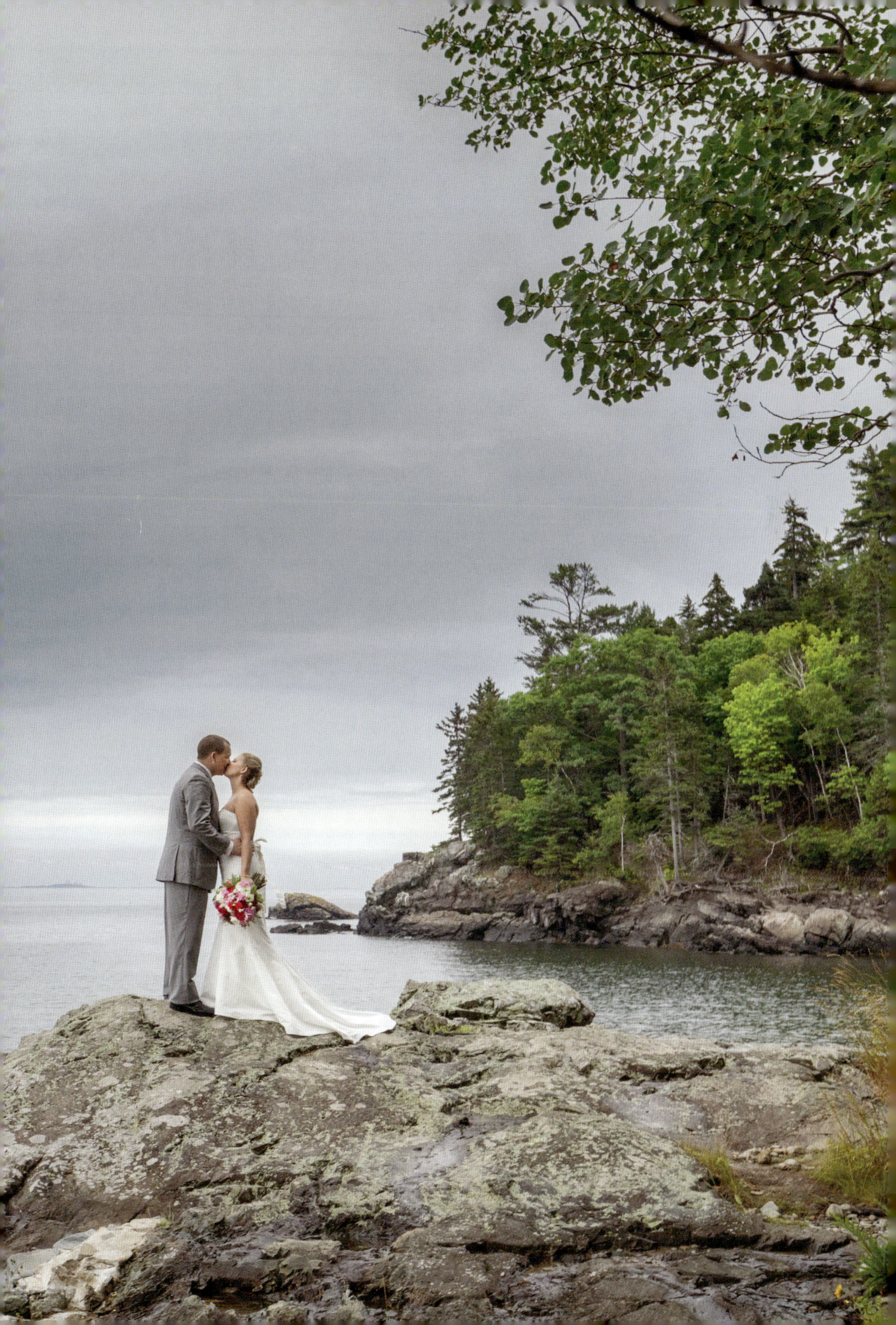

Your Investment in Time

All too often, especially among those starting out, we see photographers failing to consider the true investment in time required to complete the process of photographing a wedding. For example, for now, and without getting into detail of what's included, let's say that a wedding photographer offers an eight-hour-coverage package for $3200. Time and again, we've heard the photographer (or others) proclaim that they're "making $400 per hour!" That's absolutely not the case. Here's why: the eight hours of actual photography time on a wedding day is but a small fraction of the overall time that $3200 wedding sale took to complete from start to finish.

Write down the time each step takes, and don't be afraid to think of the worst-case scenario for each step.

Let's do an exercise. Think of the entire process of a wedding contract sale. Start at the very beginning, way back with the initial contact from your website form or the first phone call. Write down to the nearest one-tenth of an hour (six-minute increments) how long each activity related to that sale takes. Your client interaction could easily involve many emails and phone calls, Skype sessions, coffee shop meetings, and other back-and-forth before the couple even asks you for a contract. If they do,

great, but that takes more time, too. Write down the time each step takes, and don't be afraid to think of the worst-case scenario for each step. When the contract comes back, you'll have administrative work, accounting, and banking. Then it's more emails back and forth about what to wear to the engagement session, and figuring out when to schedule. Then there's always the possibility of having to reschedule. How many emails back and forth are you up to now? Write it down. Document everything you can imagine: the packing of your gear, the charging of your batteries, the preparation of your memory cards, the research of where to go shoot, and the time to drive there. And you're just at the engagement session. Don't be quick on this drill. It's critical that you consider your time in the all-important cost of goods sold category, which is what we're doing here. When you've got it all listed, add it up. Even efficient, experienced photographers who've tirelessly studied and streamlined their workflow are often startled to see that the time investment for that eight-hour wedding can add up to 40, 50, 60, or more hours. Yes, this is the often-overlooked reality.

Overhead

In running a business, there will be a host of costs, whether a sale is made or not. These are fixed costs we'll call "overhead." These considerations include office space, office supplies, your cell phone, credit card processing, supplies, insurances, website, Internet connection, computers, software subscriptions, electricity and other utilities, hard drive storage, backup storage, marketing (note that we didn't say advertising—more on that later), and the like. And don't forget the wear and tear on your camera gear. Overhead is often not considered for all its invisibility, but it is real, and it can be a huge hidden cost that you've got to keep at the forefront of your mind.

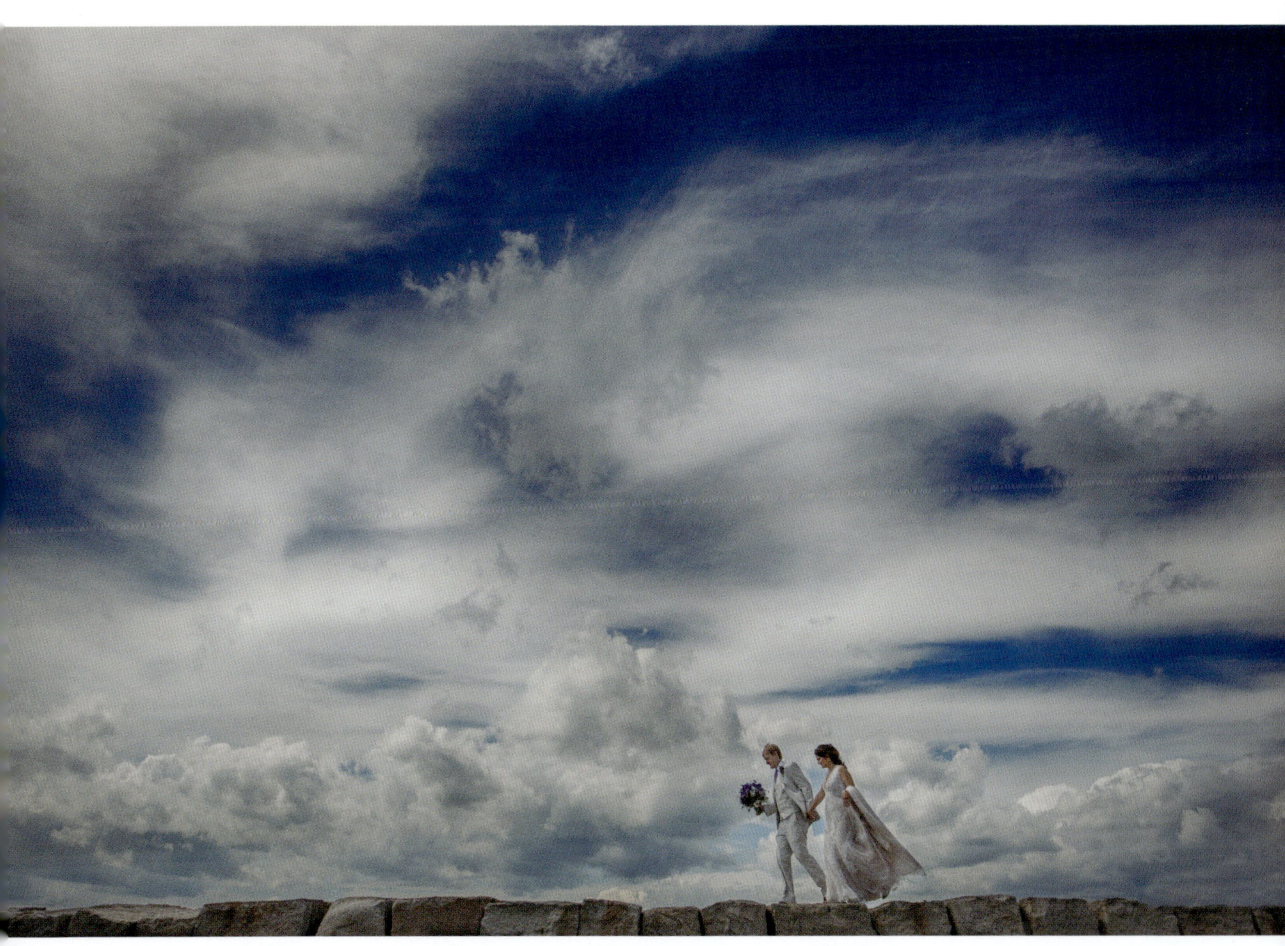

Your Bottom Line

In addition to the time and overhead costs outlined earlier, there will be material costs associated with the completion of the wedding contract. These may include things like media drives, packaging, thank-you cards, marketing materials, postage, travel, and lodging—not to mention the major material costs incurred when there's an album or other tangible goods included in the package.

There will also be outside labor costs when you hire others to help in the process. Is there a second photographer whom you'll have to pay? Do you outsource your photo editing? Do you have an assistant? In the case of second photographers, be 100 percent certain to check state and federal laws regarding the often-misunderstood and frequently highly scrutinized differences between the people being considered employees versus subcontractors. Be sure to understand, with the help of your insurance agency, the liability insurance implications of having this second person working for you. Do you pay for this? Or do they? We'll talk more about insurance in a later chapter.

While every situation will be different, the intent so far is simply to be sure that you keep your eyes open to the real investment you're

There will also be outside labor costs when you hire others to help in the process.

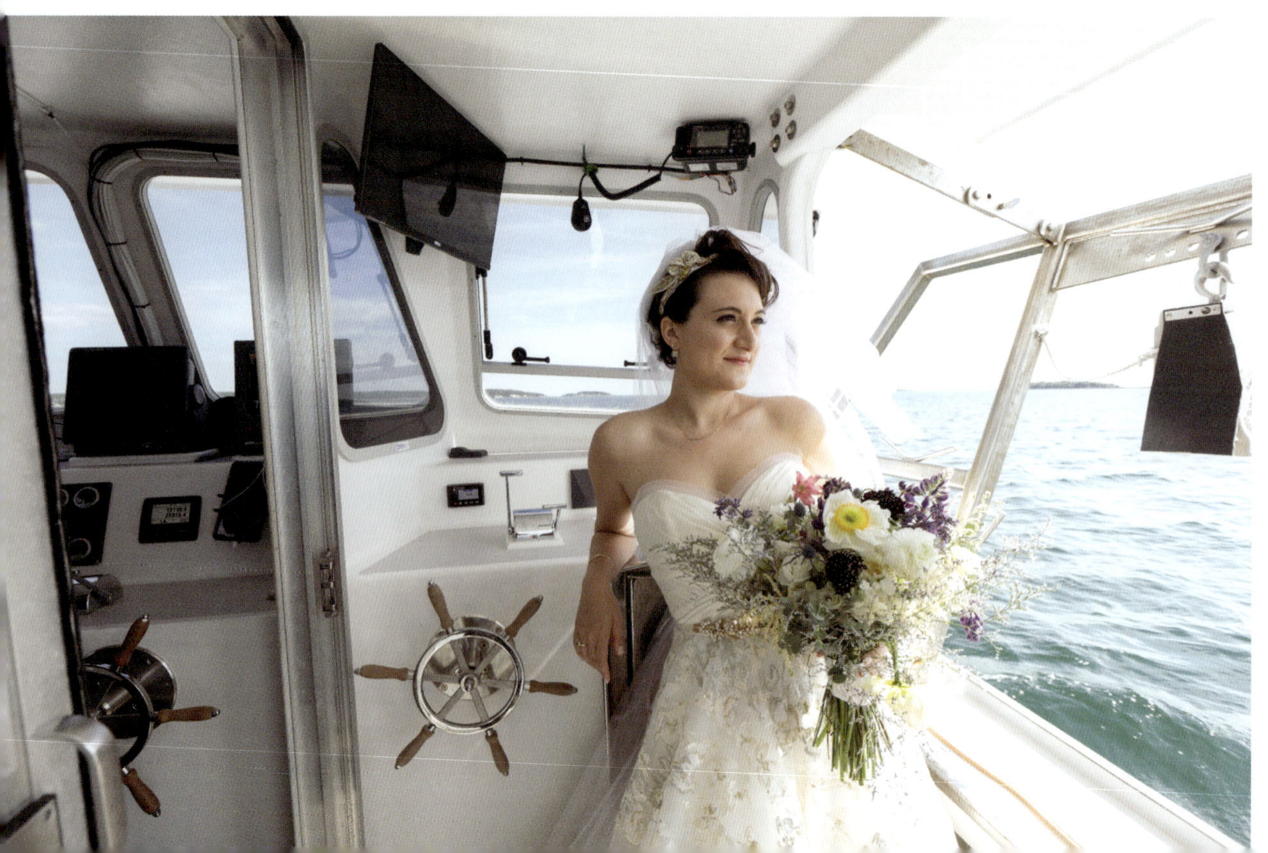

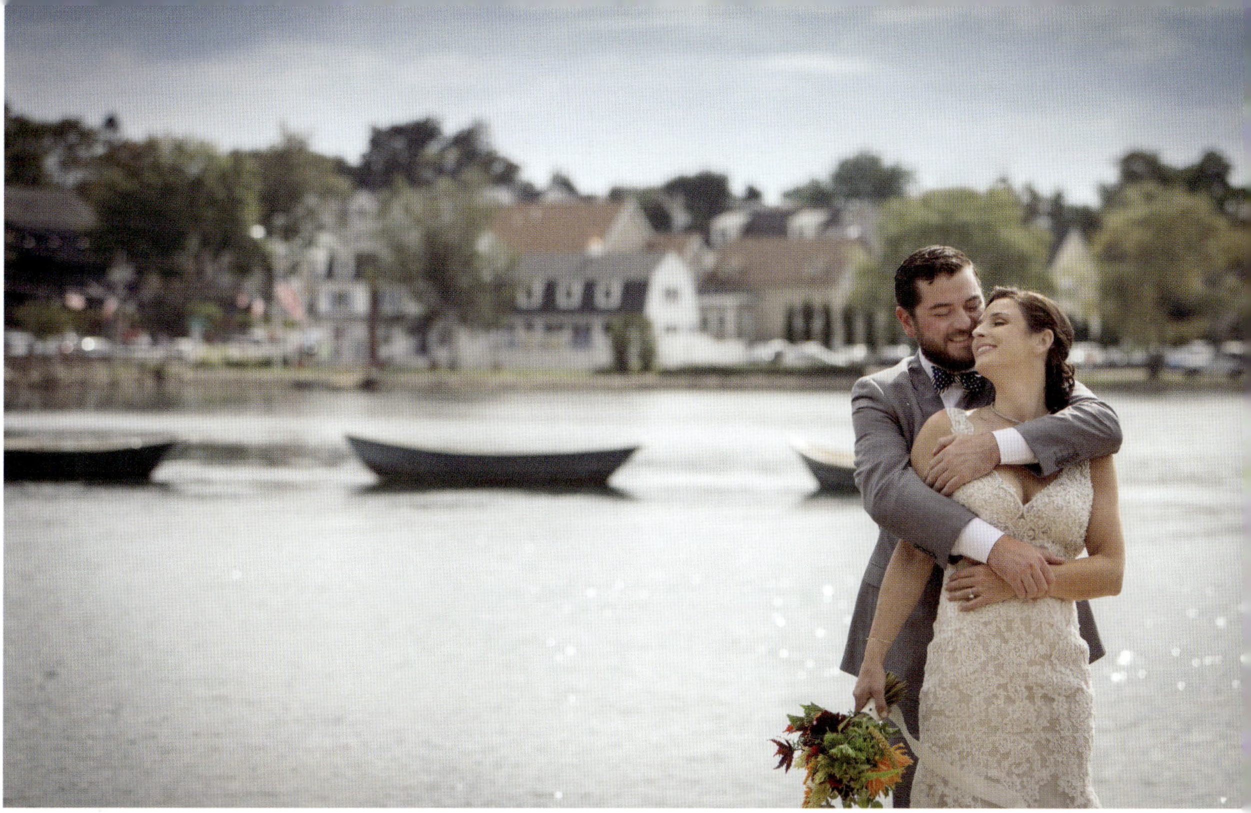

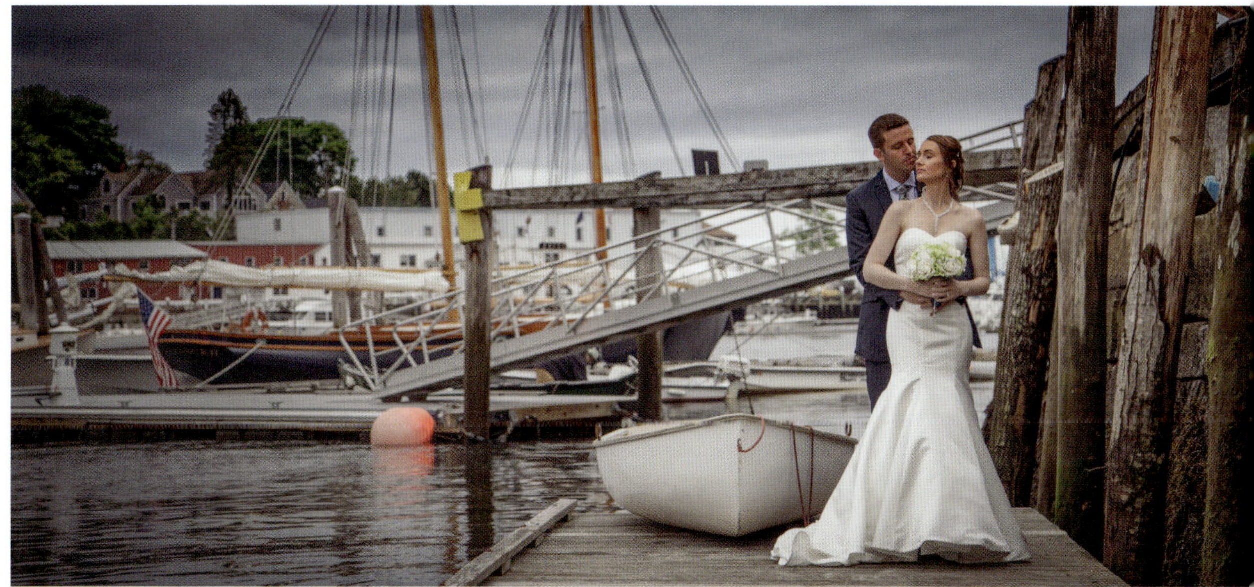

making that's associated with, say, a $3200 wedding package sale, and that this number does not *at all* reflect your actual profit.

So, with overhead costs plus the material costs of goods sold, your $3200 sale/$400 per hour profit, after taxes, may be closer to $20 or $25 per hour. Make a careful assessment and determine what amount makes sense for you to charge for your wedding photography services at the front of the process.

Remember, there's a lot resting on your shoulders as a wedding photographer. You are

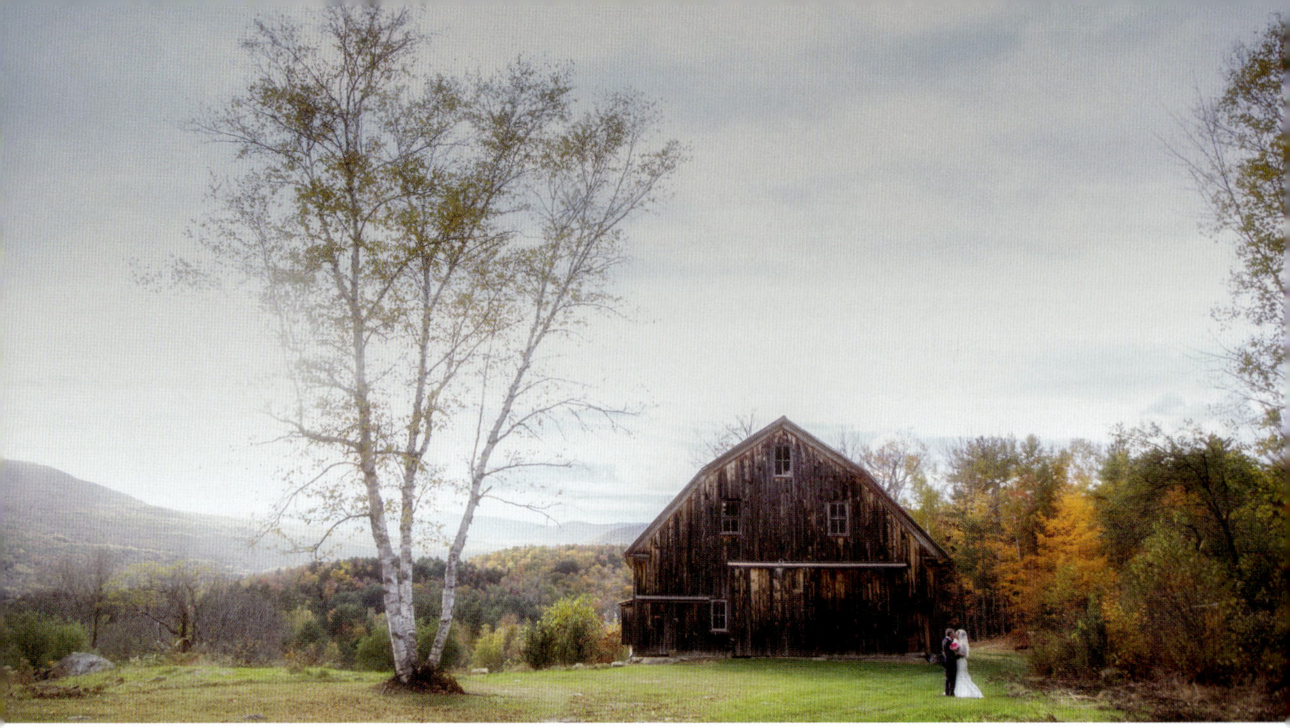

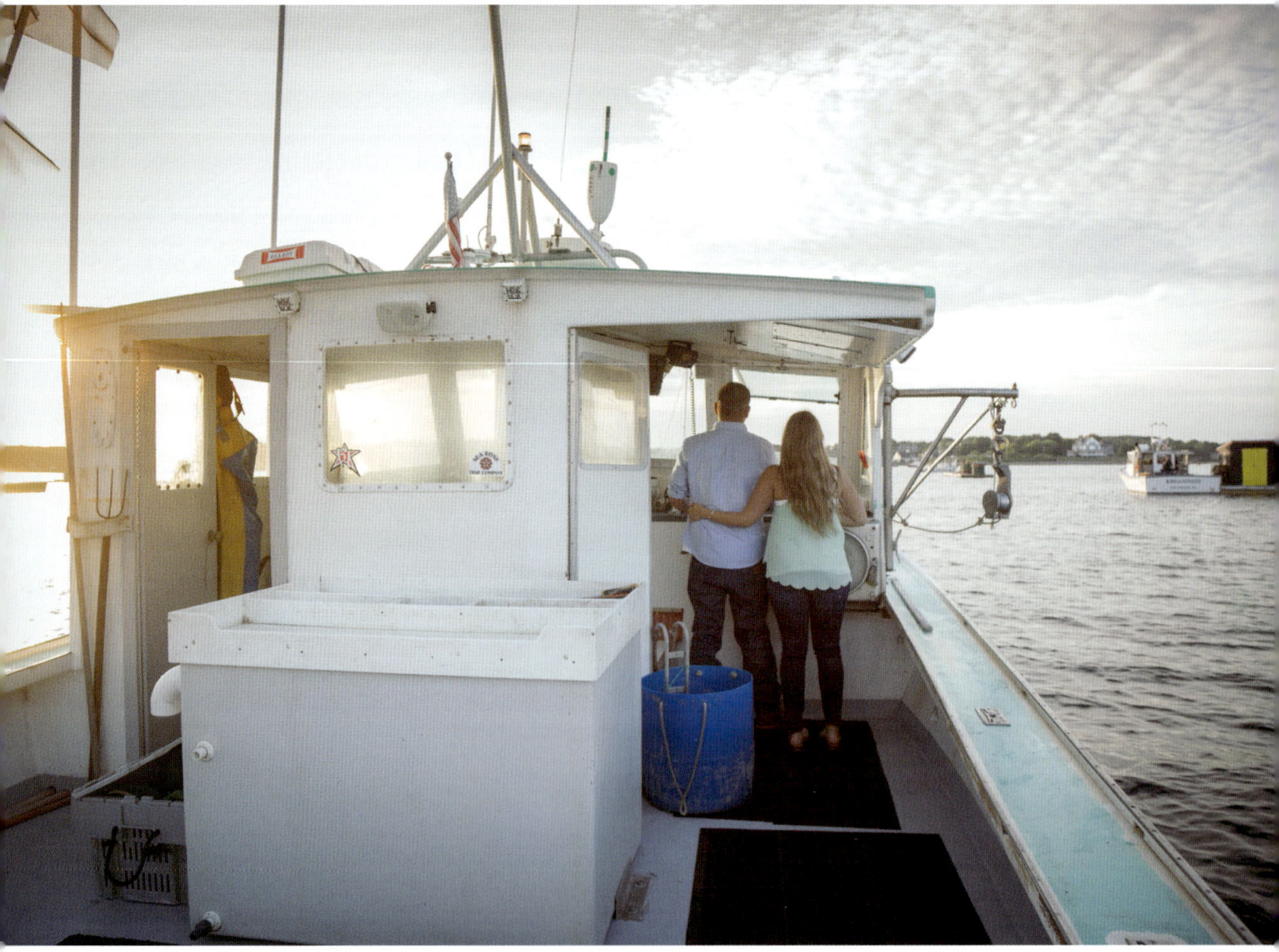

photographing something that has to be done right the first time; there are no second chances.

No one will ever know how many well-meaning and talented wedding photographers went out of business for thinking they were making several hundred dollars per hour and realizing that it was many times less than that, all the while having to do a great job photographing what many consider the most important day in the couple's life.

All of this isn't meant to scare anyone away from following their dreams to be a wedding photographer. Rather, we don't want to see wonderfully talented people not be able to follow their dreams for lack of proper consideration of the fact the wedding photography business is just that—a *business*—and has to be treated as such. It can be made to work.

Hopefully, you can now see that there are many reasons why high-quality, professional, and skilled wedding photography *isn't* inexpensive, and that cutting prices to earn work is a fast race to the bottom. Let's not be a part of that game. Let's be a part of the smaller group of photographers who are in it to win it.

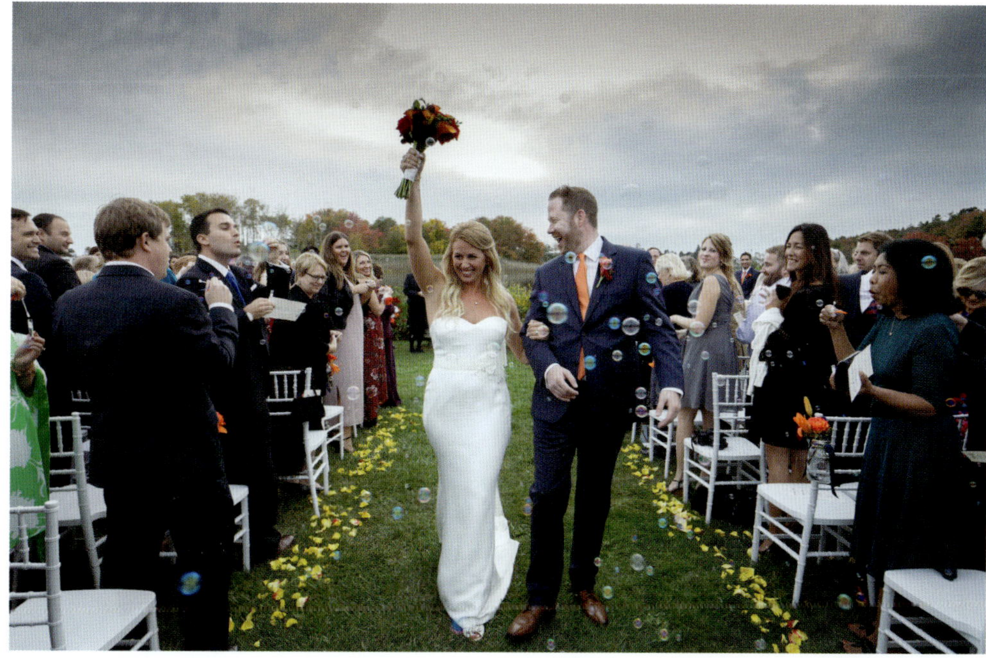

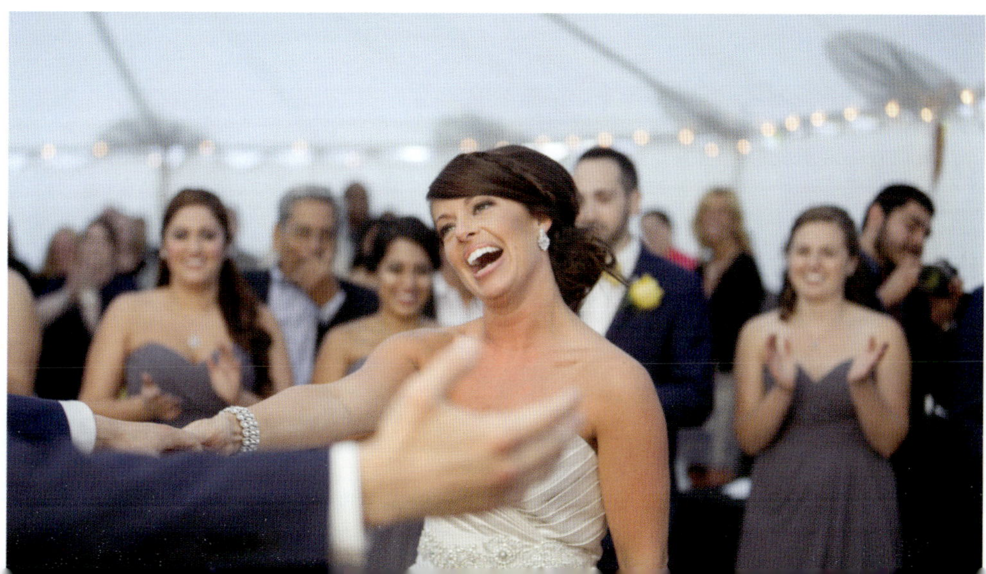

Price Lists and Catalogs

At this point, you should have an idea of your time investment and overhead/material costs for providing wedding photography services. Now it's time to develop a price list to provide to potential clients so they'll know what you offer and how you offer it.

It'd be prudent at this time to have an idea of what your local competitors are offering and charging for their presumably similar services. Aim to know what's being offered by those you perceive to be at a higher, similar, and lower tier in terms of both experience and the quality of their wedding images. A good way to gather this information is through networking and becoming friends with these folks. We like to say that in this business, it's friendship and collaboration first, competition second.

If there were only one bit of advice we could offer (but not to worry, there's more than one!) for what options should go in your wedding catalog, it would be to keep it simple. Create packages that are both what your clients will want and what you want to sell.

Keep in mind that some clients don't know what they want or need when it comes to wedding photography. They will depend upon learning this from you (and your competition). Make your catalog informative, and ensure

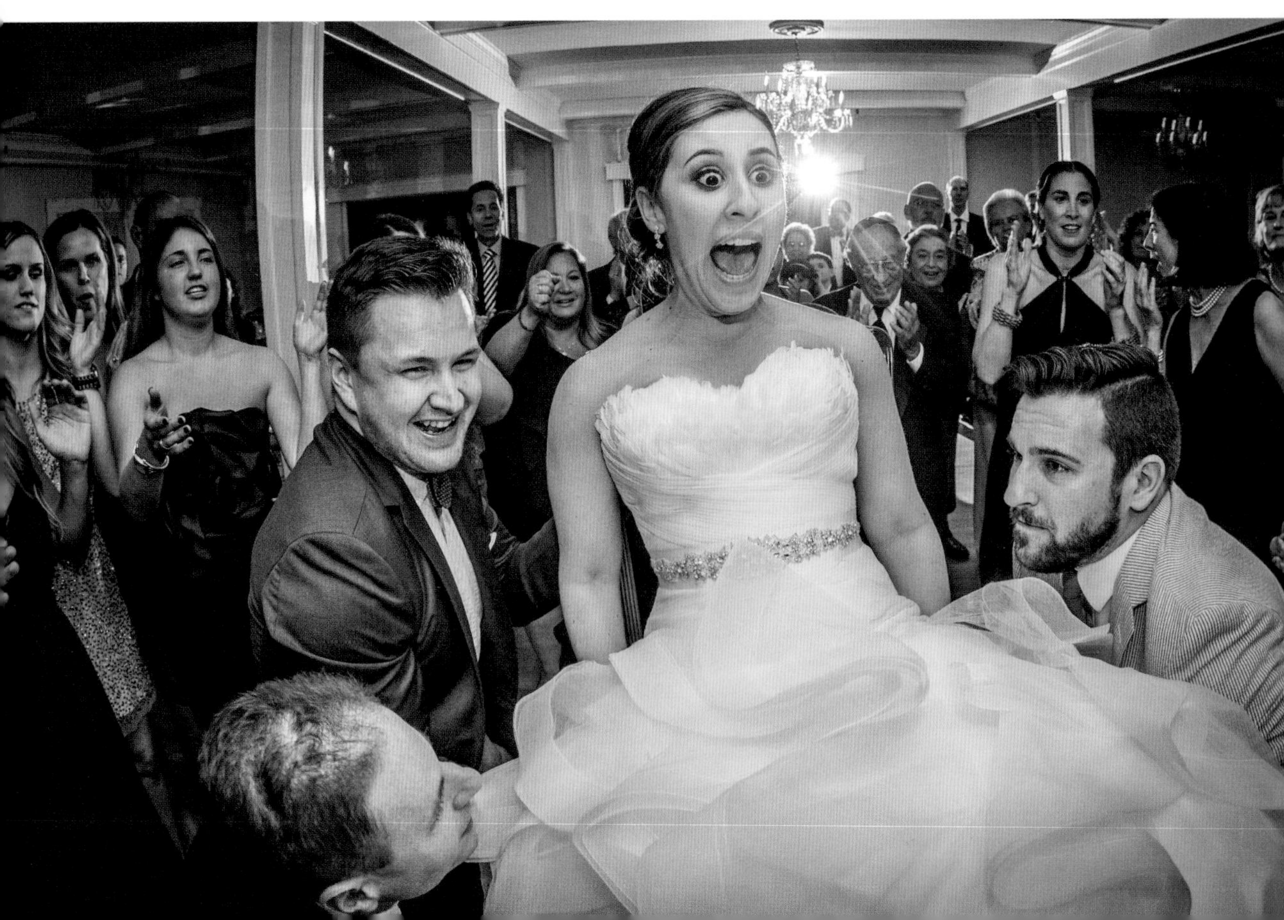

that it is a useful resource for your prospective clients.

The vast majority of the weddings we're asked to photograph are well suited to our eight- or ten-hour package. Do we offer smaller packages? Sure, but not for in-season weekends (Friday, Saturday, and Sunday), unless it's a last-minute request for a date we'd be unlikely to sell. Lesser packages are fine for Monday through Thursday for smaller weddings or elopements.

Make your catalog informative and have it be a useful resource for your prospective clients.

Speaking of elopements, when you sell coverage for one, be sure to have some language in the contract that specifically defines what constitutes an elopement versus a small wedding—especially if you offer a lower price for the simpler circumstances of the elopement. Be sure to state that the contract is only valid when those conditions are met. This isn't intended in any way to trick the client; it's to protect you against the circumstance when your services are secured for an "elopement" for $x instead of your small wedding package for $y, and the client says, "Oh, at the last minute, we decided to have a few friends and family join us! That's okay, right?" The good thing is that this is a rare occurrence, but it can and does happen.

Including a set of digital files in the wedding photography packages we offer is the norm in our market area, so we build that into the cost of our packages. Again, we don't

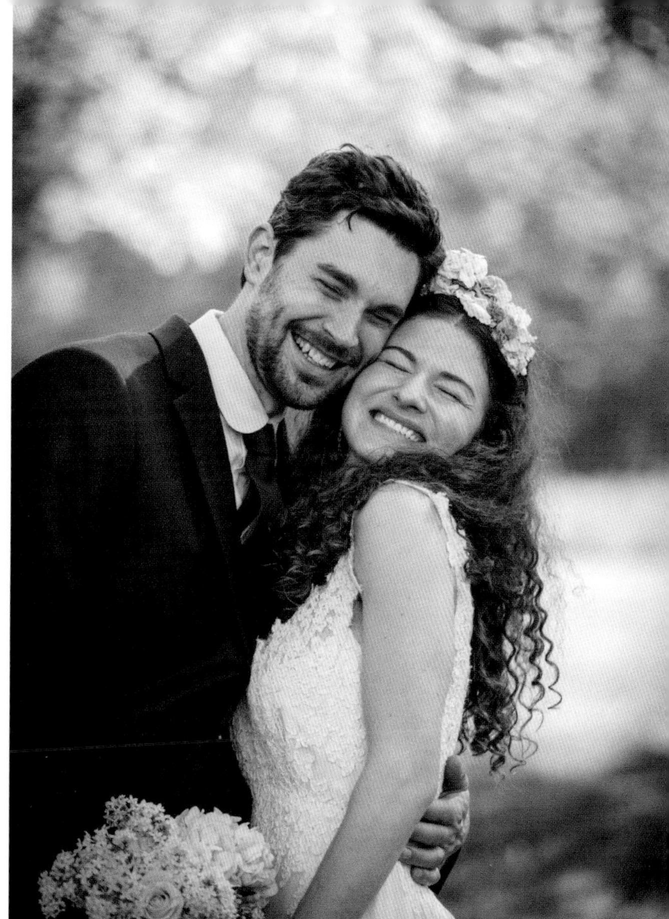

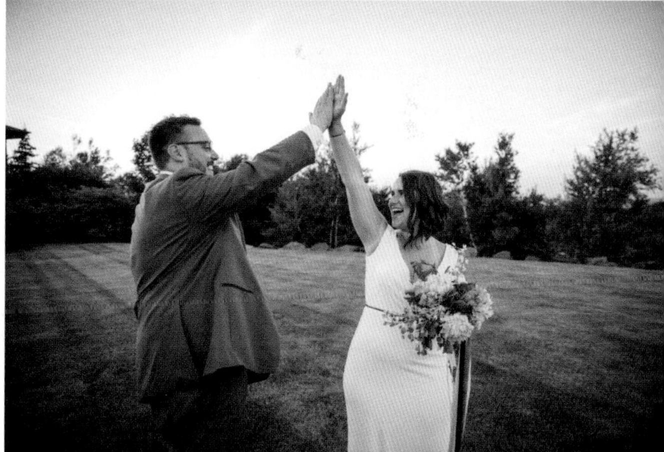

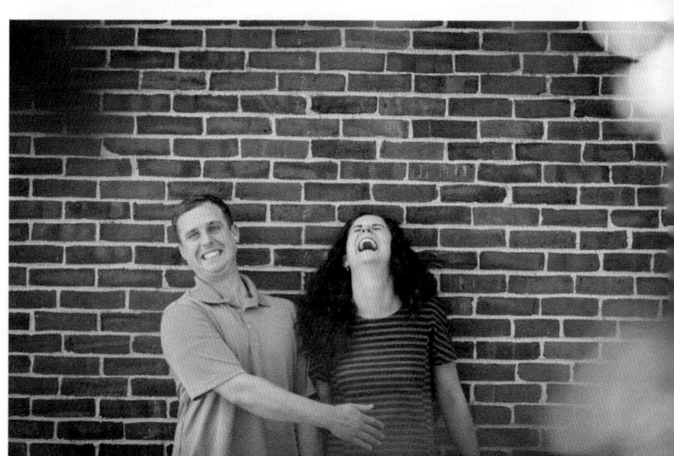

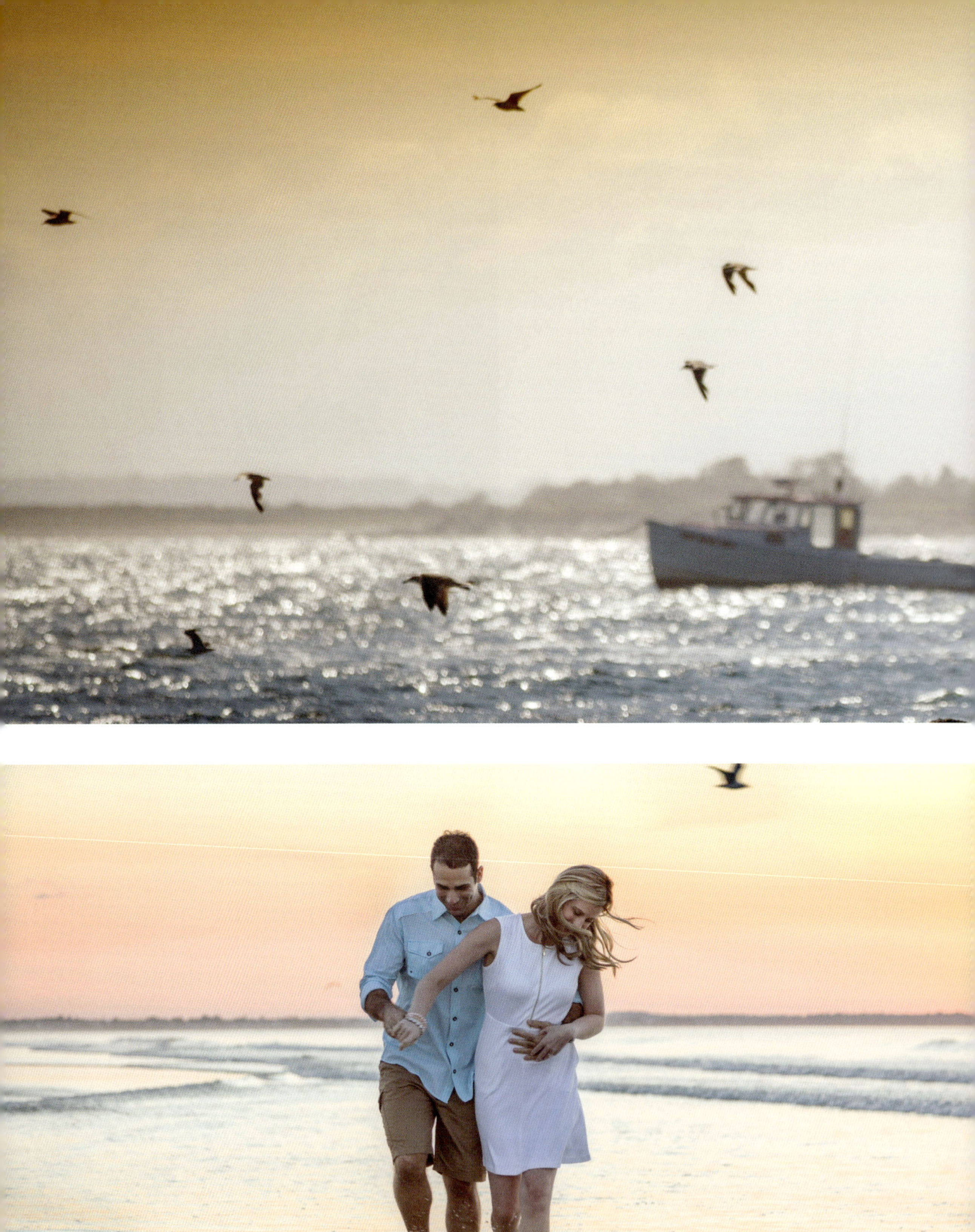

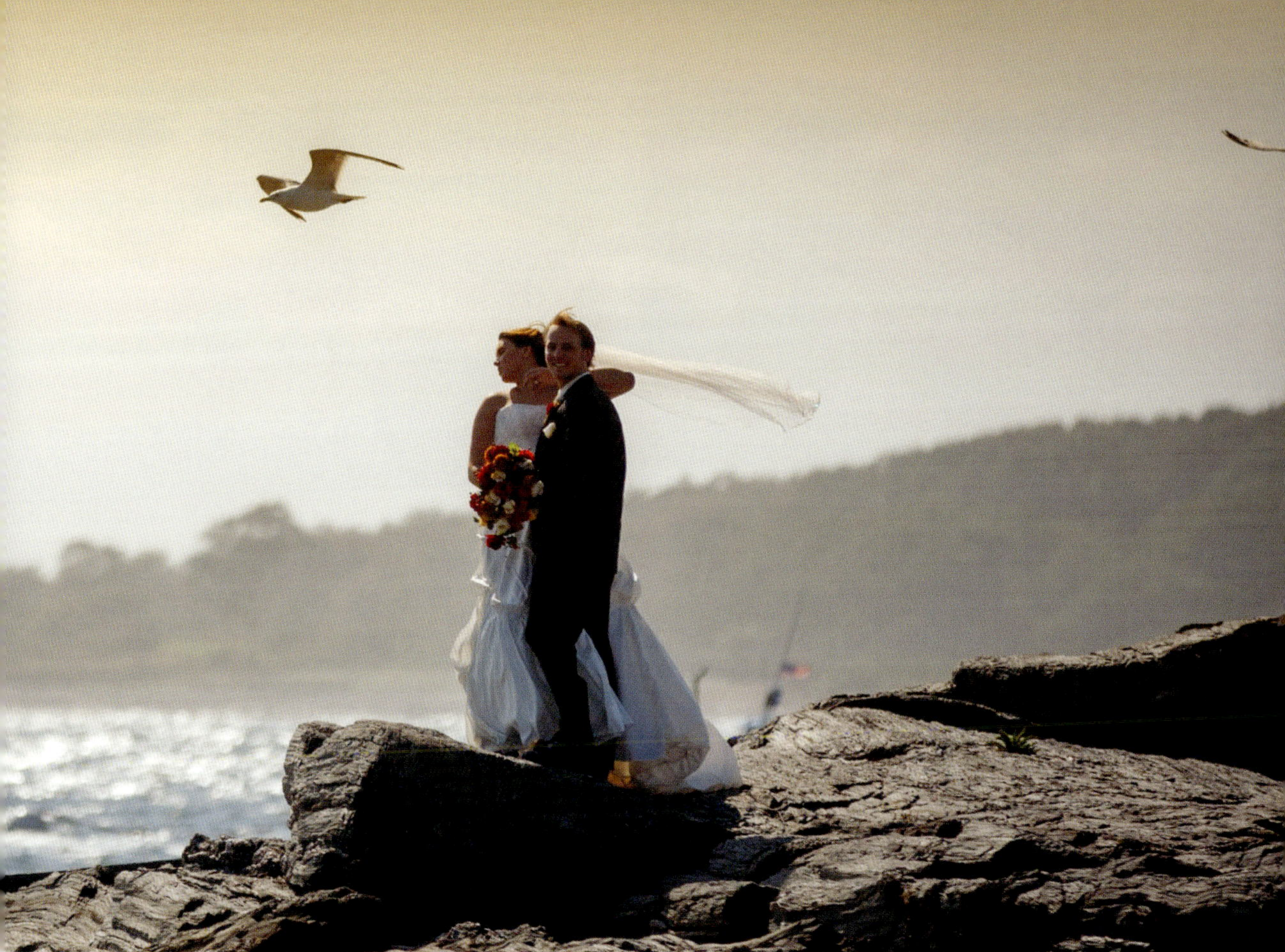

want it to be confusing for the client to choose a package. Simple is best. We want to offer what we know people will want to buy. We try to put ourselves in the mind-set of our clients as often as we can.

Be careful about including items in a bundle that people will try to have you remove to

We don't want it to be confusing for the client when it comes to choosing a package. Simple is best.

achieve a lower price. For this reason, as much as we love doing engagement sessions, we only include them in our largest package. Some folks say the engagement session is "free," so that if the couples don't want one, there isn't anything to refund. That works sometimes, but there's still a potential negative effect when anyone leaves something behind, but still pays the same amount of money.

When it comes to packages, it is important to offer three: a low, a middle, and a high. A burger place may offer a single, double, and triple cheeseburger. The double costs just a bit more than the single, but a lot less than the triple, right? That's because the restaurant has strategically priced the double cheeseburger to generate a good profit, while providing the customer a satisfying choice. So, pricing the single to be close in cost to the double results in

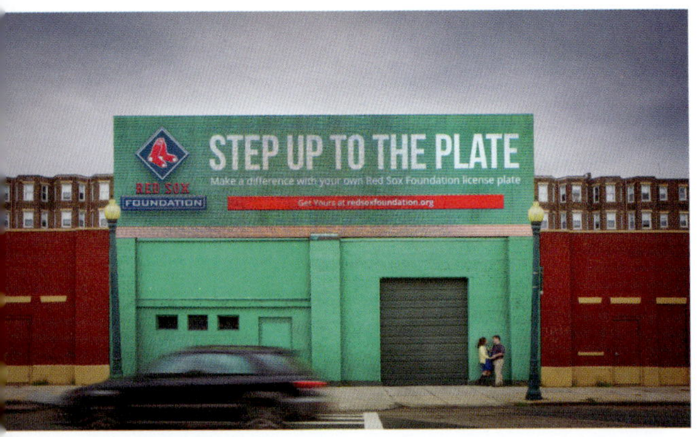

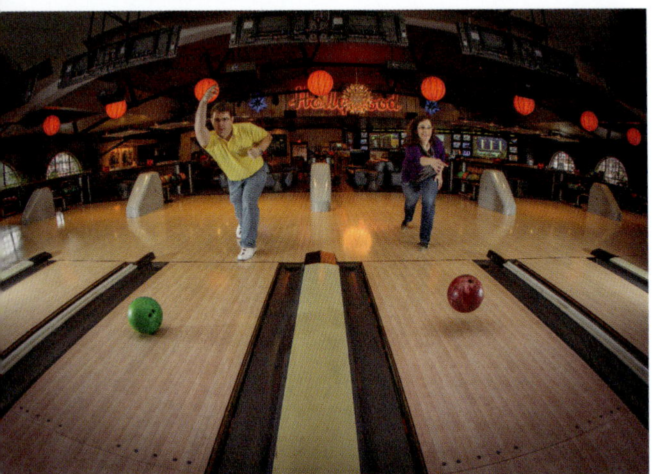

few opting for it, while making the price of the triple high enough makes the double the obvious right choice. And, hey, guess what? Every now and again you may actually sell a triple, and that means extra money. People love not buying the base level of something, and they

People fear that they will miss out when they think most people buy something more than they've chosen.

often don't want to feel guilty for choosing the most elaborate or most costly option. Often, they'll feel that they've made a good decision in sticking to the middle. Marking this middle

option as your "most popular" in your catalog is big, too. People fear that they will miss out when they think most other folks buy something more than they've chosen.

So, the low and the high packages are each there to point to the attractiveness of the middle package. Priced right, you'll still be very pleased if you sell the low or the high package, but they mainly exist to make the middle package the one to go with.

What about á la carte pricing? It works for some, but we've had time-tested success with packages. Our clients love the simple nature of the bundles we offer. Of course, you'll have separate pricing for items that you don't want to include in the base packages, such as engagement sessions, albums, and other options you may offer.

You'll want to have a clear, clean, easy-to-read layout for your price list/catalog offerings. We create our own document using a page layout app and then export it in PDF format to email to clients who've reached out to us via our contact form. We also have a copy of this catalog viewable from our website; however, we choose to not list prices there, primarily so that we may have a chance to at least begin a dialogue with prospective clients. This, and the fact that the average person shopping for our services hasn't ever gone through this process before, means that there's often sticker shock over what quality wedding photography costs.

It may be best to subcontract out your website design to a graphic design and branding company, who can help with all aspects of your brand identity, too.

Package Presentation Order

Some studies show that when you offer services at various price points, it's an advantage to start with the high (so as to emphasize the value of your services), and then work downward to the lower-priced options as they're presented in your documentation. We've tried this, but interestingly enough, we keep switching back to the other way. We've seen the best results from using the low–medium–high order.

Pricing Formats

The way prices are presented is an interesting study and worth some additional research. When it comes to written prices, some studies show, at least for large amounts, it's less daunting to show the number as "4000" instead of "$4,000.00." Think of a high-end restaurant menu. How often do you see an entrée listed as "$32.00"? It's more likely to be shown as "32."

There's good reason for that: to many people's subconscious, it seems less costly. Also, there's a school of thought that it's wise to lop off $10 and price something at "3,990" instead of "4,000." Oh, and those commas! Some studies have shown that "3900" creates a perception of being a smaller value than "3,900." Also, it's argued that you should never include the decimal and pennies in high-ticket amounts.

Find what works best for your style, and go with it. Just be consistent throughout your documentation.

Find what works best for your style, and go with it. Just be consistent throughout your documentation.

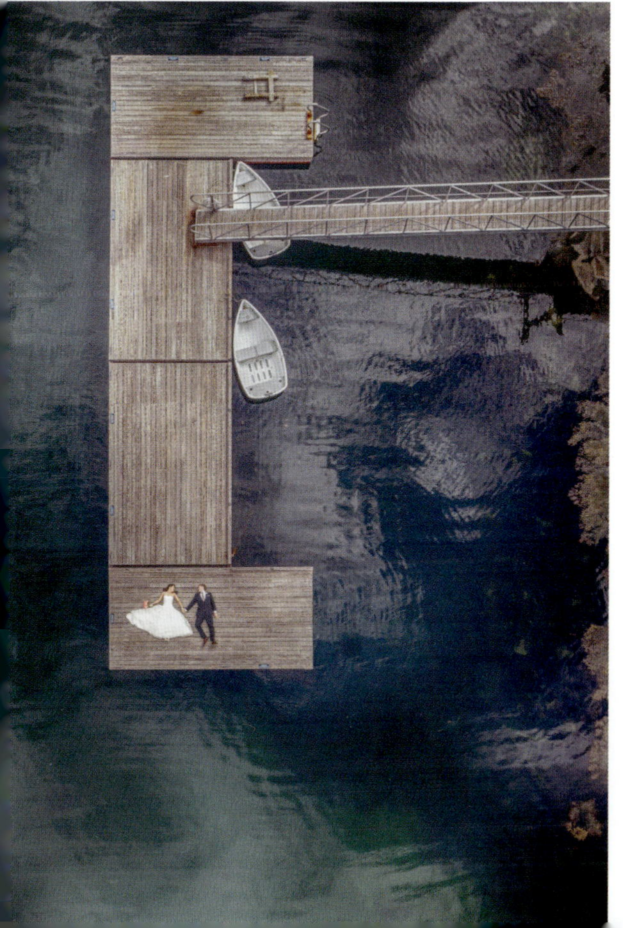

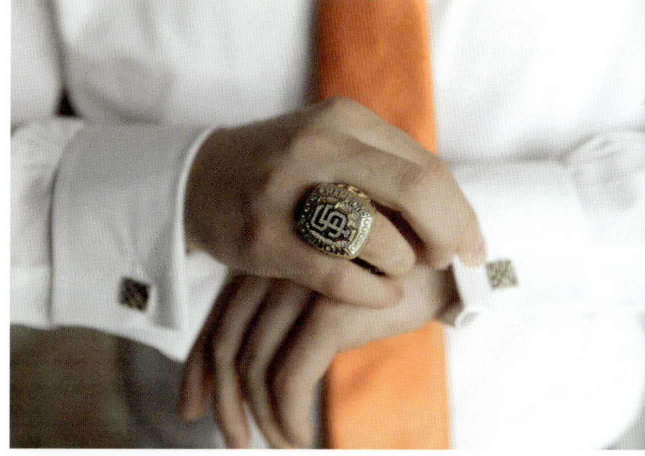

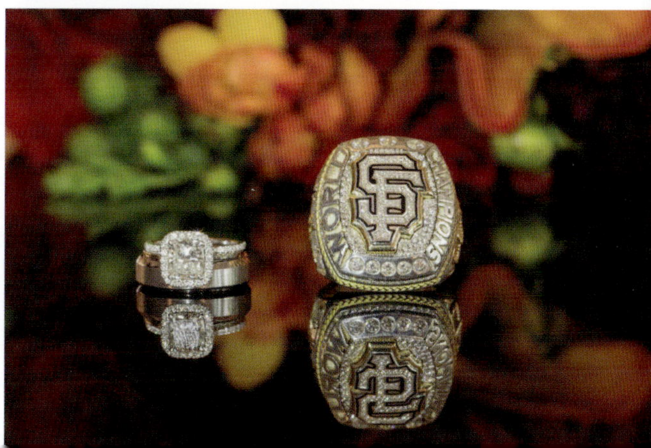

Responsiveness

The importance of making a positive first impression with clients cannot be overstated. We do this with promptness. We cannot count how many email replies we get from clients who say, "Thank you for such a prompt response!" Prospective clients requesting information from us, usually from our website contact form, are people who want to spend their money with us. They deserve a quick, courteous, and professional reply.

Now is a good time to bring to the table the topic of work–life balance. There are two schools of thought here. One is that emails, calls, inquiries, and business matters aren't handled off-hours, but are taken care of the next business day. The other school of thought is to reply to inquiries immediately, regardless of the time of day or day of the week, within reason.

We try to reply to inquiries quickly, regardless of the time or day of the week they come in. Doing so works for us and shows our clients that we are highly responsive, but we know it's not the right approach for everyone. Some may opt to maintain stricter "business hours," and that's fine. We send a short and personal reply, as soon as we can, to acknowledge that the

The importance of making a positive first impression immediately with clients cannot be overstated.

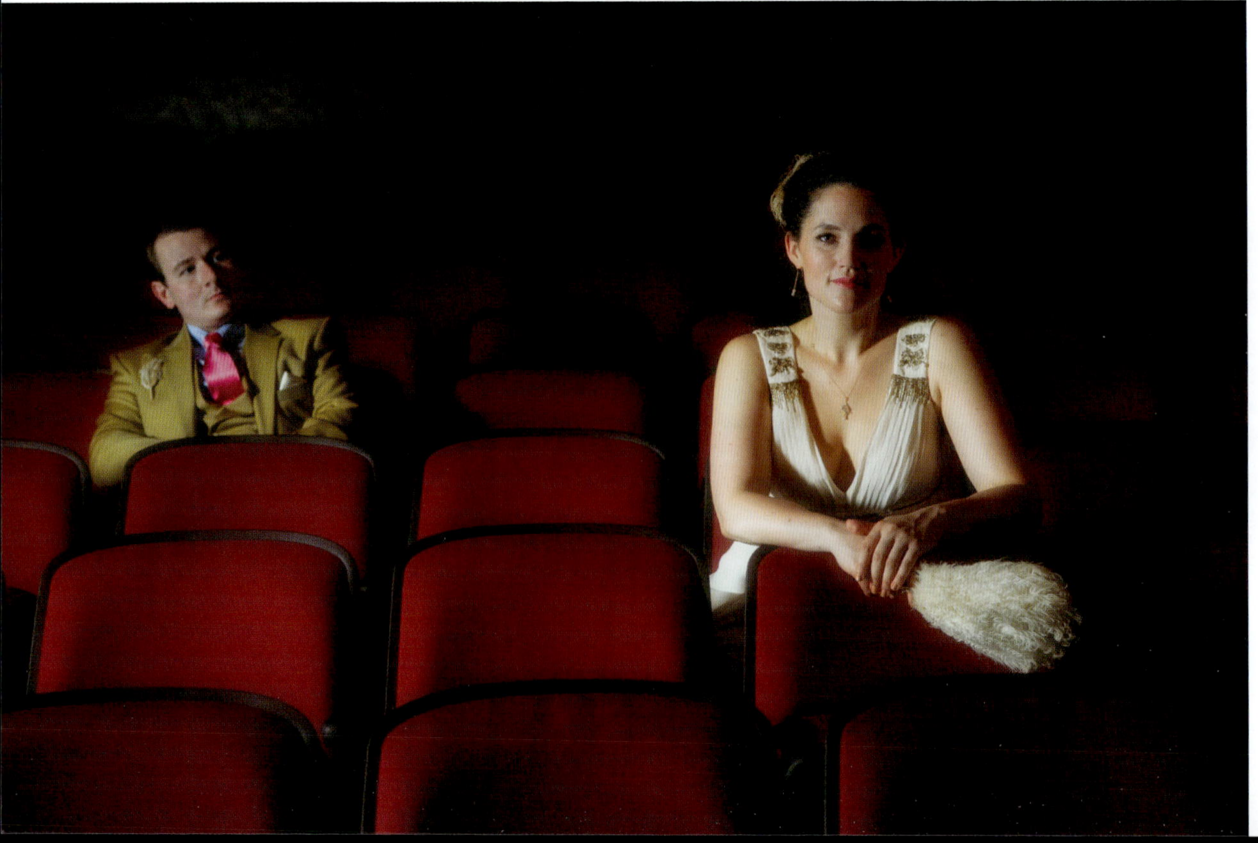

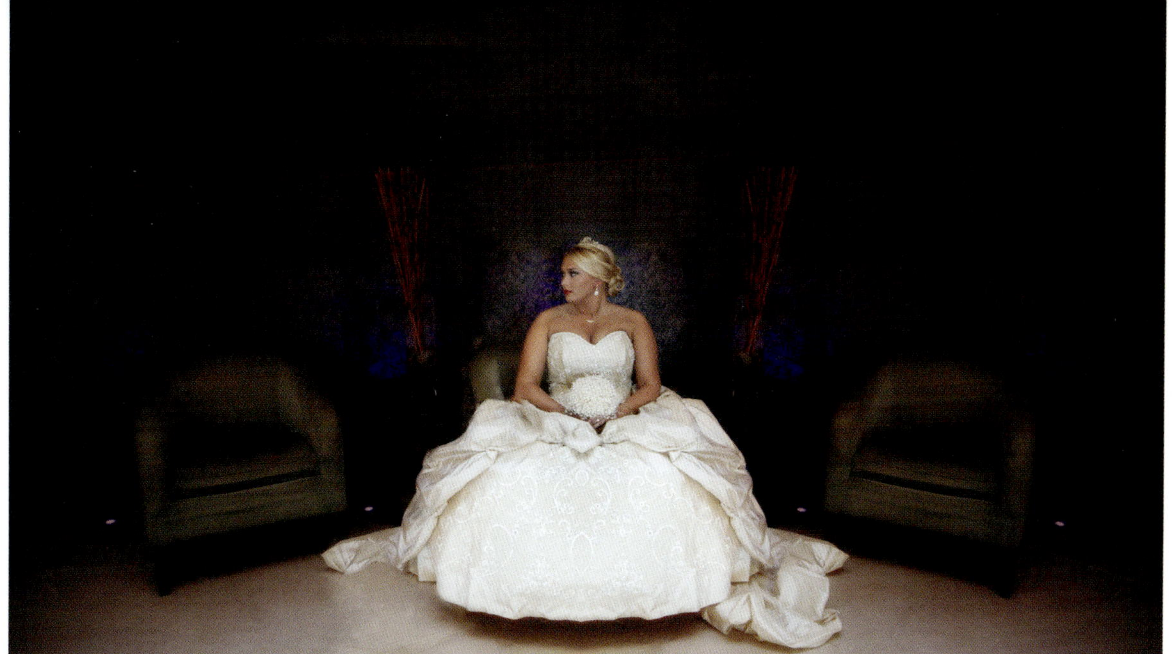

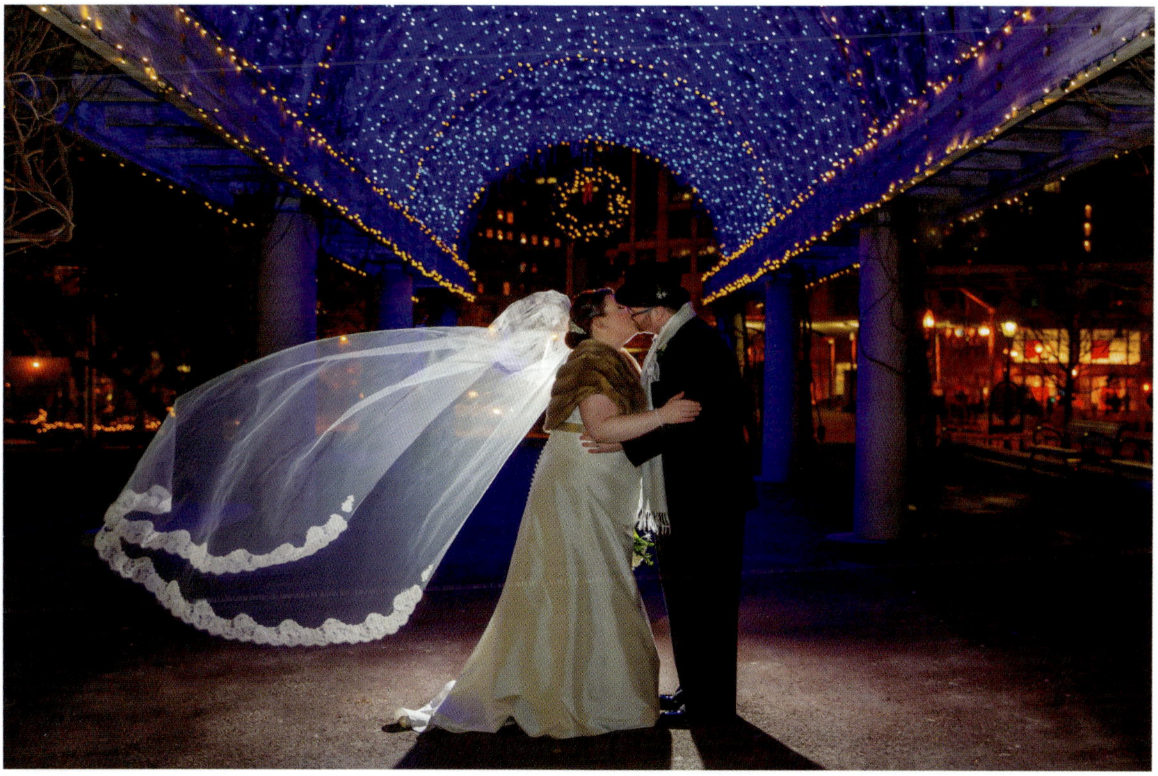

contact was received, and we promise that the prospective client will get our full information as soon as we get back to the office.

By the way, we recommend avoiding the use of "auto-responders" (a.k.a. out-of-office notifications) for email inquiries. They sound too much like, well, auto-responders. They're cold and impersonal. We don't like receiving them, so why should we send them?

Studio Management Systems

There are several software apps available to help photographers manage and organize their businesses. Even though we're a busy wedding photography studio, the systems we have put in place have never left us wanting for more, and, thus, we don't use a studio management app. We maintain our data using Microsoft Excel spreadsheets. Our accounting is done with Intuit Quick-Books. Our email server is Microsoft Outlook. We use the electronic calendar in Google, and maintain a paper-based calendar, too.

We encourage you to look at the many integrated studio management suites available today that are customized for photographers. But, be sure to approach this as a solution to a real data management and time savings, rather than a solution in search of a problem. Be sure to consider the monthly or annual costs of using these products, too.

Most email apps can create "signatures" for dozens of common communications tasks. If what we're saying is something that we'll likely say again (to other clients), we make a "signature" of that

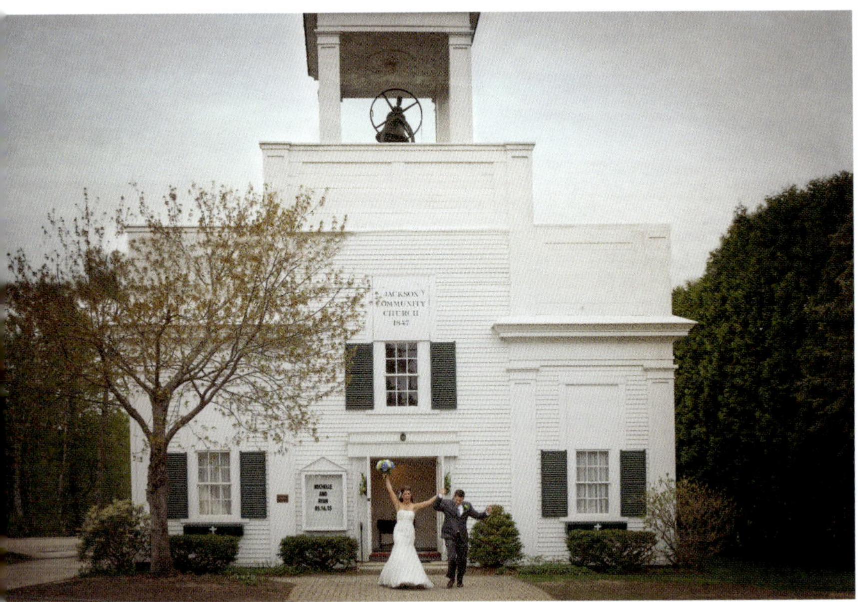

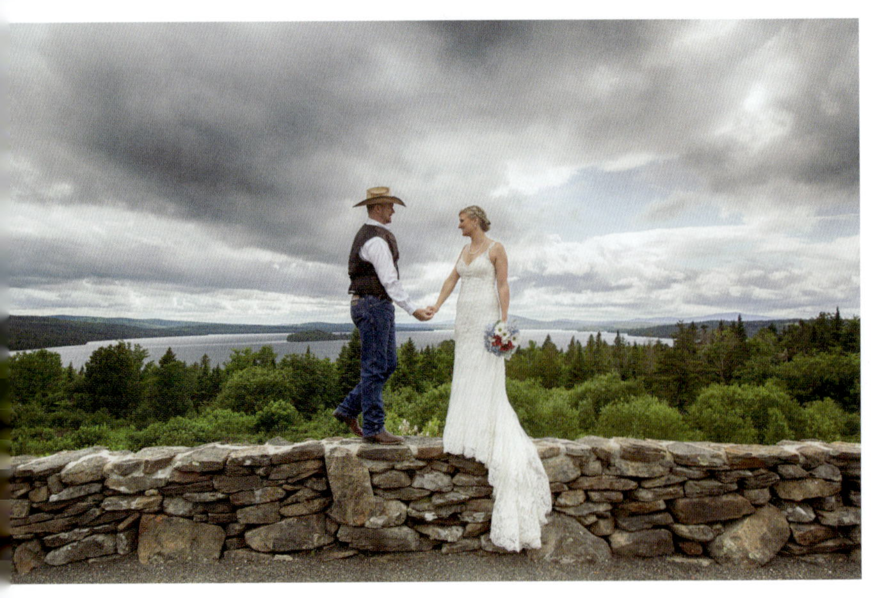

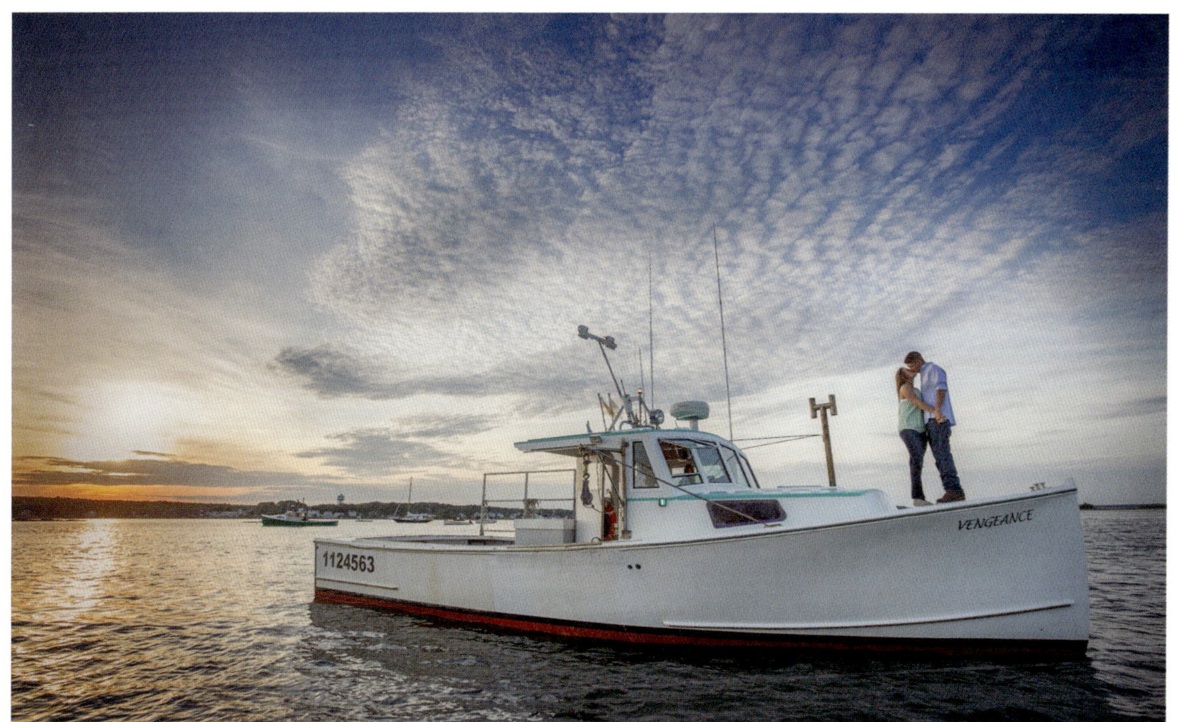

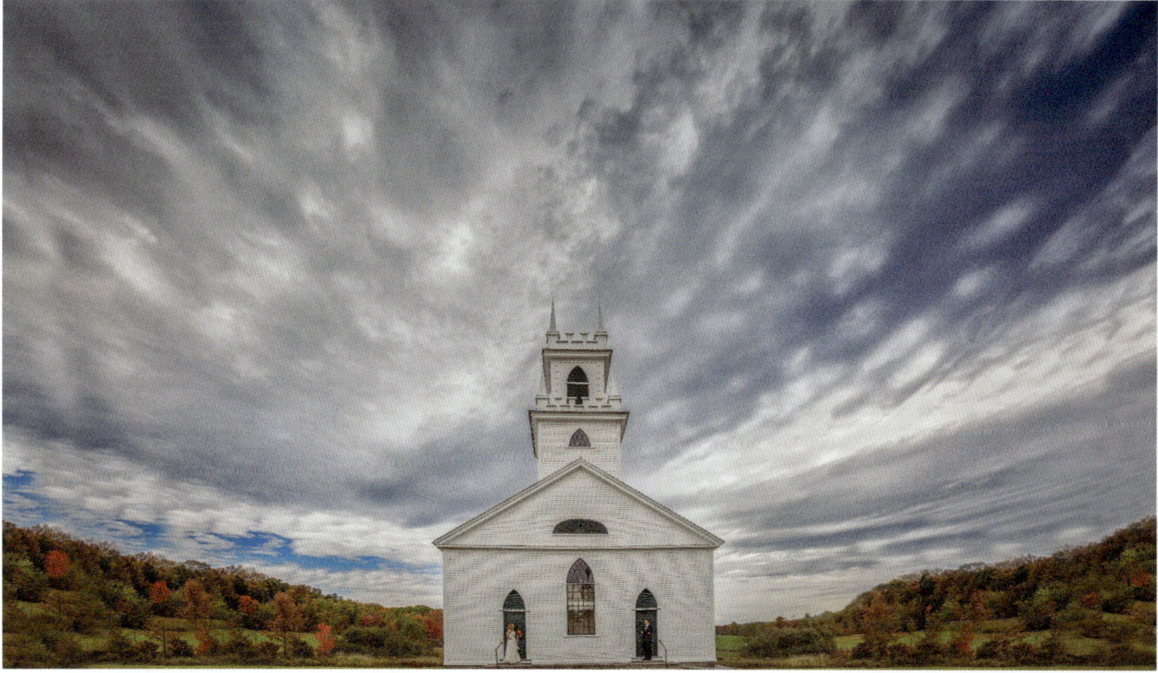

text. Think of signatures as reusable templates. At most, minor editing and personalization is all that's needed for effective and prompt communication. Our most-often used signature is the one we use to reply to an inquiry from clients using our website contact form.

Keep Track of Your Data

Our main Excel spreadsheet keeps track of many things for us. Its main function is our wedding database, using a separate worksheet for each year. It lists the date of the event, the date the contract was signed, names, venue, how the client heard about us, and other data for each wedding. We also use a separate page that tracks every inquiry we receive, and where that lead came from. Yet another page tracks by date (January 1 to December 31) how many weddings we've booked for the current year and for following years. It's an excellent barometer to measure the health of our business and the industry each year. Patterns sometimes emerge that can be very useful for planning purposes.

We sync this spreadsheet/database over Cloud storage so key information is always in reach when we are out of the office.

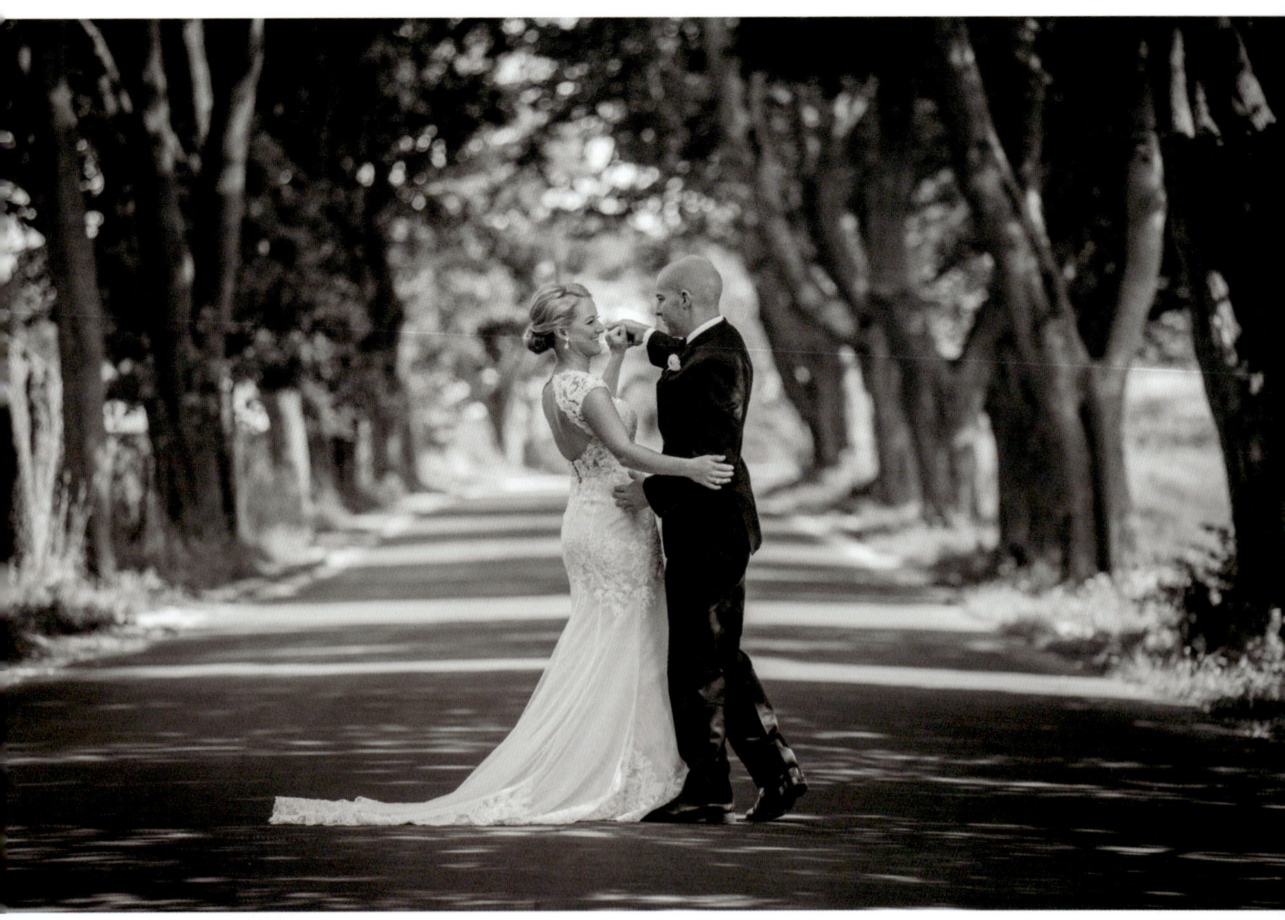

Insurance

We'll jump into insurance now because you can't continue in this wedding photography process without it.

Newcomers often believe they're covered for insurance purposes by existing household policies. Did you know that in most cases the moment you do photography for anyone and collect even a single penny in the process, your homeowner's policy does not cover you for that session? That's because it's now a business activity. You need specific business insurance. We're not only talking about insuring the value of the gear; much more importantly, you need to be covered by liability insurance.

Liability insurance protects you against (potentially really large!) lawsuits in the event you do something that causes someone else harm or injury (like someone at a photo session tripping over your camera bag and breaking a leg or countless other mishaps).

Your local insurance professional is your best resource. They can shop around and help you through what would otherwise be a confusing process. If you travel with your gear, that usually means you could benefit from carrying additional insurance, often called an "inland marine" policy. Your agent will know best.

This all sounds really expensive, doesn't it? The good news is, it's more affordable than you may think. You can often set up a payment plan that will allow you to pay monthly or quarterly.

Insurance is a necessity! We like knowing our coverage inside out. I'll often write to my agent with some "what if?" scenario to verify we're covered adequately.

We suggest taking a trip to your agent's office and having them go over everything with you. We recommend that you listen to their advice on what you need, without being excessive.

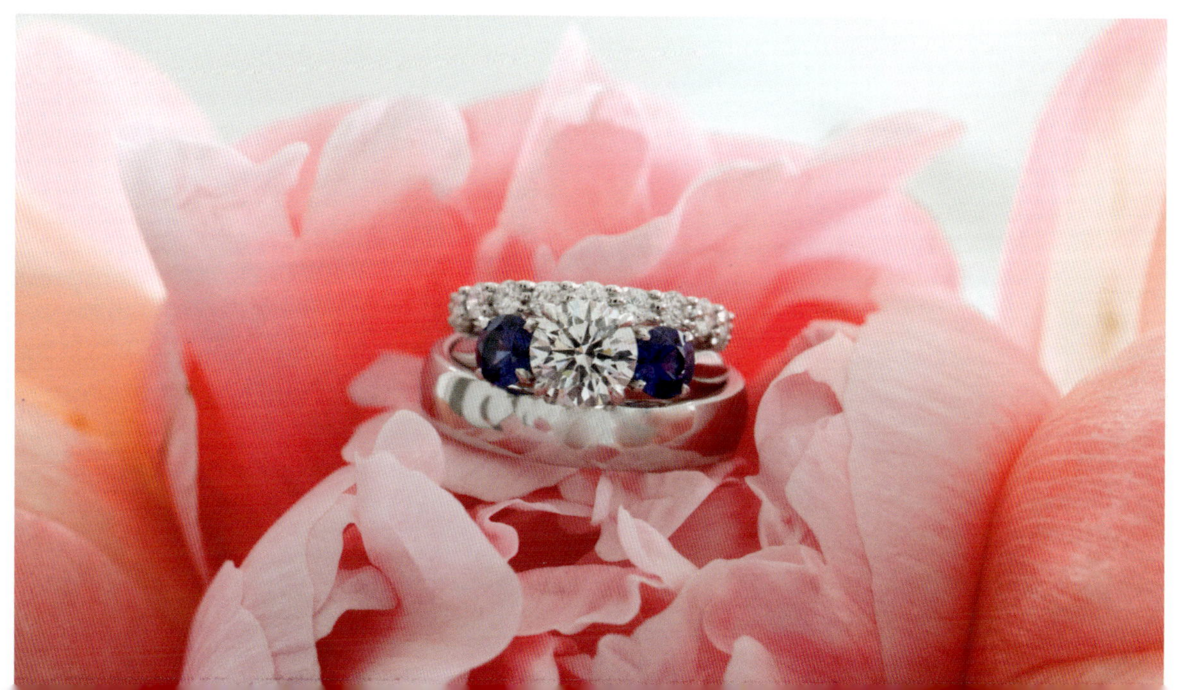

Attracting Clients

To run a wedding photography business, you need clients. What are the main ways we attract them? The chart below shows our four key sources for securing clients: Google, past clients, venues, and other photographers. It's important that you do all the right things to keep each of the four aspects working optimally.

Google

For Google and other search engines, it is critical that you learn about, and then start working on, Search Engine Optimization (SEO). Having great SEO results means clients will find you sooner and more frequently because you will show up in the first few results for a given search term.

Ideally, you'll seek some professional help here, as this is an ever-changing, complicated game. Is there a SCORE chapter in your city? SCORE is a service of the U.S. Small Business Administration and provides entrepreneurial assistance for low or no cost to small business owners. It's likely that the chapter in your area will be an invaluable resource.

In general, keeping your website relevant, updated frequently, and with regular blog posts will be a good start, but there's much more than this involved. Also, making your website an industry resource for a variety of wedding topics may help drive traffic and increase your SEO ranking.

Paying for ads to help you be on "page 1" of Google for the most relevant search term for your business is an option, but ideally you'll want to achieve high rankings "organically" (i.e., on the merits of the content of your site).

Past Clients

Providing top-notch customer service before, during, and after the wedding day is a fundamental value for us. Treat your clients the way you want to be treated. You want your past clients to think of recommending you the moment they hear that a friend is newly engaged. Offering incentives like a free canvas wrap or a print might help, but that's not really what you're after. You want your past clients to refer you because you did a great job, helped make the

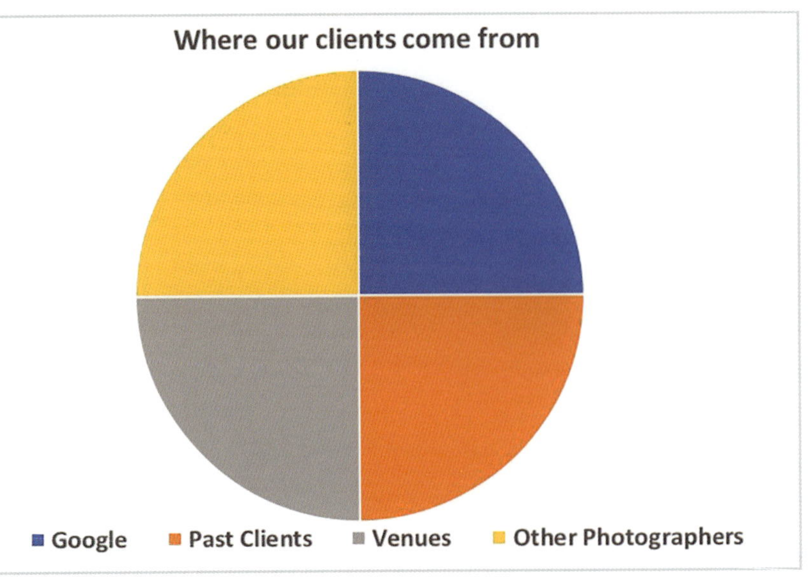

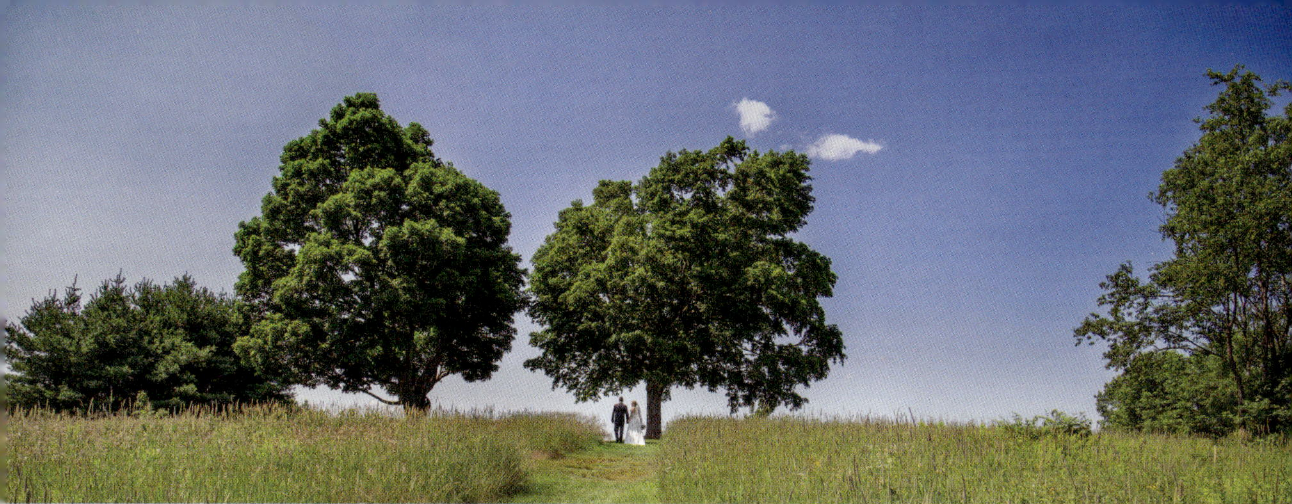

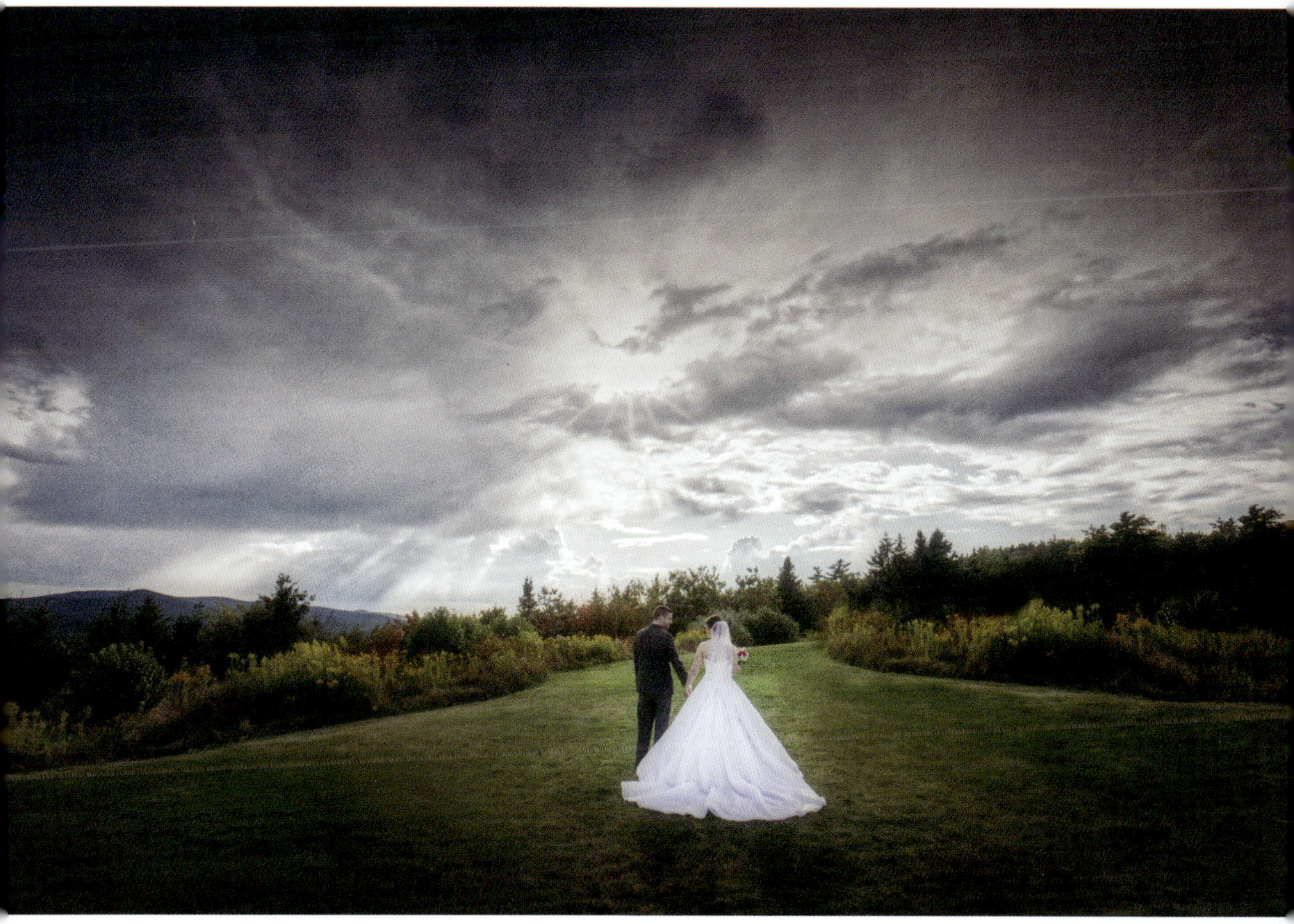

...lay run smoothly, made the bride's interests
your #1 priority, were kind and responsive
through all of your communications with your
clients—and, oh yes, and for the great photographs and memories you gave them.

Venues

Working exceptionally well with the event coordinator at the venues where you photograph
weddings is a huge first step to getting your
name on that venue's recommended vendor

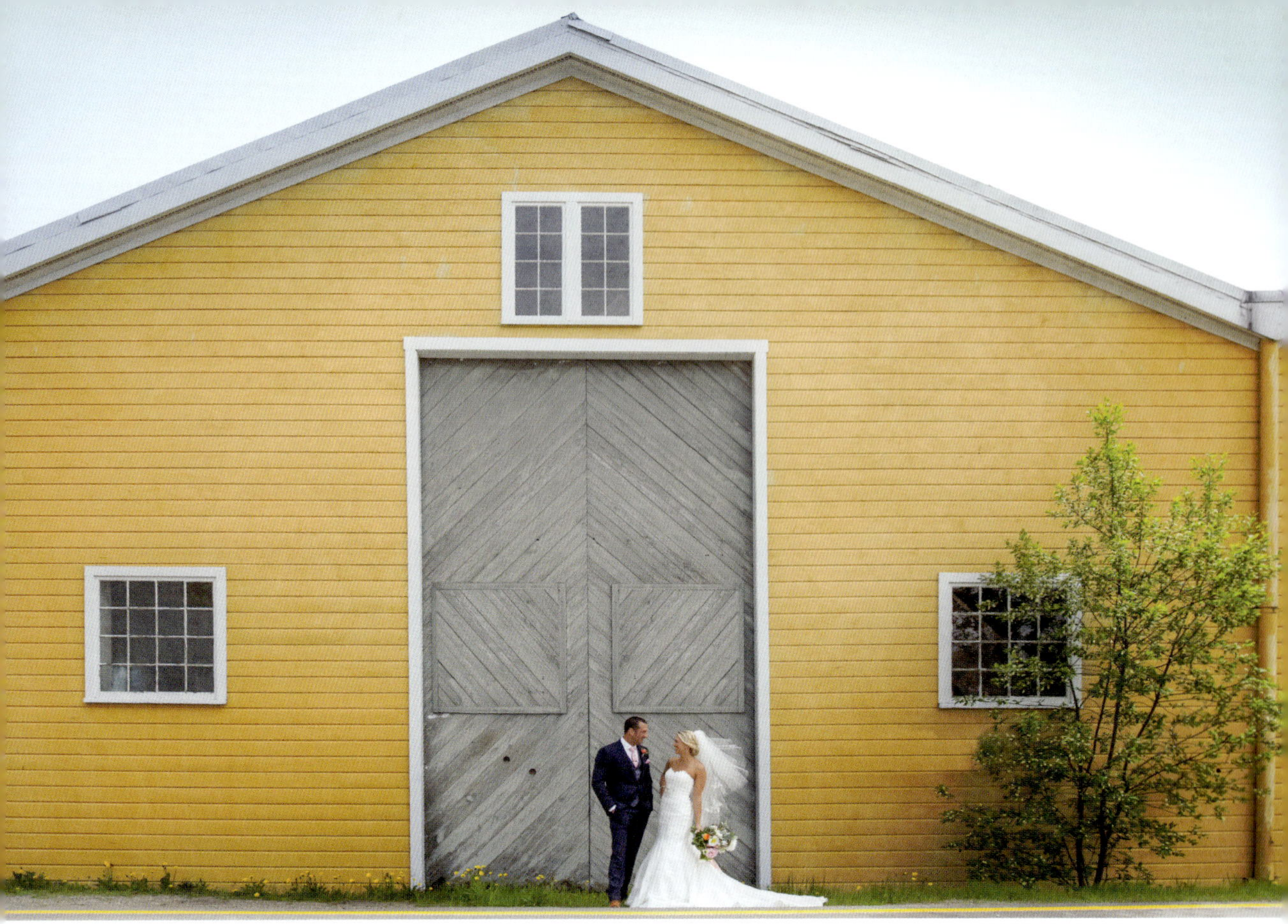

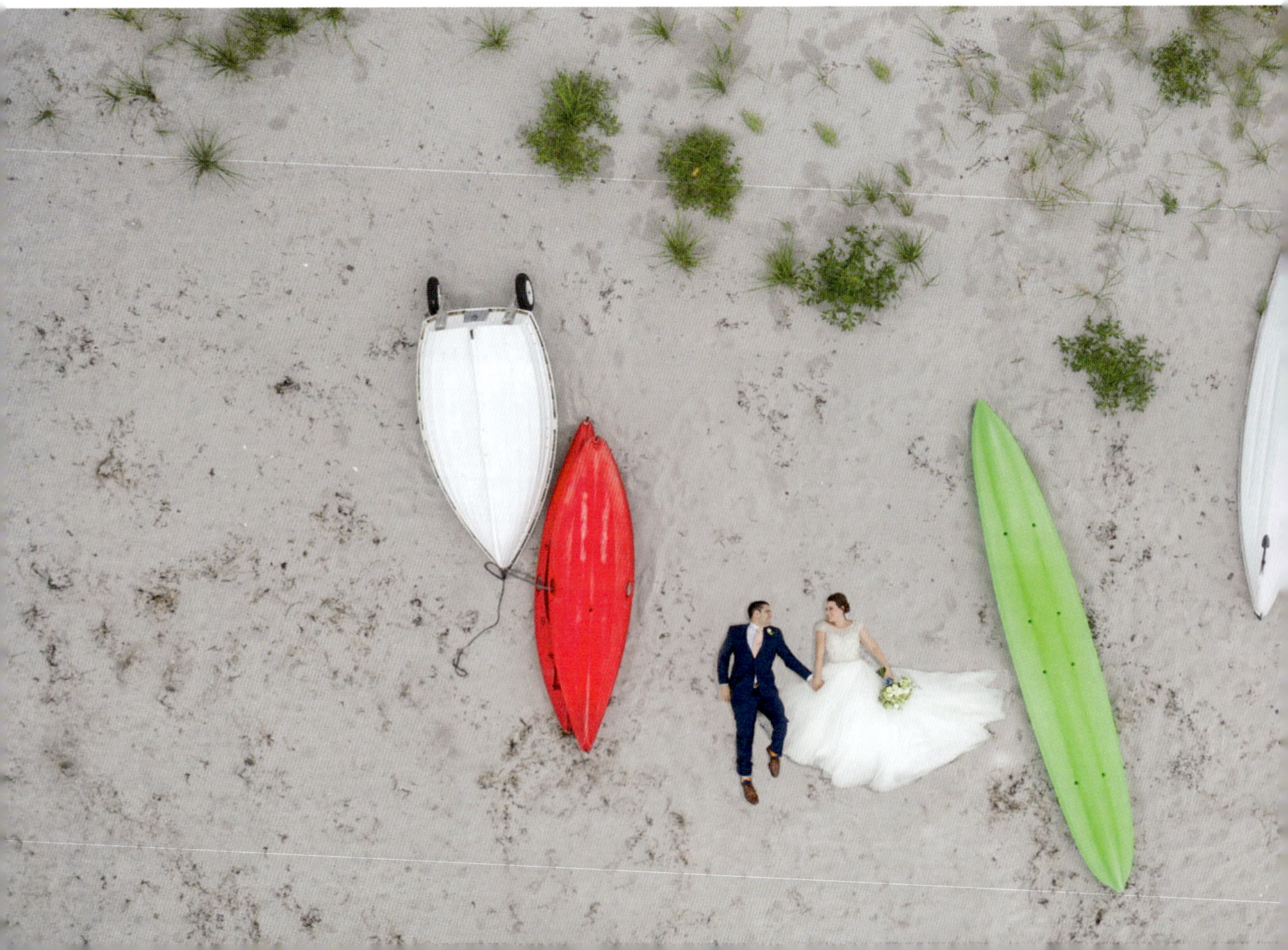

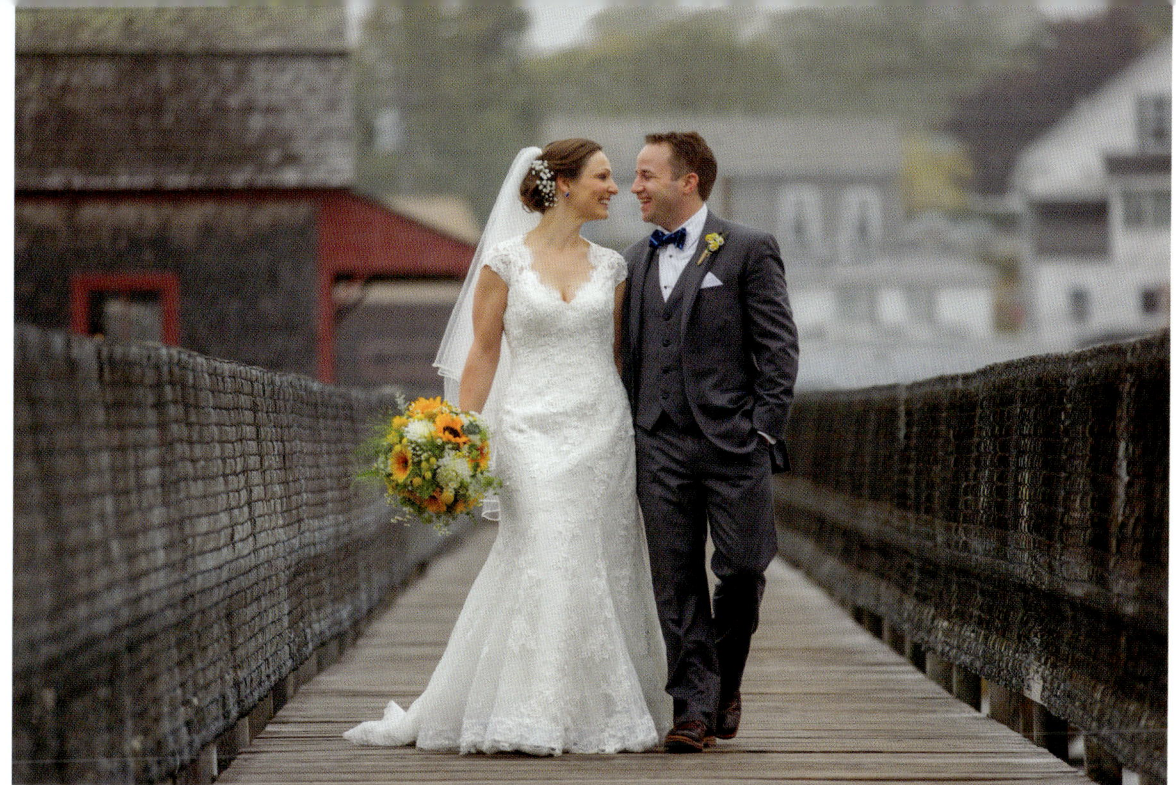

list. When meeting a new coordinator (and, yes, they do tend to change often), get to know them, ask them what you can do for them, etc. Be their friend. Treat these folks like gold; it'll turn out to be one of the very best and least expensive marketing methods you employ.

Other Photographers

Set up a referral network with a small number of like-minded peers with whom you most closely identify. When you receive a lead for a date for which you are unavailable, you can check with the others in your circle, based on whom you feel would be a great fit, to see if they're available. Then send their name(s) along, suggesting to the client that they contact the photographer sooner than later while they still have the date open. Include in your circle only people you trust and would hire without question. You'll have the favor returned to you by them, so it's a win–win.

Advertising

In the chart on page 28, there's no mention of paid advertising in print or on mega wedding websites. This isn't an oversight. Our experience has shown us that print ads aren't a cost-effective marketing strategy for wedding photographers. Your results may vary.

Business Cards

Business cards are still valuable today. We give ours out everywhere we go: we hand them to servers at restaurants, people we meet at networking events, etc. The nicer your business cards, the better the impression you'll make. Ours are printed on thick stock, and we chose a square format to differentiate our business. When we hand out our card, recipients invariably say how impressed they are by its feel and substance. People have even said, "You must be a great photographer with a card like this!"

Handling Requests for the Same Date

Let's say that you've had the fortune (and you will—if not now, eventually!) to end up with two different potential clients who want to hire you for their wedding—and both are on the same day!

After reviewing your offerings, let's say that couple #1, Alex and Sam, write back to say they're interested in moving forward for their wedding on October 20, 2020. Here's what we do: we ask the couple which package they want and then prepare a tentative contract. We return it to the clients to review with the understanding that they aren't under any obligation to accept it. We give the client three days of a "soft hold" on the date. What this means is that while they're reviewing the contract, in the event someone else (couple #2) comes along who also wants the same date, and they're ready to pay the initial fee, we'll give couple #1 a right of "first refusal." Were this to happen, we'd contact couple #1, advise them of the situation, and give them 24 hours to confirm that they're going to accept the contract and to make the first payment.

During this time, we'd tell couple #2 that the date may or may not be available depending on couple #1's decision—and we tell them exactly when we'll be able to let them know.

Without a sound and specific system in place as described above, were the situation to occur of two couples wanting the same date, you may find yourself sounding like you're playing one couple against the other—and that could easily backfire by sending both couples away, never to contact you again, if neither was exactly at the point of being ready to commit. Just be clear, straightforward, and honest to ensure each couple that you're not making a sales ploy.

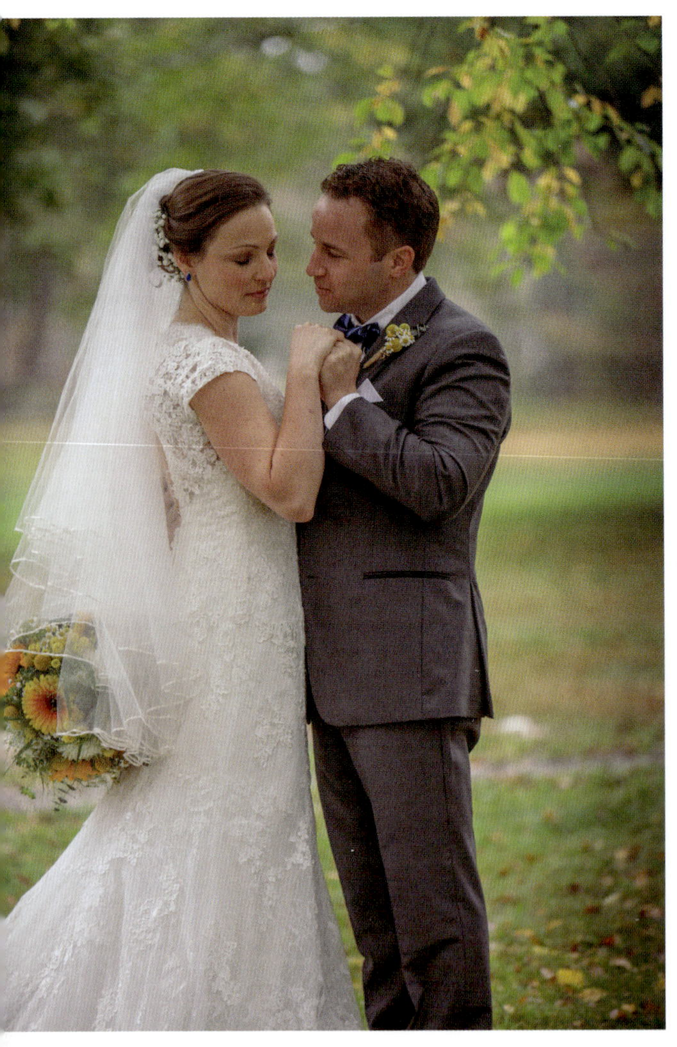

Contracts

Having a well-written contract is as important to the client as it is to you. It's the "script" that dictates and legally solidifies the who, what, when, where, what ifs, and price as it pertains to you photographing the couple's big day.

Depending on whether or not you use studio management software apps (most of which can take care of contract generation and management), the contract itself can exist in a variety of ways. We've had great results with our contract being maintained as a Word document. We keep a template version of it called "blank wedding photography contract," and each time we need to generate a new contract, we save it with the client's name and date in the format "smith 09 07 19" and in a folder specifically for contracts, by year. This folder is kept on a Cloud drive for easy access and redundancy. When it's time to send the contract to the client, we do it in PDF format.

We've had great results with our contract being maintained as a Word document.

The Basics in the Contract

We start, naturally, with the client's name, date of the wedding, day of the week it falls on, location of the ceremony, and location of the reception. To this, we add the name or description of the package the client is buying, what it includes, the total cost, and when the payments are due.

The base pricing should include a reasonably generous travel fee. If the location to which we need to travel for the wedding is beyond a comfortable driving distance, we add a cost to cover time and mileage. If the location is far enough away and we can't get back home at a time we're comfortable with (midnight?), we'll add in lodging costs.

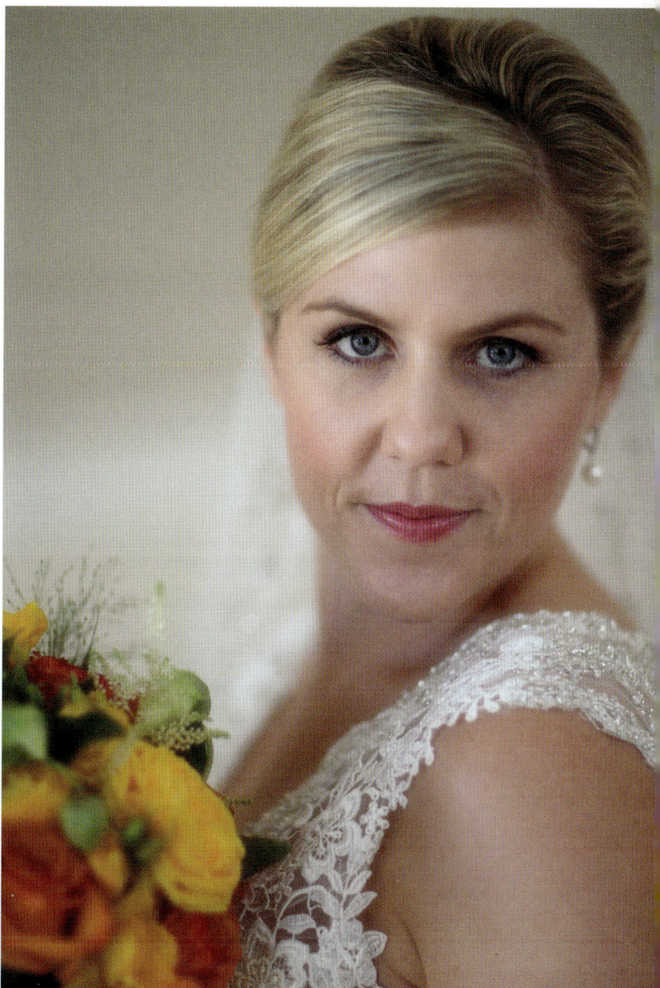

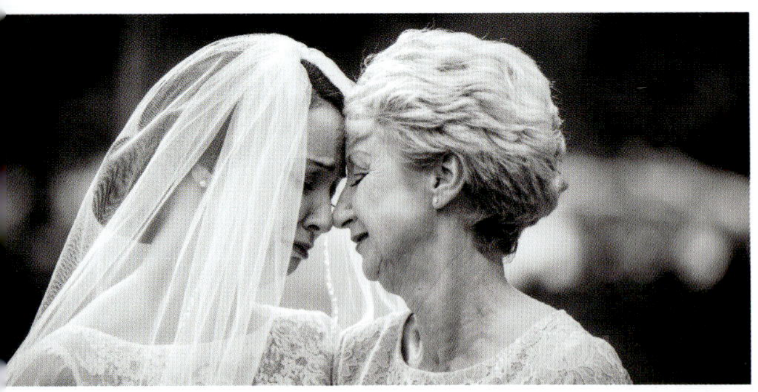

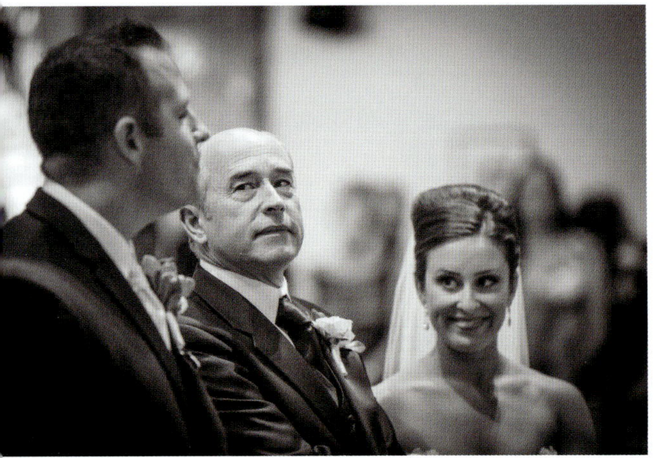

We remove as many opportunities for prospective clients to go to someone else as we can, while ensuring we are fairly compensated for every aspect of the wedding photography process.

For consistency, we always use the name of one of the people getting married as the client.

There's a lot more to talk about in this section, so let's continue, one point at a time.

For consistency, we always use the name of one of the people getting married as the client. This generally means the bride. Regardless of who's paying, we want this key person to be the one with whom we're contracting.

Of course, listing the date of the wedding is essential. So, why does the contract also expressly mention the day of the week of the wedding? We've been told the incorrect date more than once, but couples never say the wedding is on Sunday when they mean Saturday. So, we'd catch this showshopper of an error and check back with them right away.

The contract specifies the dates that installment payments are due for the contract. To help level-load our cash flow, we take the total and split the amount into four payments due before the wedding, as follows: (1) with the contract signing; (2) nine months before (3); six months before; and (4) two months before the wedding date. We call the first payment a booking fee, not a retainer or a deposit. It's applied to the client's balance, of course. The reason why we use this terminology is that, were it to come to a court of law, retainers and deposits will more likely be deemed refundable, despite what your contract may or may not say about refunds. We use these words to explain the booking fee:

> *At the time the contract takes effect, the Photographer reserves the date for the Client and will refuse other requests for services from others for that date. For this reason, in the event the Client cancels the contract for any reason, the amount shown as the booking fee, plus any subsequent payments made shall be retained by the Photographer to offset the loss of business.*

There are many sound reasons to schedule the four payments at the staggered points in time. First, were the wedding to be canceled, the amount paid increases as the time draws near, proportionate to the loss it's likely you'll take for the lack of work. Next is the smoother cash flow. Another is that under no circumstances do you want to collect money on (or even close to) the wedding day, because the first thing you'll hear is "Oh, I don't have my checkbook or cards with me!" Our clients have a 100 percent on-time payment track record, but if that were not the case, having two months before the wedding day to sort out any remaining balance would be essential. In no case do you want to wait until after the wedding to collect any of the fees associated with your coverage or time. If there isn't enough time ahead of the wedding to use these payment points, adjust them to suit your needs, but always ensure you are paid in full two months before the wedding.

We're very good to work with in all regards, but we're always quick to send reminders of late payments, in the rare cases they occur, starting at the first moment a payment was due and not received. People tend to first pay the people with whom they know they don't have any slack.

We send electronic reminders of upcoming payments at two weeks and one week ahead of the due dates. Invoices were already mailed more than one month but not more than two months in advance.

We send electronic reminders of upcoming payments at two weeks and one week ahead of the due dates.

Studio management software can do all of this for you. However, our system works well, there are no monthly fees, and most importantly, it allows us to keep a finger on the pulse of our business. We'll consider a studio management app when the day comes that we cannot manage the data for the number of weddings

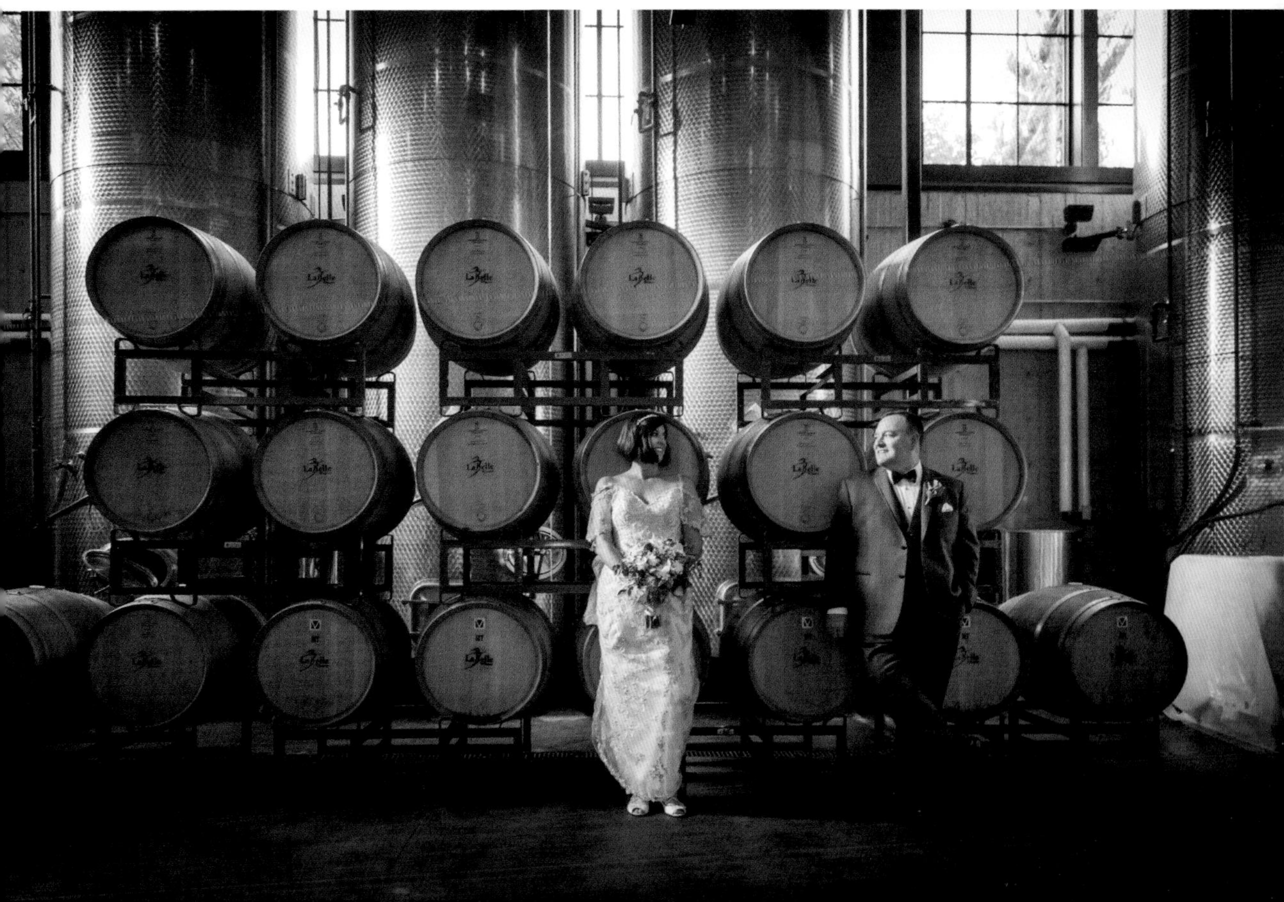

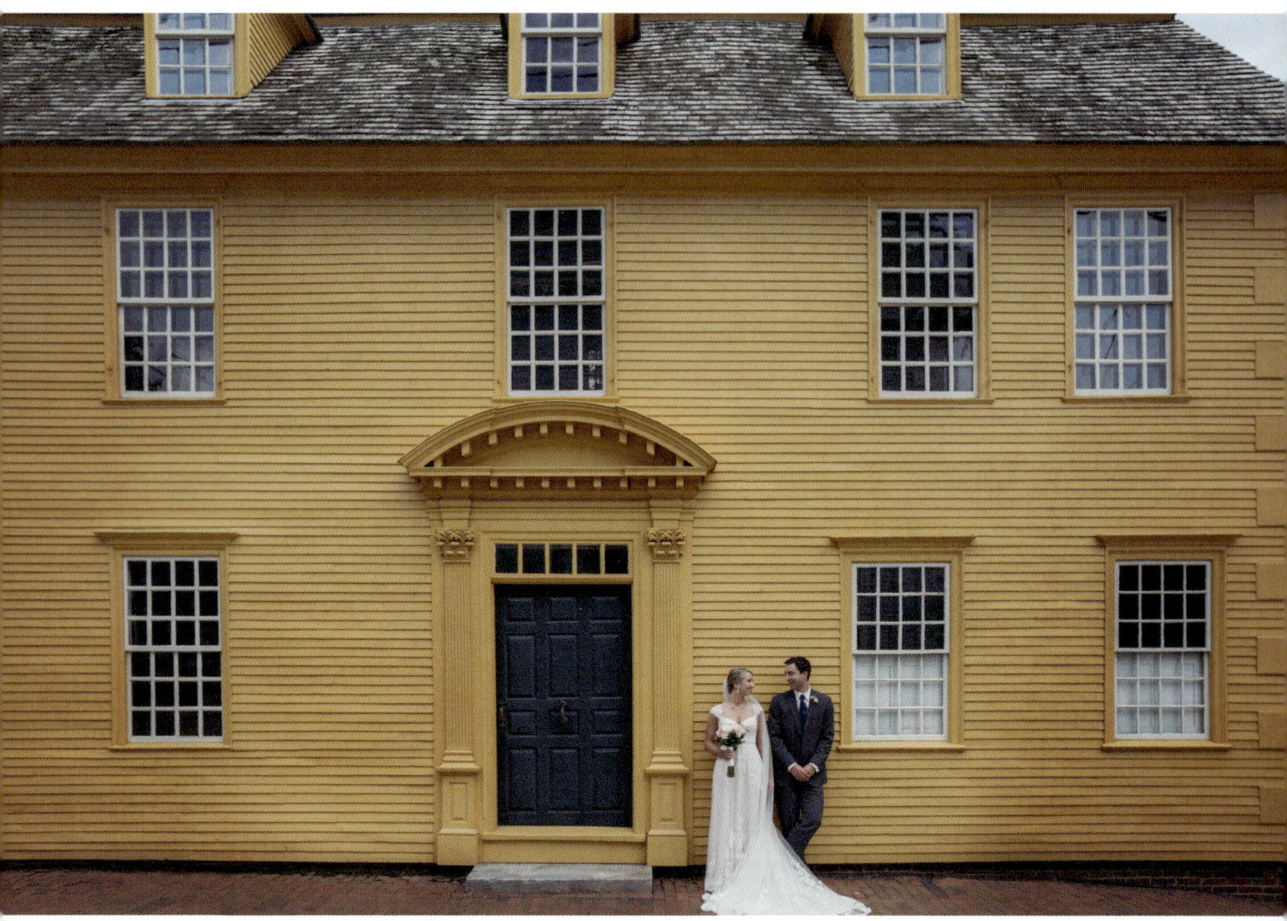

we photograph each year, but so far, that hasn't happened.

Credit Cards

Processing credit and debit cards comes with fees that add up surprisingly fast. We accept cards for only the first of the four payments for a wedding contract. We clearly spell this out in our contract and in follow-up invoicing.

Other Contract Details

The wedding photography contract covers a wide variety of important topics that must be clearly stated to avoid confusion, complications, potential image misuse, and to set clear expectations and responsibilities of everyone involved. Let's take a look, in general terms, at the main things that should be included.

In virtually all cases, a photographer owns the right to the images he or she takes.

Copyright Licensing. In virtually all cases, a photographer owns the right to the images he or she takes. You don't want to give up that right in any way, so for weddings, you, as the copyright owner, will license (but relinquish your rights to) the images to the client for their unlimited personal use. Here, too, is where you'll spell out that you retain the right to use

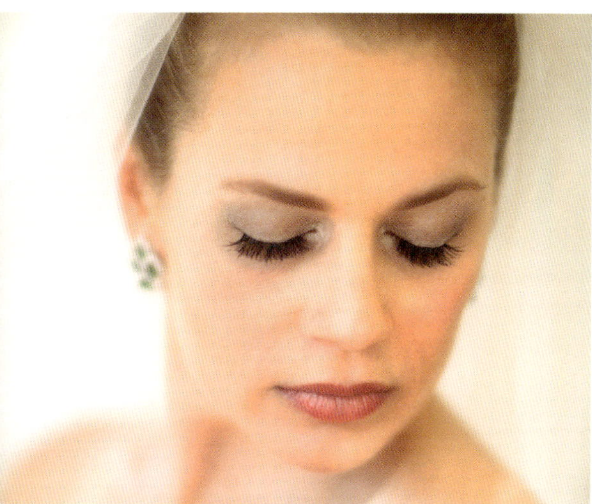

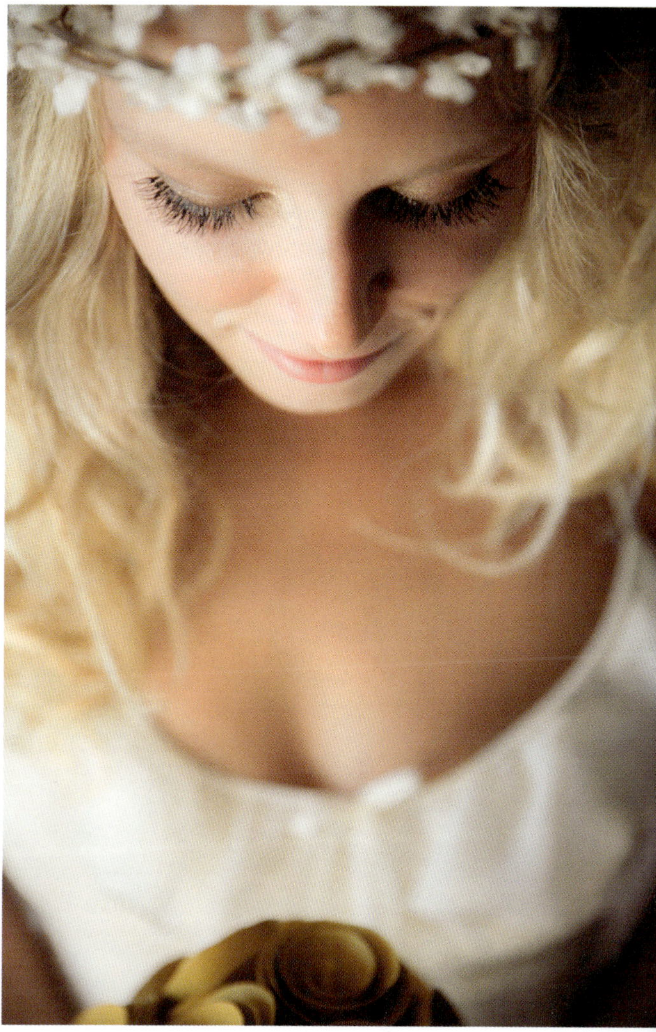

images for promotional (and perhaps competition) purposes. This personal-use license specifically prohibits the use of the wedding images for any commercial purposes. Clients seeking commercial use would need to obtain a separate license to do so, with an appropriate fee charged.

Image Delivery. We build the cost of a full set of digital image files into our wedding packages. That is all spelled out in the contract. You'll want to specify the format (JPEG; don't deliver Raw files) and the type of media download or drive you'll be using for delivery. Don't ever promise an exact delivery date, as unexpected things can happen. Do state something like, "We generally deliver your images within eight weeks of the wedding." We also clearly state that unless the client purchases archiving options from us, the delivery of the images constitutes transfer of the original set of files from us, the photographers, to them, the client. Your contract should specify if you'll be delivering full-resolution JPEG images, or images with an intentional size restriction, such as low- or medium-resolution formats. We'll detail archiving and sizing options later in this book.

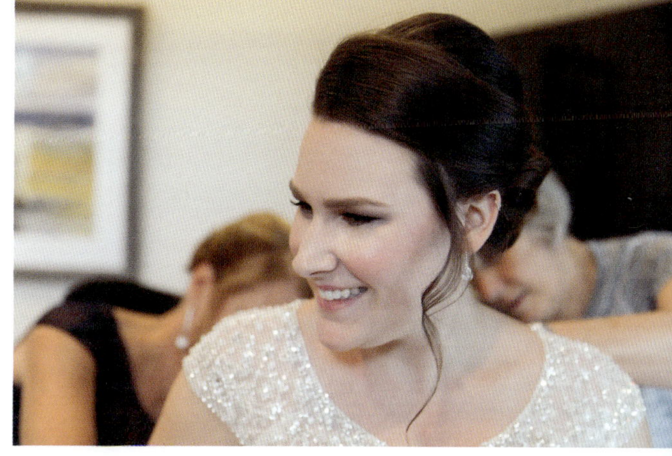

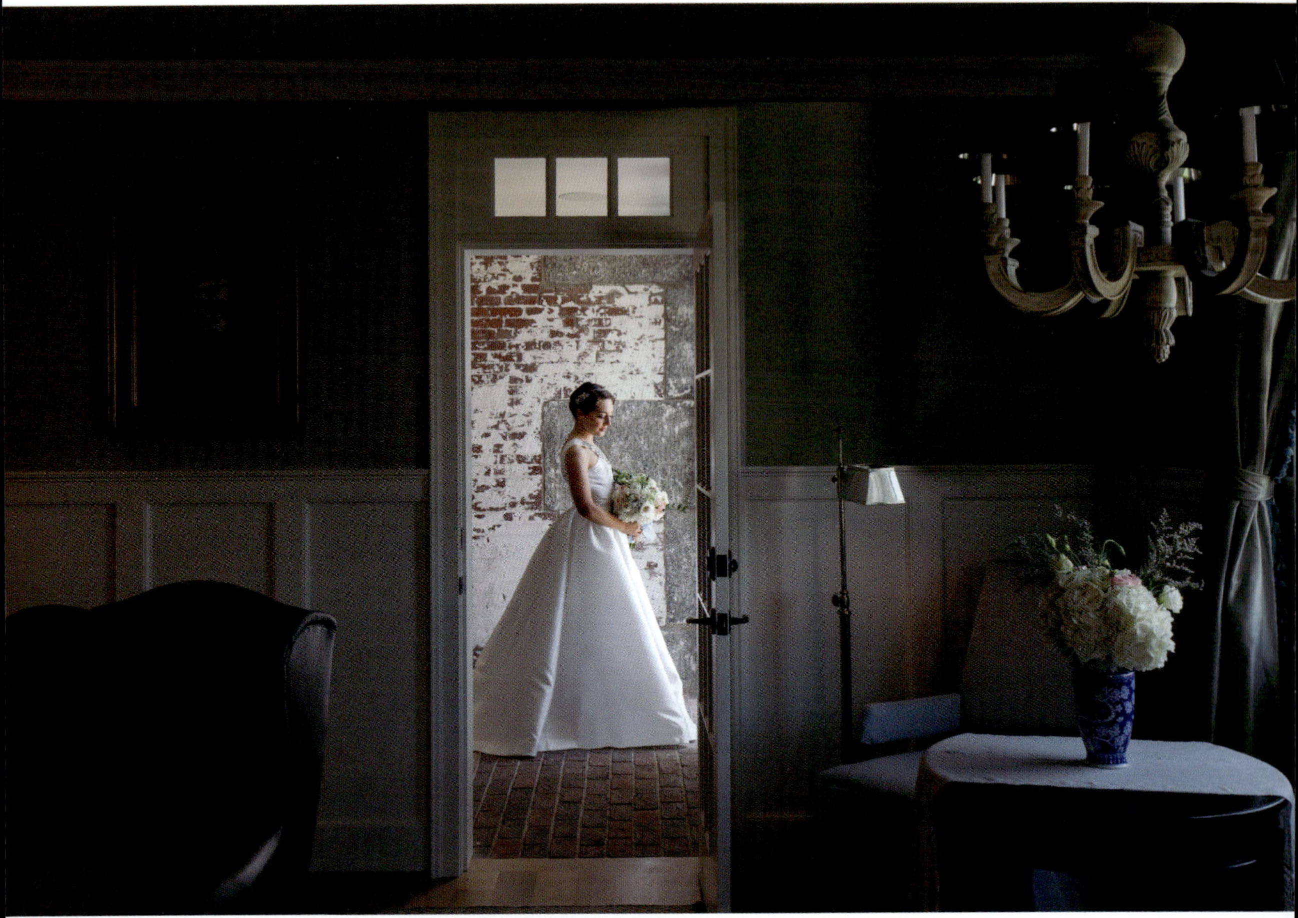

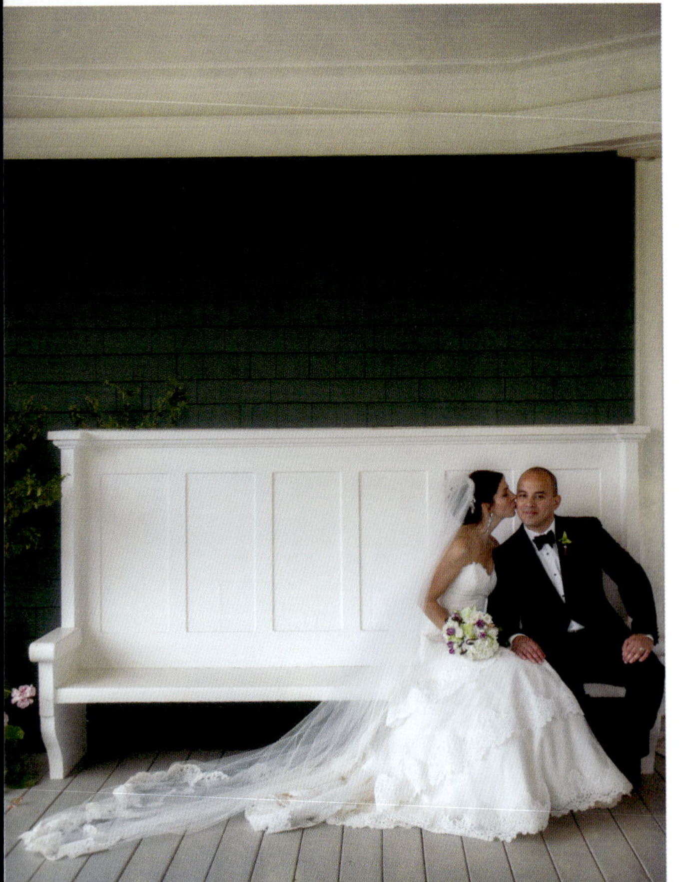

Image Editing and Culling. Let's review this carefully, as it's very important.

You'll want to clearly state that you edit images for photographic correctness (exposure, cropping, reducing highlights, increasing shadows, straighting horizons, and the like). You'll also want to clearly state that editing for things that are out of the photographer's control may be available at an additional cost.

Now, keep in mind that you have the full right to additionally process your favorite batch of images from the wedding to a higher degree. And yes, you should do this. What does this mean? Well, for each wedding, we go through and select an assortment of our favorite shots from the start to the end of the day—about 50 to 75 photos—to feature in our blog post for that wedding. These generally receive some level of "artistic touch" editing, meaning things like the exit sign that you could not possibly be responsible to edit out in all the images *does* get edited out for that amazing first-dance shot where it's visible, in all its glowing red glory, behind the couple. Those distracting power lines in an otherwise gorgeous outdoor shot? Gone! This is done in Photoshop. Not good or kind of rusty with Photoshop? Take classes and practice. This is a key tool of your trade.

Another important point, and one we'll talk more about in a later section, is culling. Culling is when you choose the "keepers" from the full set of images taken. Resist the temptation to be quantity based, and instead focus on being quality based. We include at least one of

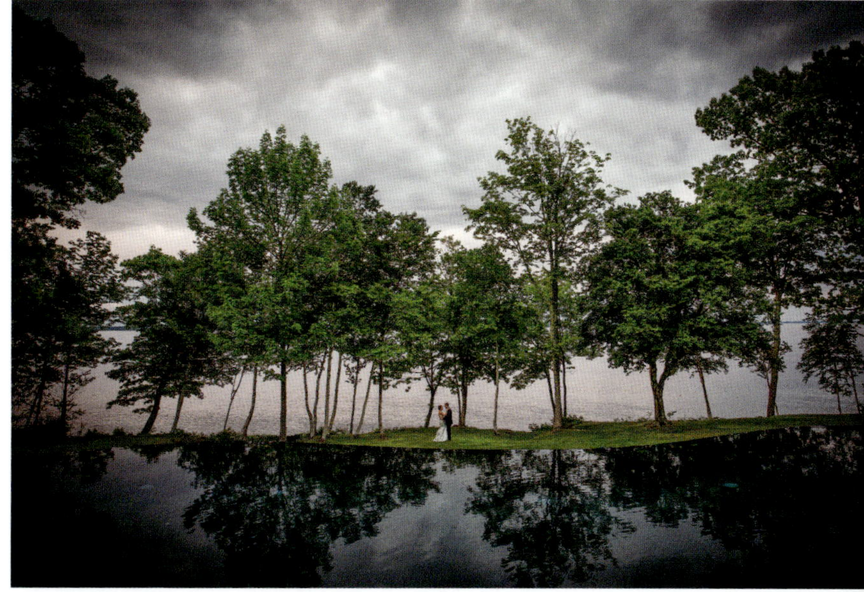

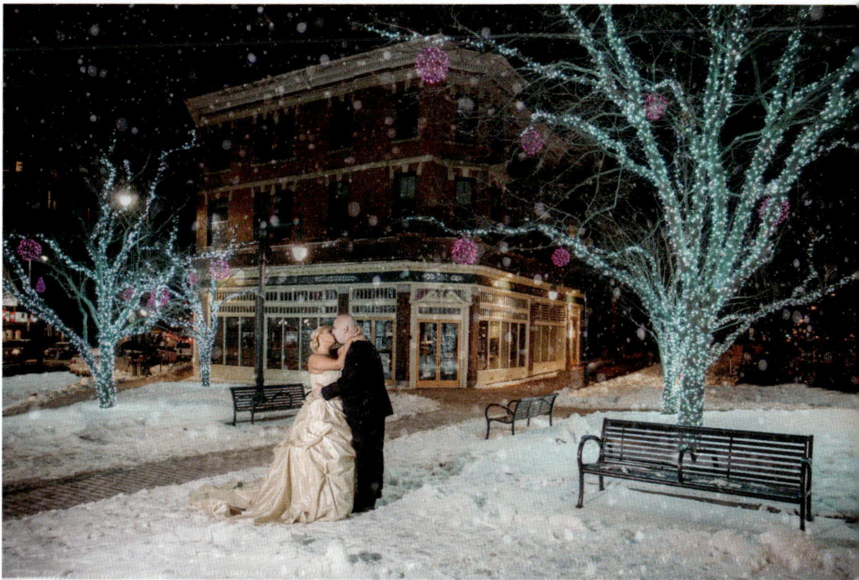

the best images from everything we set up, like bridal portraits, for example. But in the creation of that one amazing shot, we may have taken a dozen or three dozen more; we only pick the one best. Sending clients multiple similar photos will overwhelm them and give the appearance of slipshod editing on your part. You'll want to include a much higher percentage of the candid and journalistic images you took, as they vary more. Be deliberate in your shooting, and as you gain experience, you'll ease back from "spray and pray" rapid over-firing. You'll thank yourself for coming back with very thorough coverage with half the number of overall images as you once may have had. Keep in mind that until you gain a high degree of proficiency with culling and editing, you'll

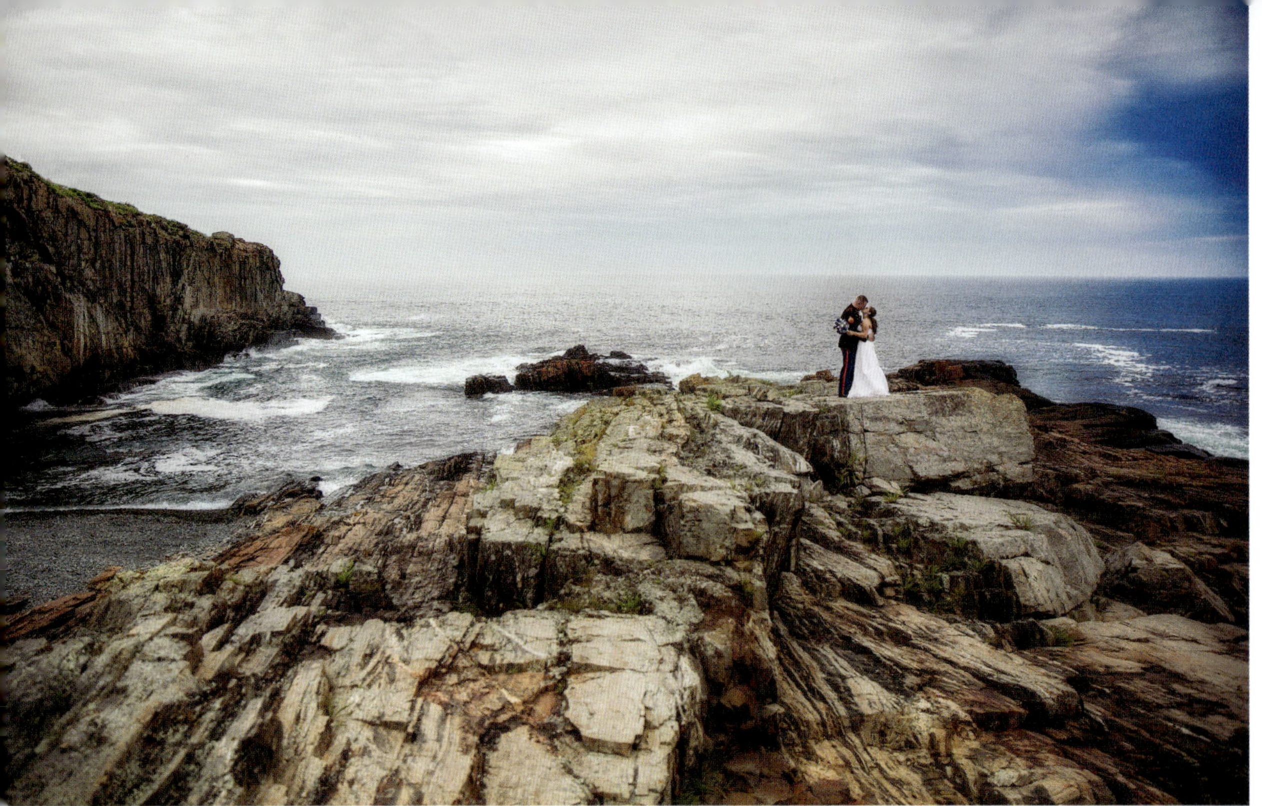

likely spend in the postproduction process at least the same number of hours as the wedding itself took.

Never promise that a certain number of images will be delivered. Doing so will set you up for not being able to meet your own contract language, and/or including images that don't deserve to be included. Do, however, provide an indication of what your couple is likely to expect. We say, "Most weddings yield between xx–yy delivered images per hour of coverage (including the images by the second photographer), but every wedding is different, so it's not possible to guarantee an amount." Modify to suit, but you get the idea. For us, this range is 50 to 60 images per hour of coverage. Occasionally, the amount is higher, but it's almost never less. Since this represents a delivered set of 500–600 images from a ten-hour wedding day shoot, we're rarely, or ever, for that matter, pressed to answer the question, "Are there more?"

Lastly, it's imperative that your contract states that you, the photographer, have the exclusive right to decide what to include and exclude and to determine how the processing is handled. Just be sure to give the client at least one image from every different shot you set up. Be consistent, and deliver images that represent your style and what is shown in your portfolio.

Be consistent, and deliver images that represent your style and what is shown in your portfolio.

Style. Speaking of style, it's a good idea to have a paragraph in your contract that states that the client acknowledges their familiarity with your photographic style and "requests services in accordance with that style." Why? If your style is clear, natural color, with spot-on exposure, you don't want clients asking you to process their images with a desaturated and under-exposed mood, do you? Stick to and show the work in your style, not that of someone else.

Photography By Others. You might want a paragraph in your contract that puts reasonable "controls" on photography by others. Mostly, this is to ensure that your work is not impeded by others. We mention that photography by guests at the ceremony and reception is allowed, but photography by other professional photographers is not. Also, we don't allow anyone to "shoot over our shoulders" for things we set up or direct.

Ideally, your clients will opt to have (perhaps on your urging) an "unplugged" wedding—or at the least, an unplugged ceremony. It'll keep the chaos to a minimum and let the guests concentrate on what they are there to witness in the first place.

In the event that rampant and errant photography by

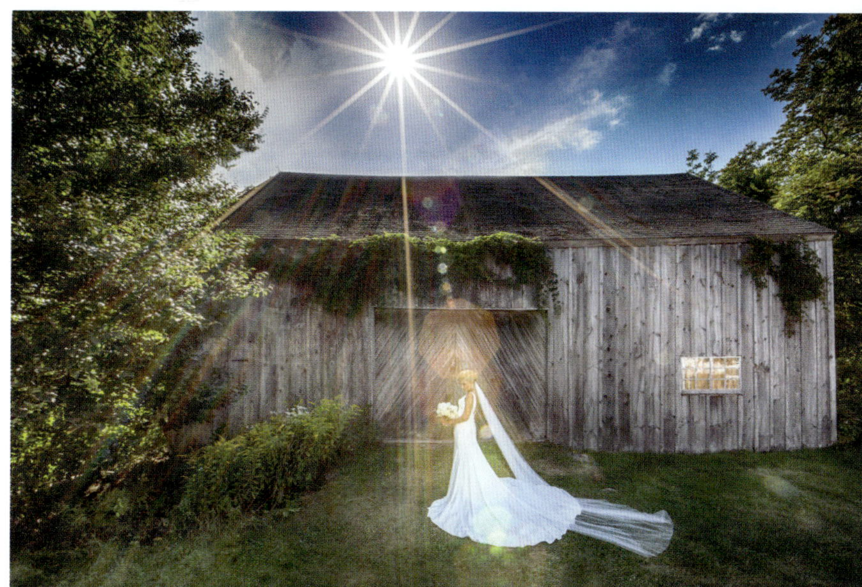

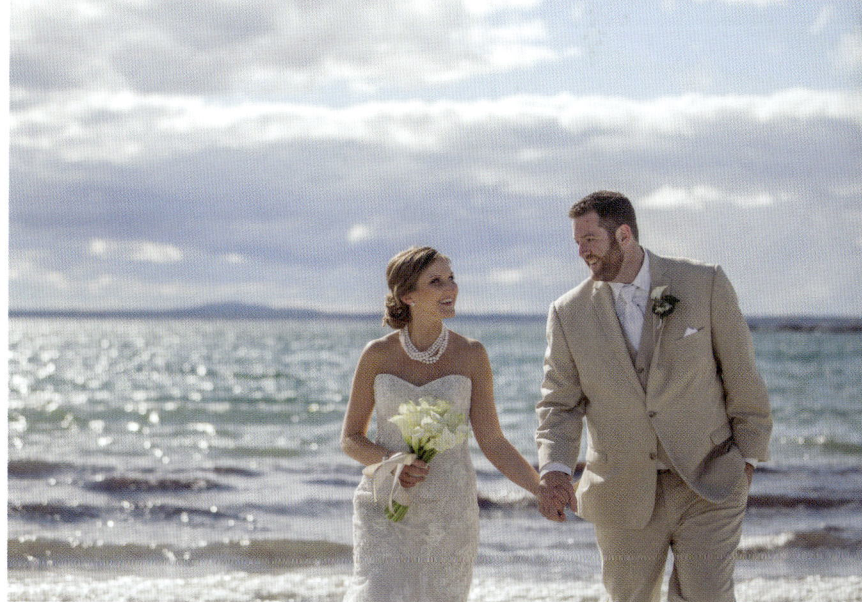

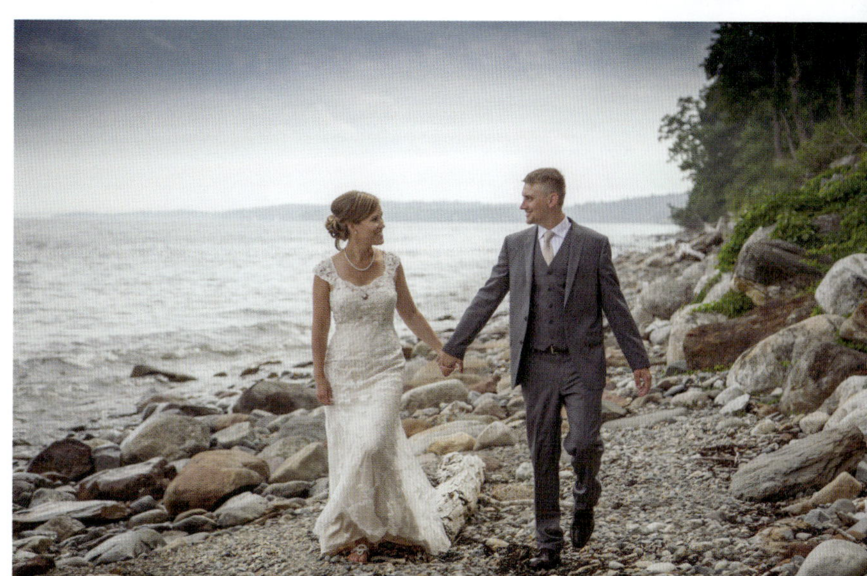

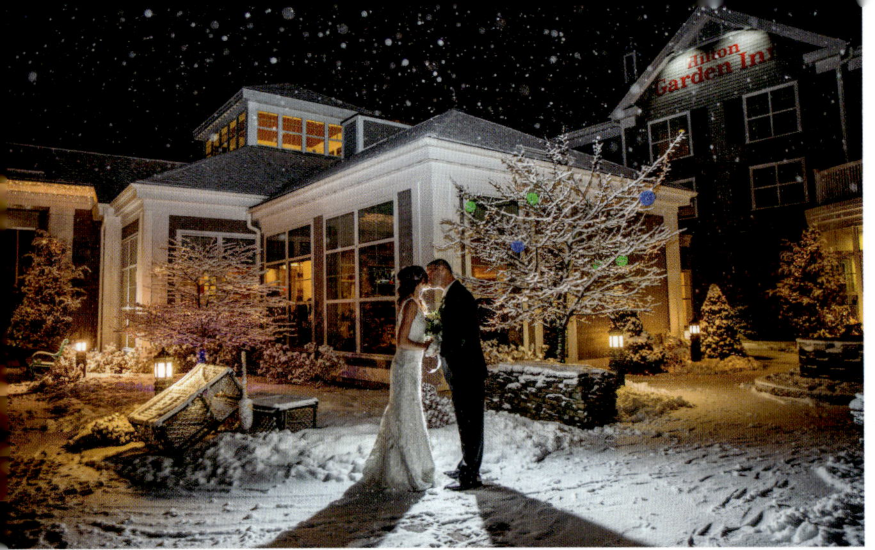

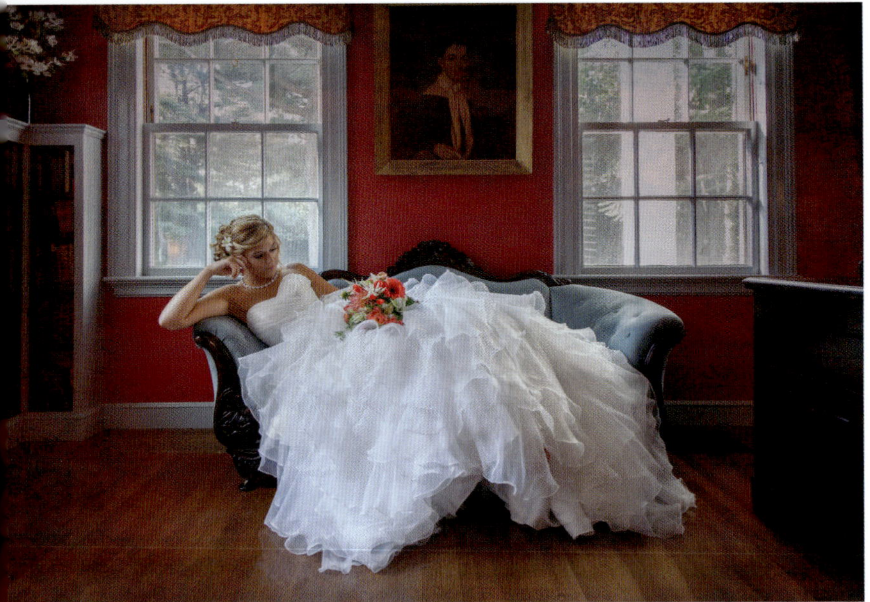

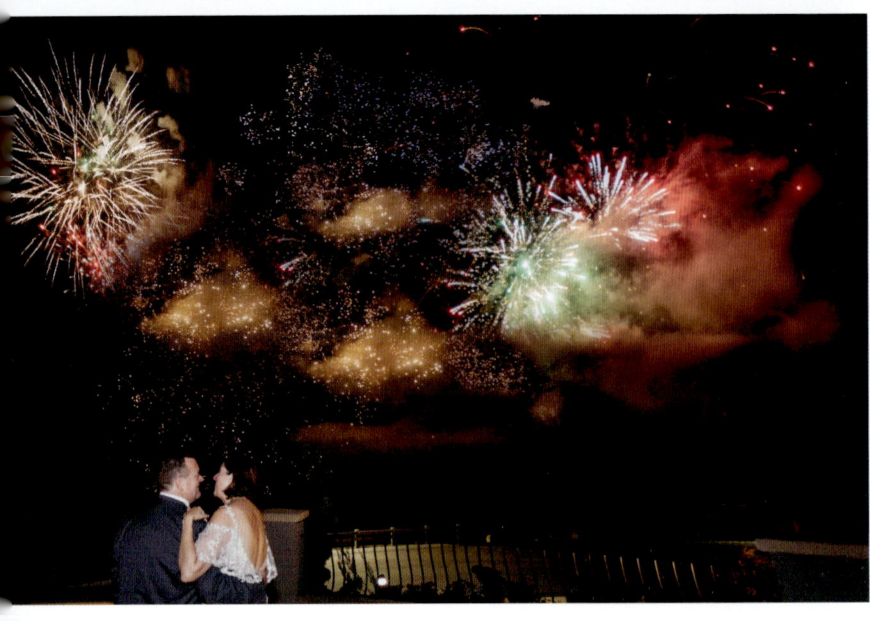

others occurs, you'll need to be in control. Handle any issues that arise professionally and firmly. You have a job to do and a limited amount of time in which to do it. You don't need unnecessary distractions.

Videographers. Also addressed in our contract is the topic of outside videographers. If the videography will be provided by your own company or someone you're subcontracting, then the considerations here really won't apply, because you'll get to call all the shots. If that is not the case, however, it'll pay big dividends to have your clients select a videographer from a list you provide of professionals who will "play well" with you as the photographer, and vice versa. At a minimum, ensure that the contract states that when there's an outside videographer and a conflict for who-gets-to-go-where arises, you, the still photographer, will take precedence. We are always respectful. Each of us has a job to do, and we can support each other, because in the end, it's our mutual client who matters most. We play nice, and professionally.

Albums. If the contract with your clients includes albums, spell out the details of how you handle that. Indicate a finite number of minutes/hours or rounds of revisions the client will be given for edits to the design. Without this, you have a potential "leak in the dam" that could cost you far more in time than the value of the album sale. You may also want to stipulate a time period after which proposed designs are discontinued because, oddly enough, clients tend to drop the ball on approving album designs. Some have been known to resurface years later.

Coverage Hours. Your contract should clearly state the number of hours of coverage by each photographer and list the lead and second photographer (if any) by name, if known at this point. Indicate how you handle requests for added time on the wedding day, and the associated charge.

Our on-duty time on the wedding day is contiguous, and yours should be, too. Once we start the clock, it doesn't stop until it's time to leave. We clearly explain this in the contract. If a wedding contract is for ten hours of coverage, our end time is exactly ten hours after we begin—all in accordance with the timeline we've developed together. (More on that later.)

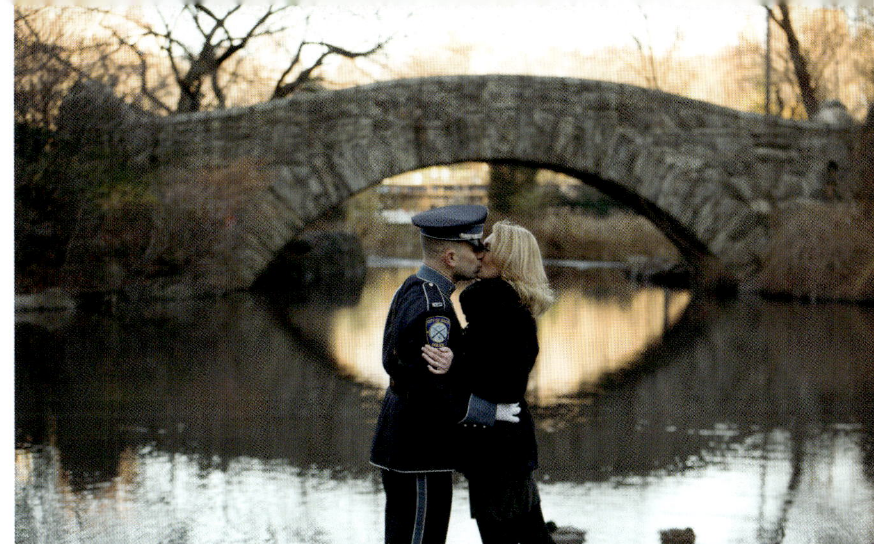

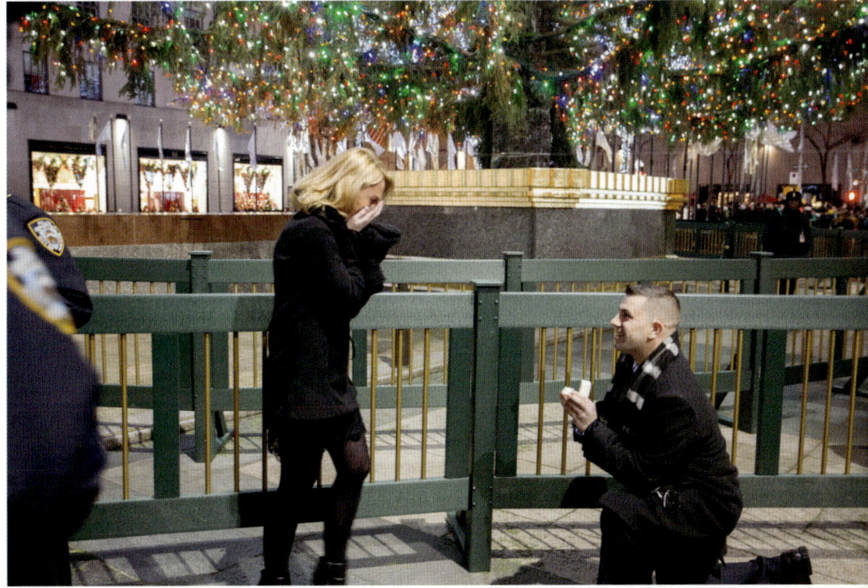

The clock doesn't stop for anything. This is really important. We're careful in our planning to be sure that the time we'll be there is adequate to cover all the key phases of the day. If a client has opted for a package with fewer hours than other packages you offer, do not put in any

If a wedding contract is for ten hours of coverage, our end time is exactly ten hours after we begin.

overtime without being compensated. If you were to do so, it would be unfair to those who purchased longer coverage, and unfair to you to work uncompensated. Again, it's all about planning to ensure you never find yourself in the awkward position of it being time to leave, though not everything has yet happened that needs to be photographed. We're helping you run a real business here.

We rarely suggest that there's a need for us to stay until the end of the reception. There's usually no reason to do so. Having 30 minutes of dance/party photos is typically more than sufficient to tell the story of the day. The time is better spent capturing the things happening earlier in the day. There may be exceptions, so be ready to recognize those cases.

Meals. Indicate in your contract what your meal requirements are. Almost more than anyone else at the wedding, it's the photographers who've often not eaten for many hours. Point out that your meal must be served when the wedding party is served so that you're up and ready to get back to actively photographing as soon as the couple and the wedding party are done eating. Besides, there's no graceful or otherwise acceptable way to photograph people who are eating. You're going to want your clients to expressly state these requirements to the caterers or venue. Otherwise, your need to eat will be on the back burner.

Payment Terms. State payment terms clearly. Say what will happen if a payment is late. Also, indicate that if substantive elements of the wedding change (e.g., the date or other important terms), it may be cause for cancellation of the existing contract. How you handle the financial implications is up to you, but be sure to address these issues in your contract. You must guard against any lost opportunity for income.

Replacement Photographer. It's important to address what would happen if, for some reason, you—the lead photographer—could

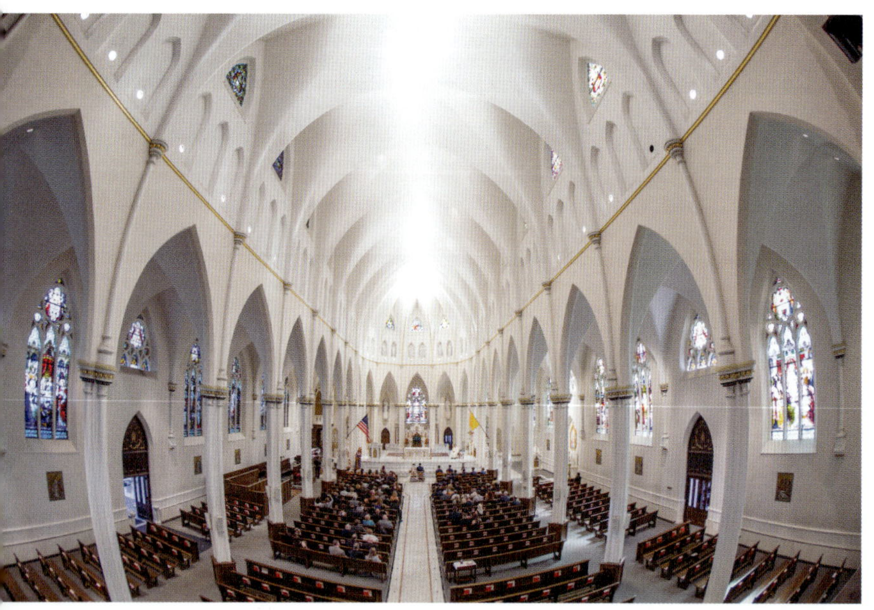

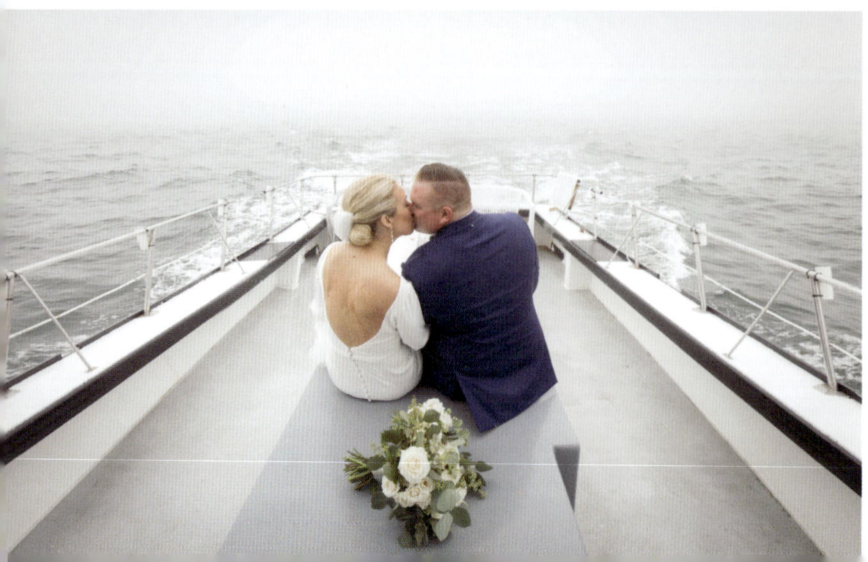

not attend on the wedding day. Our contract states, "In the event the lead photographer is unable to attend due to illness or an unforeseen emergency, the photographer shall send a replacement of similar skill." You should also state in your contract what would happen if the backup photographer could not attend. Have a plan in place. Determine who you would call if you couldn't attend a wedding for which you're contracted.

These are the main topics we feel every wedding photography contract should include, but there may be others. We recommend that you say what you need to say, as pleasantly as possible, and keep the client's interests in mind. That said, don't say anything more than you need to. Keep things simple. An overly technical, complicated, long-winded, not clearly written, or overly restrictive contract could lose you a potential client. It's first-hand experience speaking here.

You'll probably want to hire an attorney to

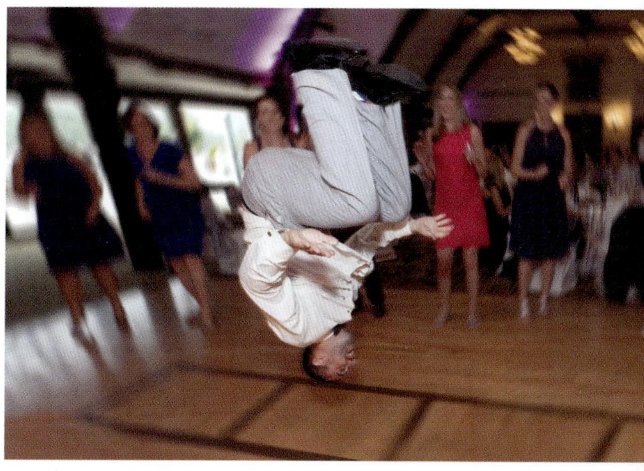

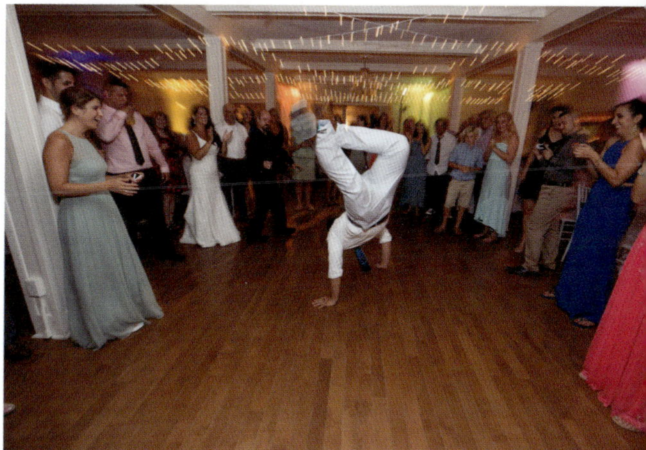

> You'll probably want to hire an attorney to review and approve your contract . . .

review and approve your contract, but do avoid filling it with excessive legal jargon.

Client Information Form

Within the contract, we ask clients to handwrite a few things over again that are already well-known to everyone. These include the date and day of the week of the wedding. Having the couple write the information yet again is another cross-check and provides a measure of insurance against errors.

When we obtain the client's email information, we ask them to provide an address that they'll continue to monitor after the wedding. This is because many couples set up a special email account that they use solely for wedding-related business. We communicate perhaps even more after the wedding, so we want to be sure we have a good email address.

Client Relationships

We like to treat our clients and prospects with professionalism, courtesy, promptness, and friendliness.

Another client relationship aspect we're proud of is that we set clear expectations. We

> We like to treat our clients and prospects with professionalism, courtesy, promptness, and friendliness.

use precise communication and keep them abreast of where things stand and when they can expect things to happen. We also make it a habit to under-promise and over-deliver.

What do we mean by this? First, we don't promise an exact date for anything, though we do communicate an expected date for milestones. The date we propose is a date we will— barring unforeseen circumstances—be able to keep. We try our best to beat that date by a week or so; we under-promise and over-deliver. Just because you haven't promised an exact date doesn't mean you don't need to be diligent and turn things around in a timely manner.

Setting clear expectations starts early in the process. It begins with the setting of the timeline (next section), which says to the client that we care how the day will run and are here to help make that happen. It asks them to give us

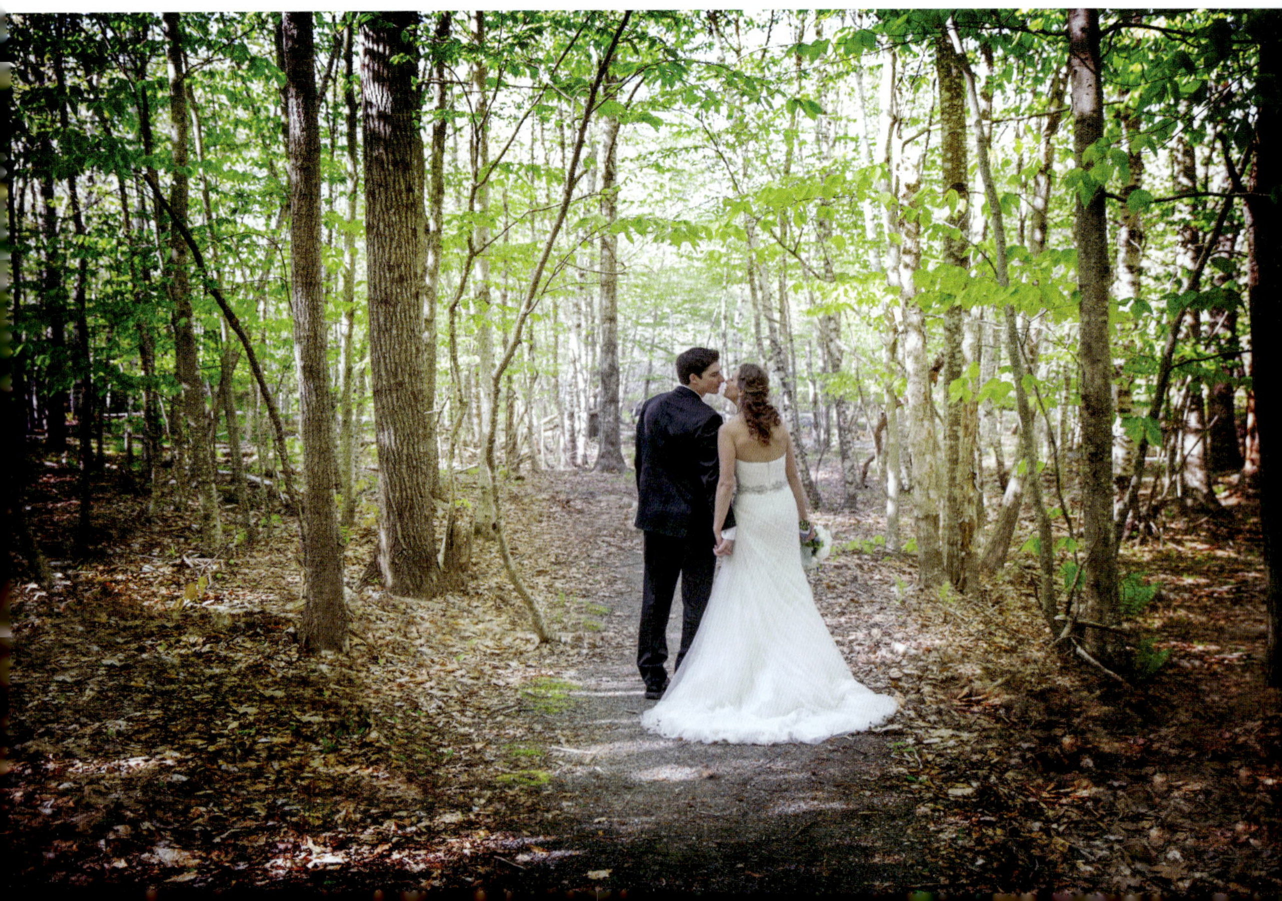

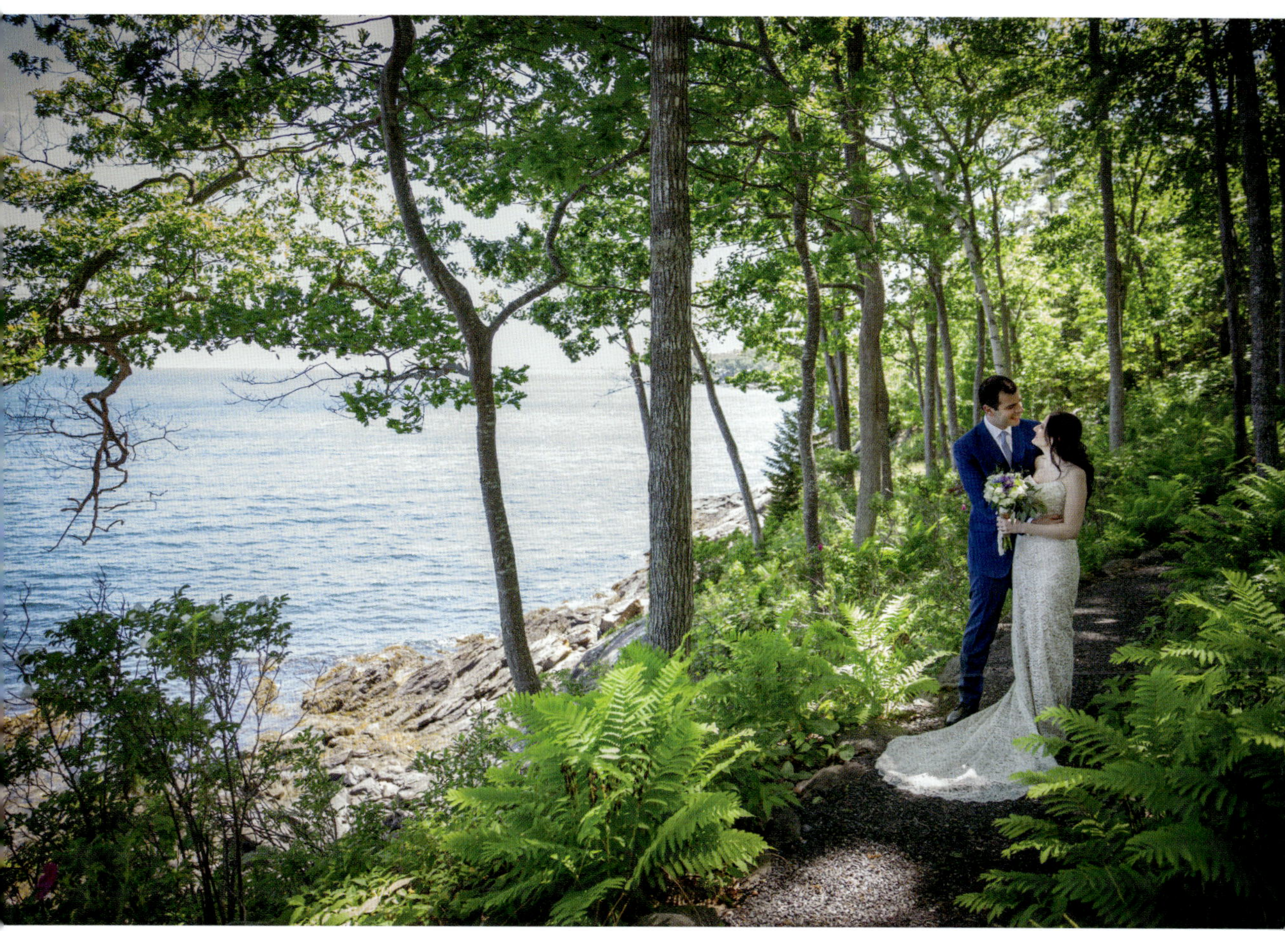

key information, which we in turn use to propose back to them an outline of the day that otherwise, in most cases, no one really would do. The give-and-take involved with agreeing on this forms a key part of the setting of expectations. The clients know what they need to do, and we know what we need to do. They learn what time the florals are needed, when the hair and makeup artists need to be done, the time the family needs to be ready, and where the need to meet. It's all the little things that are far better to have a plan for ahead of time. People are generally very happy to oblige, they just need to know what's expected of them.

You will want to do everything in your power to leave a very positive impression with your client. This includes your presentation, demeanor, timeliness, effectiveness, and all the things that define you doing your work. Having awesome photographs on its own isn't enough;

You will want to do everything in your power to leave a very positive impression with your client.

the overall (positive) client experience is a really big piece of working toward being referred by them time and again. We like to give our clients the treatment that we would like to receive were the tables turned.

Timeline Planning

Most of the weddings we photograph are at resort hotels, where the hotel staff establishes the timeline, but only from the end of the ceremony, starting with the beginning of the cocktail party. Without an external planner, who sets the schedule for all the things that happen prior to then? We do! Developing a timeline of how the wedding day will flow from the time the photography begins until things transition to the cocktail hour and reception stage is an enormous benefit to us as wedding photographers, as well as to the bride, groom, their wedding party, and families.

A well-developed timeline is one of the things a bride will remember being valuable on the wedding day—and it's equally valuable to you, as the wedding photographer.

A well-developed timeline is one of the things a bride will remember being valuable on the wedding day . . .

We developed a simple spreadsheet in Microsoft Excel that does much of the work for us in making a realistic, workable, achievable timeline that leads up to the point at which the hotel or venue folks take over. (The chart on the following page shows a sample timeline.) Since doing this, our wedding days have flowed very smoothly. We have very few schedule-related issues on the wedding day. Our clients love that, four months ahead, we've worked with them to create this mutually agreed-upon script for the day.

When we make our spreadsheet, we start with the time of the ceremony. It's one of the only "givens" the bride will know well ahead of time. We work backward from there, setting time slots needed for the things that will happen prior to the ceremony. The bride will often have an idea of the duration of the ceremony, and this allows planning to occur once the ceremony ends. You'll stay on the venue coordinator's good side by sticking to their schedule for the rest of the coverage time. An exception: Let the coordinator know if you'll need to take the couple outdoors at sunset for fireworks or a sparkler send-off. The sparkler "exit" is often best staged at an earlier hour rather than at the end of the wedding. This is because your contracted coverage times will not likely extend to the end of the night, and there will be more guests present at an earlier time. Also, the guests will theoretically be in better condition to wave the burning sticks earlier in the evening! (Speaking of sparklers: recommend that your clients get long sparklers and have a number of candle lighters handy.)

Working on either side of the ceremony start and end time, we enter the duration of various events, in minutes, and have written formulas so that Excel calculates the start and end times accordingly. Our hours of coverage

WEDDING DAY (with FIRST LOOK) TIMELINE PLANNER for PHOTOGRAPHY PURPOSES

©2019 Russell Caron Wedding Photography		*Nick & Meaghan*	
Version 2 - 3/4/19	Meaghan M		Nicholas C
	9/20/19 Friday		Unplugged y/n: Y
Version 2 - 3/4/1	Kennebunkport Hotel	Sunset: 8:29PM	Video y/n: N
	Bridal party bm+gm: 3+3 Guests:~125		Officiant: Matt Hartley
	Photographers* start at	12:30 PM	
	and end at	8:30 PM	
Bride's bouquet is needed at this time	12:30 PM		
Events:	*Event start time*	*duration (mins)*	
Photographer start time	12:30 PM	0	
details and candids will also check in with men during this time, around 12:30PM	12:30 PM	60	
bride's hair and makeup must be done by this time CANNOT RUN OVER (only the bride must be done now)	1:30 PM		CRITICAL EVENT NOTE TIME
bride down time/lunch	1:30 PM	5	
bride start into gown and fully dressed	1:35 PM	15	
bridal portraits then transition to first look location	1:50 PM	15	
first look -	2:05 PM	15	
artistic set	2:20 PM	45	
bridal party photos -	3:05 PM	20	
family photos	3:25 PM	20	
down time before ceremony	3:45 PM	15	
Ceremony	4:00 PM	15	CEREMONY
transition to cocktail hour	4:15 PM	0	
cockltail hour	4:15 PM	60	
transition to announce in	5:15 PM	0	
approx asnnounce in time	5:15 PM	0	
all events to be photogrqphed must be completed within 30 mins before photographer end time	5:15 PM	180	
Sunset photos	8:15 PM	15	
Photographer end time	8:30 PM	0	
*second photographer ends earlier than lead photographer			

are contiguous, meaning that we end the number of contract hours after we start, with no breaks or deductions. You need to do this, too.

About four months ahead of each wedding, an information document is sent by email to each client. It has them consider important things like if they'll see each other before the ceremony with a first look. About 85 percent of couples we work with do a first look. The advantages are many, but in a nutshell, it helps level-load the photo-related events of the day, making for less stress for everyone, especially the bride—and less stress means more happy moments and better photographs. When looking back at photos, people clearly remember how they felt at the moment that photo was taken. No matter how good an image may be, if the subjects were under pressure or stressed when it was taken, they'll remember that, and probably won't like the shot.

After the couple has reviewed the information we've sent, we have them reply using a Google document. It confirms all the basics and tells us everything we need to know to assemble the proposed timeline. See Appendix A for the questions we ask.

Note the red "warning" in the timeline chart. It's critical that everyone plays along once the timeline is developed. Ever since we've clearly communicated and emphasized that hair and makeup cannot run over, we've had 100 percent compliance. In fact, probably because our clients "pad" this time when scheduling their hair and makeup vendors, many are done ahead of time. It will relax the bride a great deal if you can comment on how organized she's been and how the day is actually running ahead of schedule. Don't rest on your laurels, though. It's rare that things will stay ahead for long. If you're on schedule,

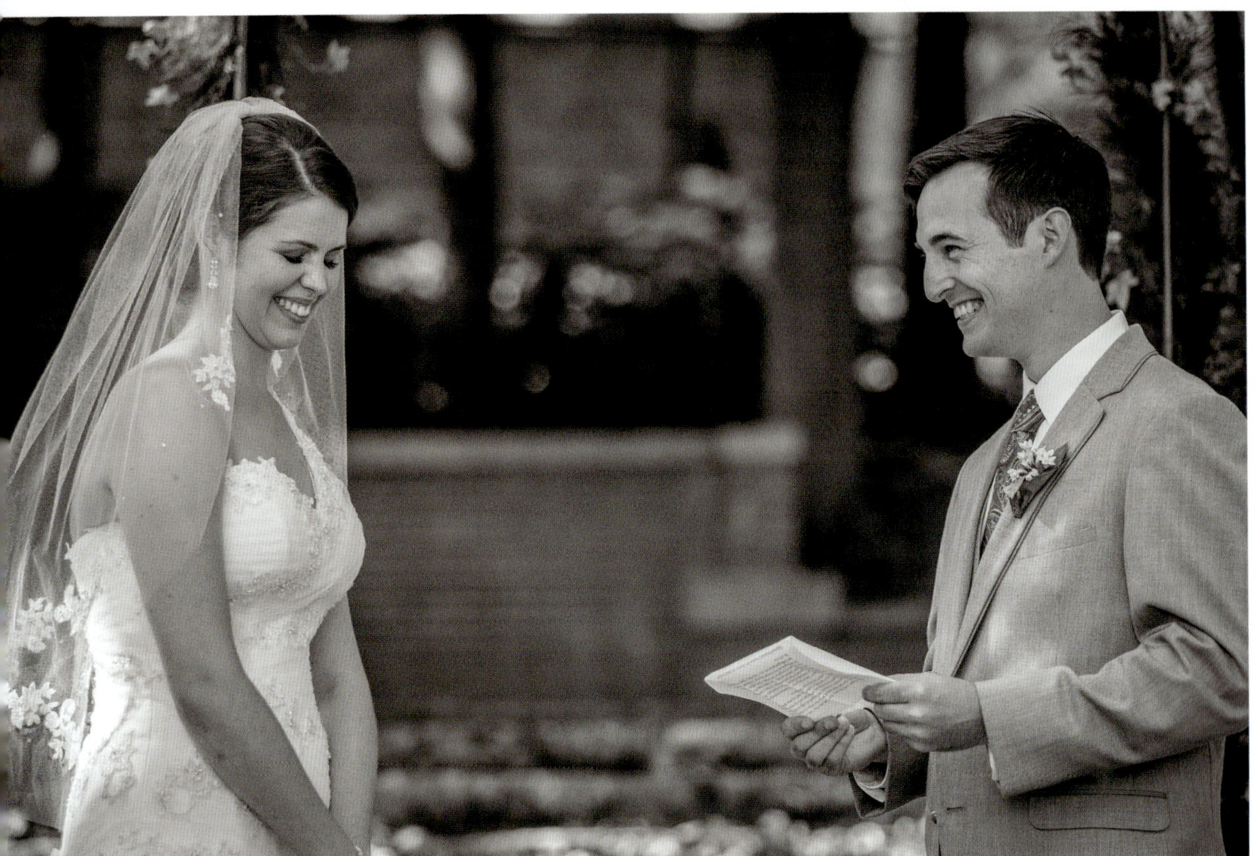

that's just fine—but don't let the day start to run behind. It's all in the planning.

When there's a first look, it's only the bride who has to be ready at the set time. Others can continue to prepare until it's time for the entire wedding party to meet after we get through photographing the what we call the "artistic set" with the couple.

Depending on the venue and area, we often take our couples off-site for what the artistic set. (Don't do this in your own car without first contacting your auto insurance agent and telling them your plans. You may need additional coverage, but it likely won't be expensive.)

Once the timeline is developed, we send it to the couple for review, any tweaking, and approval. They then have what's often the first tangible look at how their special day will flow.

If there's a planner involved, it's important to share the approved timeline with them. Emphasize that you're not trying to run the day; rather, you're simply ensuring that the photographs you're being paid to take will be made in a smooth, organized manner.

We can't emphasize this enough: having a timeline has greatly reduced potential stress for our brides. It sets clear expectations, gives us the time we need to do what we do, and provides the couple with a well-thought-out "script" for their day. Be prepared for their excitement and appreciation!

We can't emphasize this enough: having a timeline has greatly reduced potential stress for our brides.

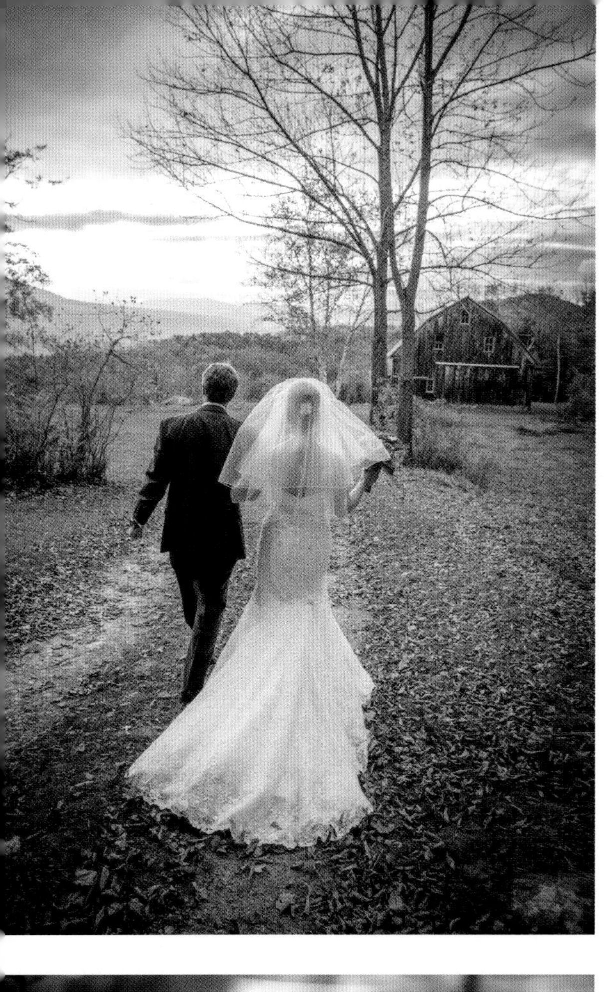
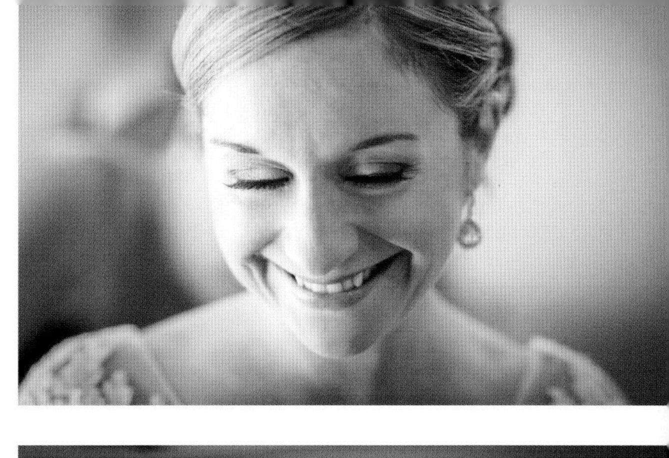
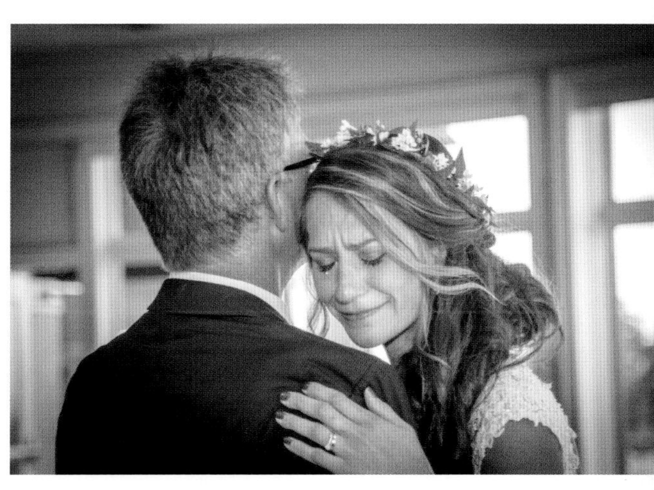
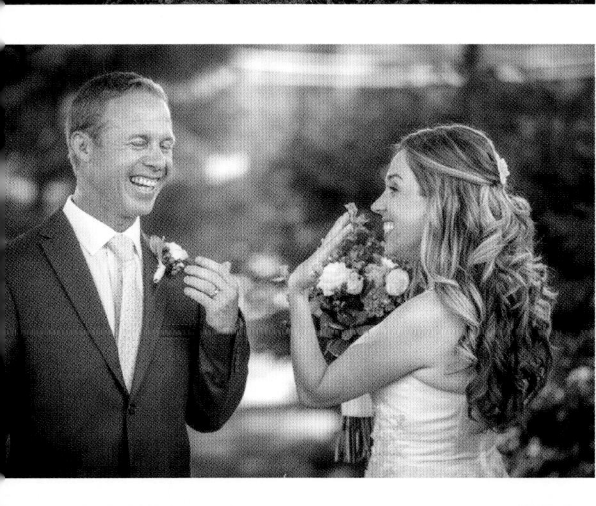
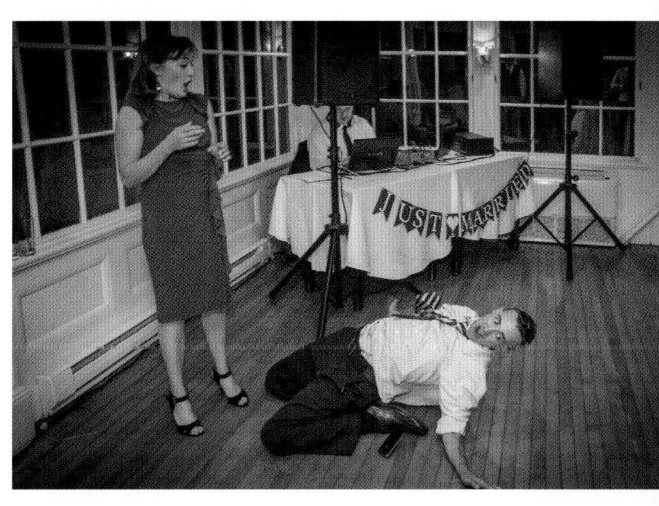
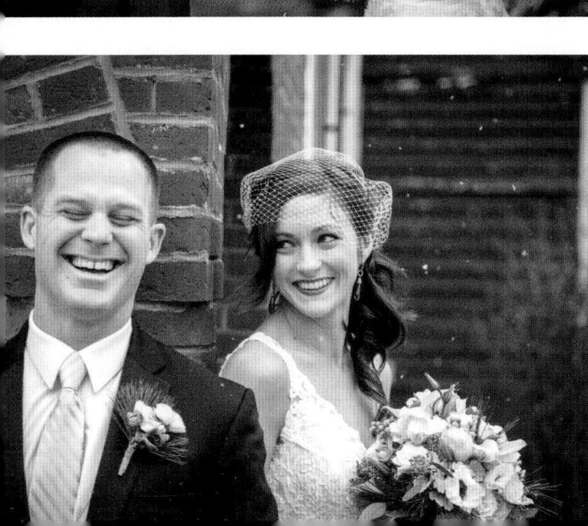
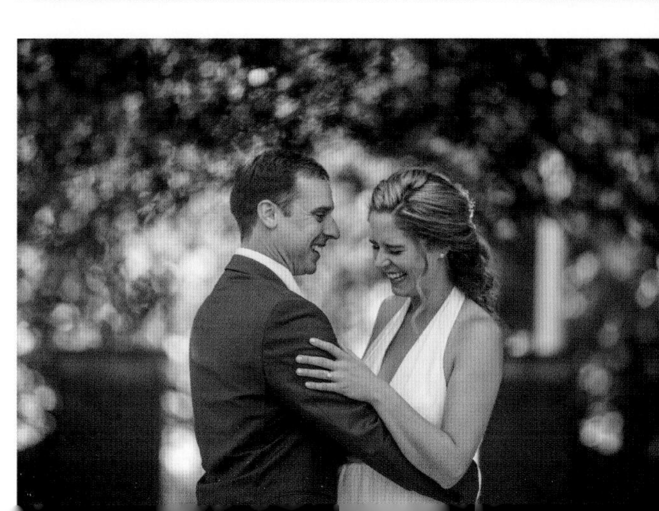

Engagement Sessions

Many of our wedding contracts include an engagement session with the couple. There are multiple benefits to doing one, in addition to the photographs that result. Many times, the engagement session represents the first time we've met our couple. While not meeting until the wedding day happens occasionally, and it works out just fine, it's always advantageous to have met the couple before the wedding. Even though our engagement sessions rarely take more than an hour and a half, we marvel at how, at the end, even the most apprehensive couples tell us what fun they've had and how they are no longer worried about the photography and are actually looking forward to it.

It's a good idea to find out, well ahead of time, when and where the client might like to do their engagement session. You'll want clients to describe the vibe they're looking for with their session, such as coastal, urban/city, park, country, field, woods, mountains, lake, etc. Within all these location types, we highly recommend that you, not the client, suggest the specific location. We love our engagement sessions to set as positive an experience as possible, and the few that didn't meet our expectations seem to have in common the fact that we (erroneously) let the client pick the specific setting. As the photographer, scope out locations ahead of time and scout for great light. Find the best time of day to work there, and

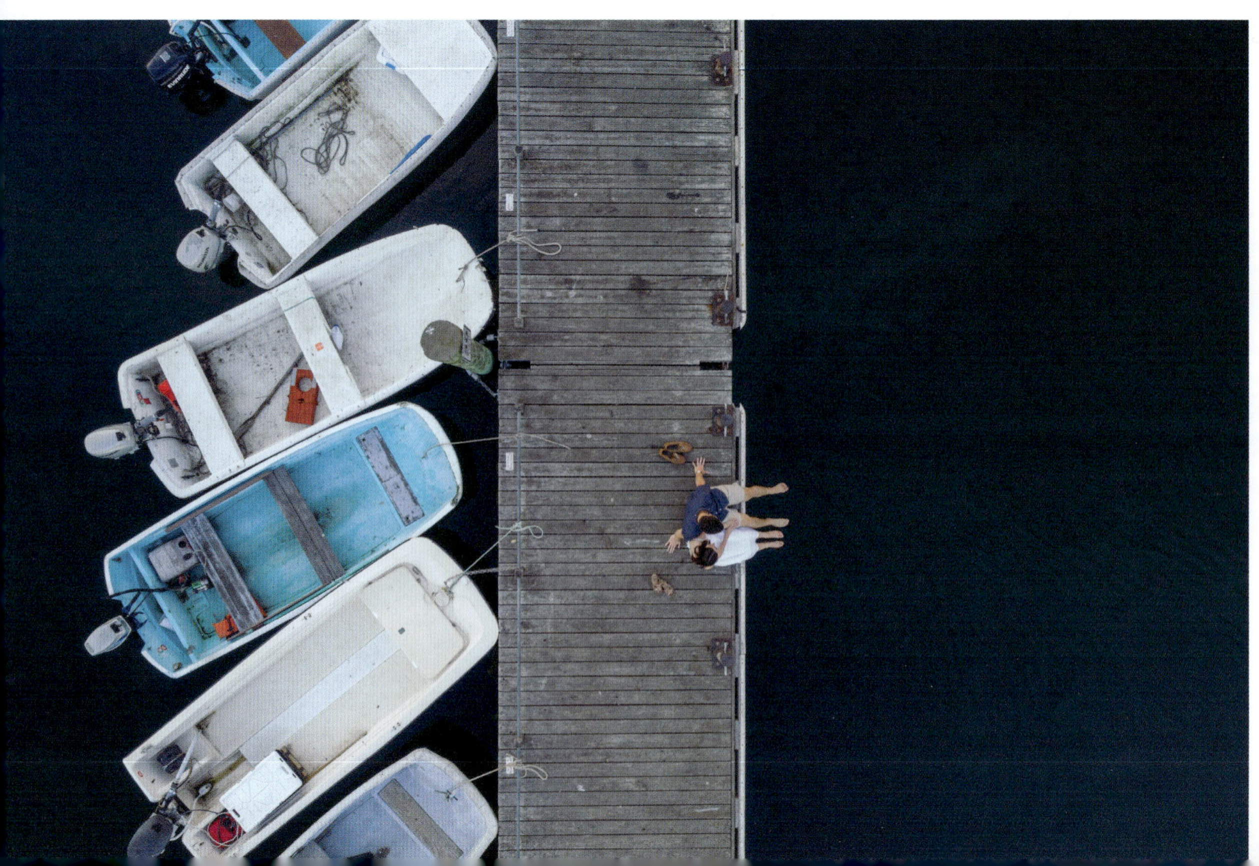

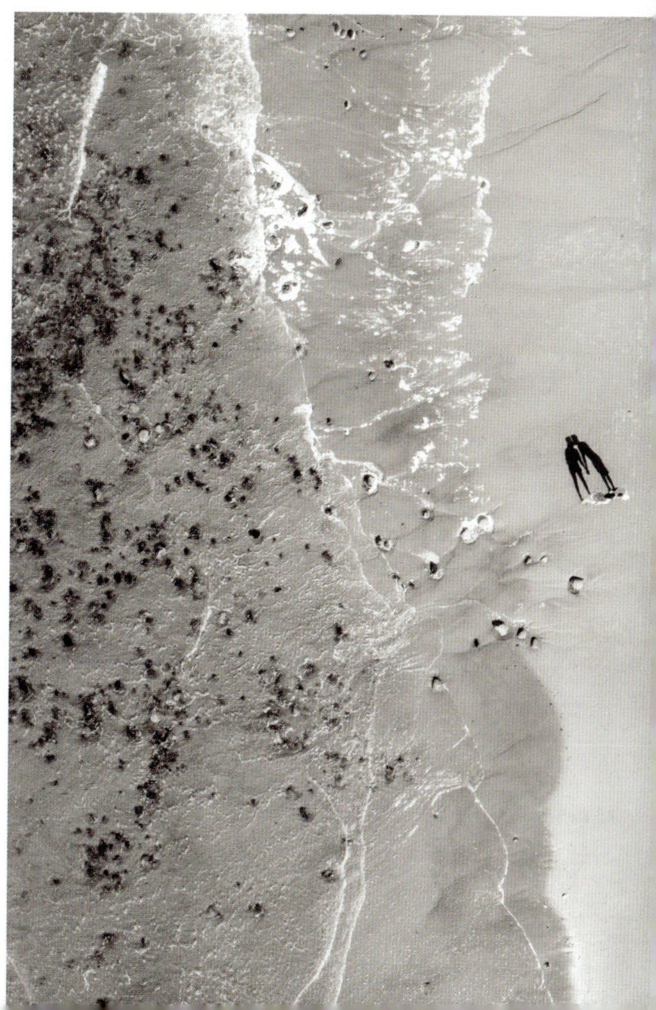

stick to that when you provide your suggestions to your clients.

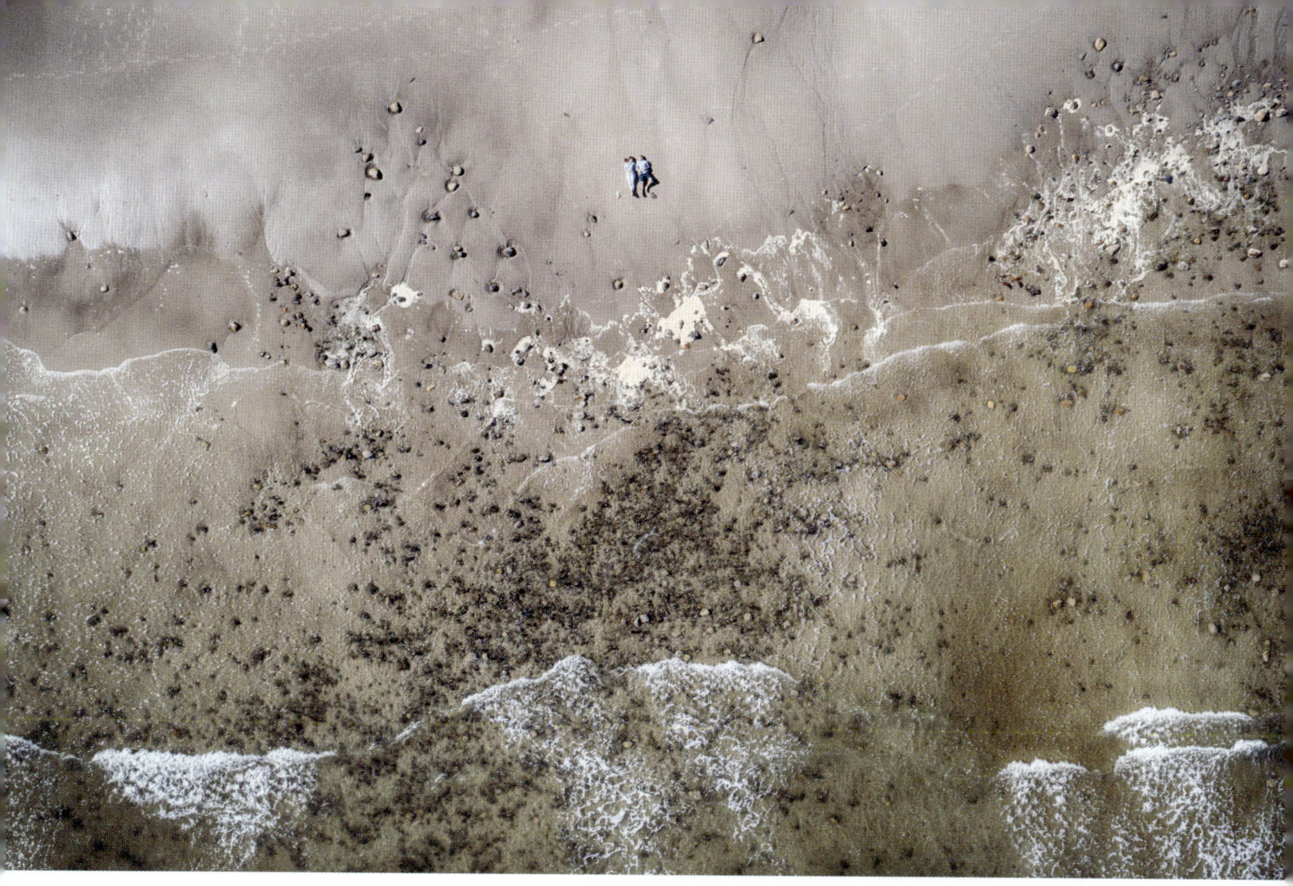

Speaking of light and time, use a smartphone app for detailed pre-planning. We like PhotoPills. It shows you the exact position of the sun based on the date, time, and geographic location.

When you first meet with your engagement couple, spend a few minutes (or more!) just chatting. It's the perfect get-to-know-them time. In some cases, it may work well to meet at a coffee shop or other social setting before heading out to start the photo session. You'll know early on how comfortable they are (or

When you first meet with your engagement couple, spend a few minutes (or more!) just chatting.

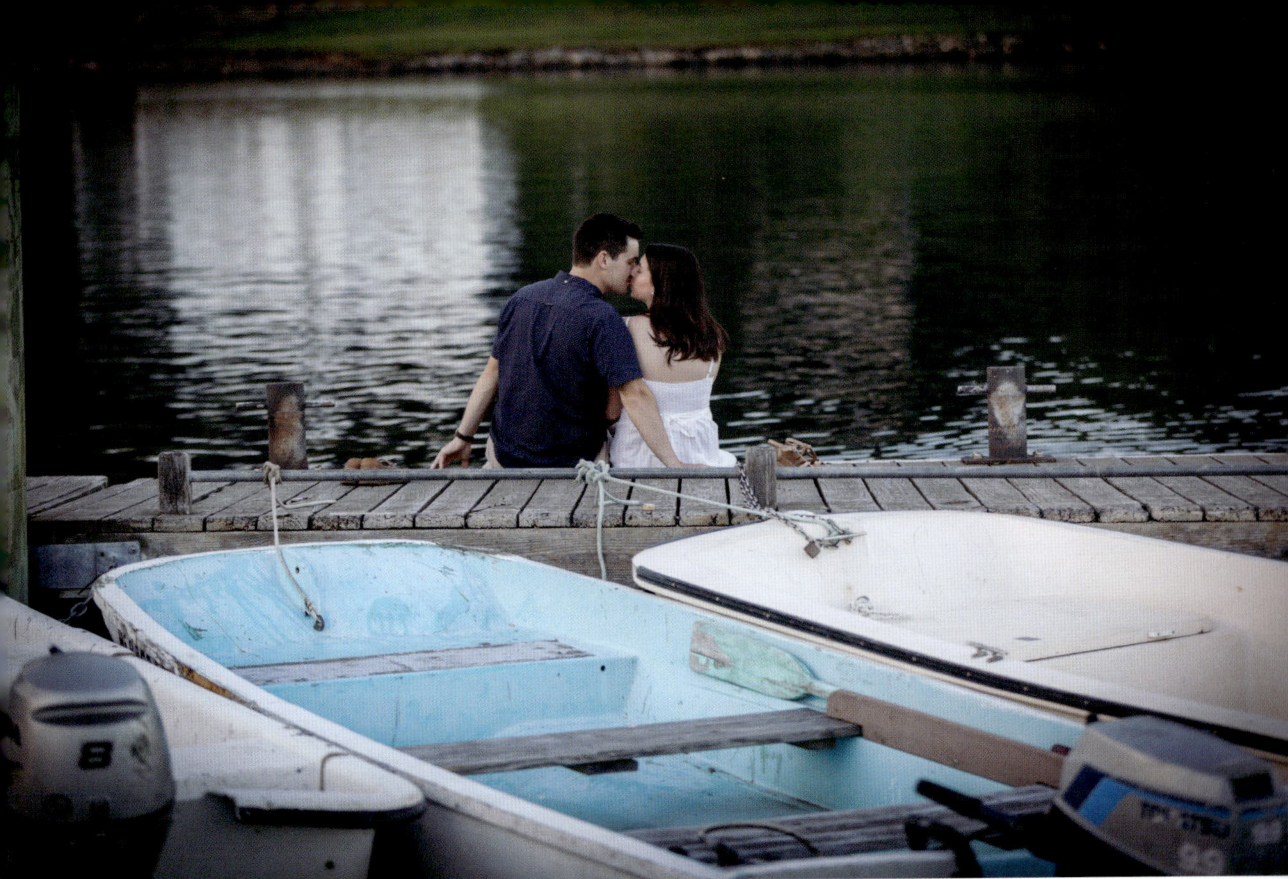

aren't) being in front of the camera. Help them relax as best you can. Keep them encouraged that they're doing well, and they're very natural, even when that isn't 100 percent the case. The goal now, even more than on the wedding day, is for them to be who they are as a couple. This is critical. Get them to whisper something funny or romantic into each other's ears. Assure them you won't hear. Be ready, and

The goal here, even more than on the wedding day, is for them to be who they are as a couple.

shoot. This is key: keep shooting after you say, "Okay, that was great!" Often, the best shot comes when they laugh and look at each other when they think the shot is over. Tell them that when they hear your camera shutter clicking quickly, it's a sign that they're really rocking things. Encourage them, offer praise, and then encourage them some more. This is your time to coach, all in the positive. Don't be afraid to model what you'd like them to do, too. We'll say, "Okay, I'll be Adam. Just lean against this wall, and Nicole is going to be right there. Just look at her and smile. I'll be photographing you from over there (point to the spot)." We don't use "left and right" to indicate where to move. Instead, we point to the direction. It's a fine balance in knowing just how much guidance is needed.

All this said, you absolutely don't want to micro manage, as this will inevitably increase the clients' tension and self-awareness. Most of the time, you'll find that the couple will naturally settle in and know what to do more organically after the first round of poses.

We find that a session of about 75 minutes is just right.

Before departing, remind your couple how well they did. This is all about building trust and confidence. Explain that the engagement session they just rocked was more intense a photo shoot than any part of wedding day. Though you'll be there far longer and take many times more photos on the day of the wedding, the actual segment strictly dedicated to the couples alone likely won't be as long as the engagement session.

Don't offer a full set of digital files for the engagement session. Rather, offer a small set (six?) of fully finished and retouched files. For an added cost, offer larger sets and the option for a full set.

Edit the files you'll deliver to professional standards. We call the style we use "precision editing." It's an important discussion, so we will return to the topic later in the book.

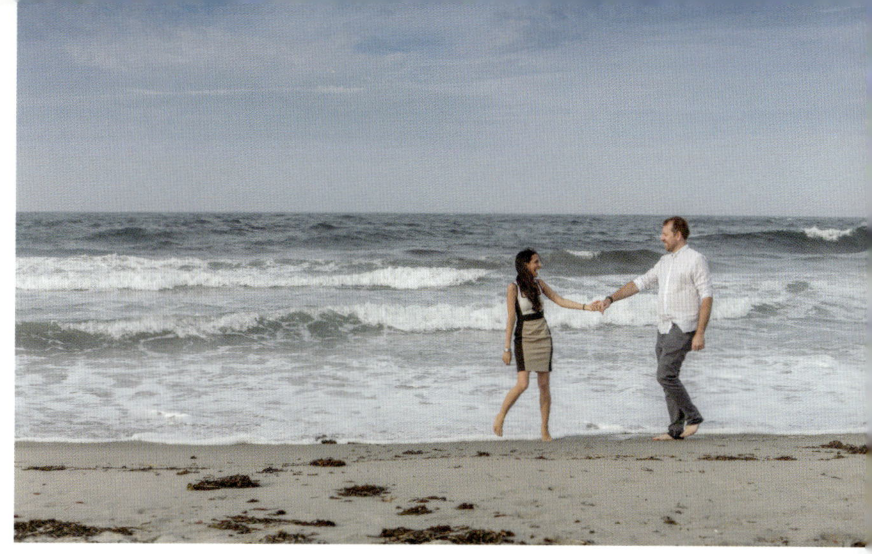

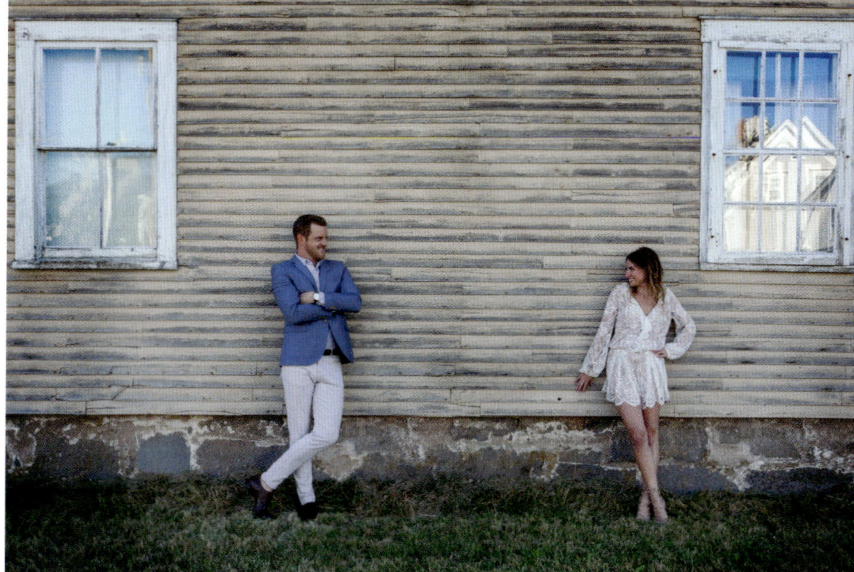

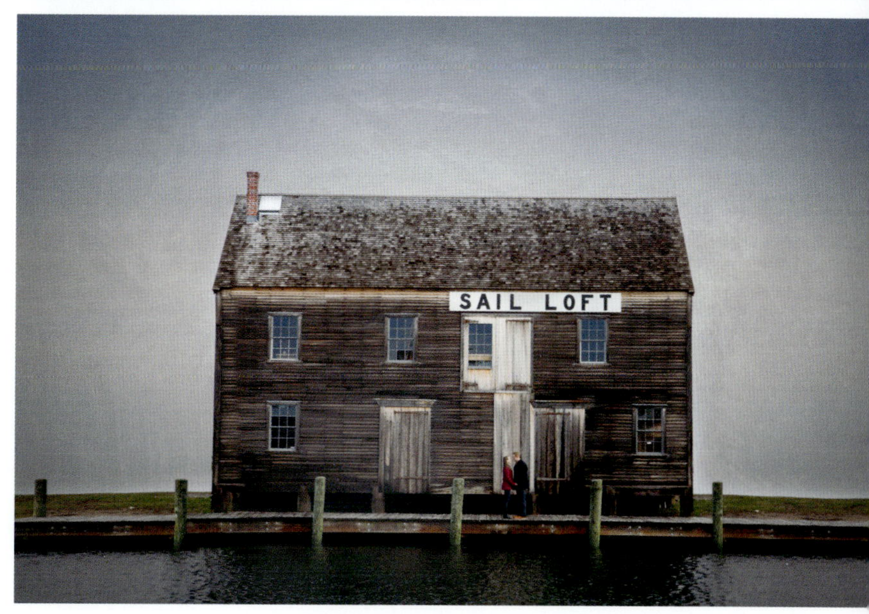

As the Wedding Day Approaches

week before the wedding, we send to the couple a document called Last-Minute Tips Before the Wedding. It provides a long list of ideas for a smooth-running wedding day. Included here is a request to have the detail items that we typically photograph on the wedding morning all set aside and ready for us (ideally, in a box). This includes the wedding bands (we assure the bride we'll get them to the best man before the ceremony); the paper suite (the invitation, RSVP card, food menu, save-the-date card, envelopes, and the like); and special jewelry, shoes, etc. In the document, we ask that the bride have her diamond cleaned by a jeweler before the wedding day. We always handle the ring with the utmost care while photographing it.

See Appendix B for the text of this document. Again, this communication is essential to setting clear expectations for a smooth-running wedding day.

A week before the wedding, we send to the couple a document called Last-Minute Tips Before the Wedding.

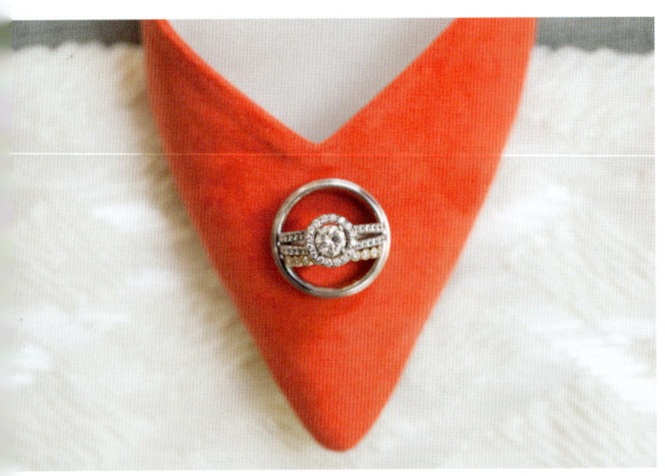

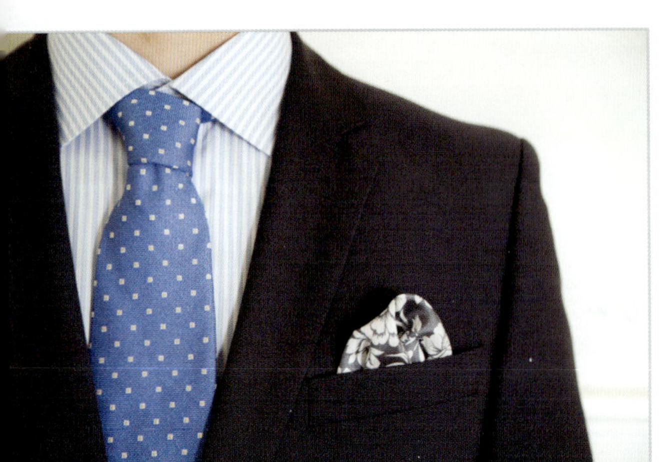

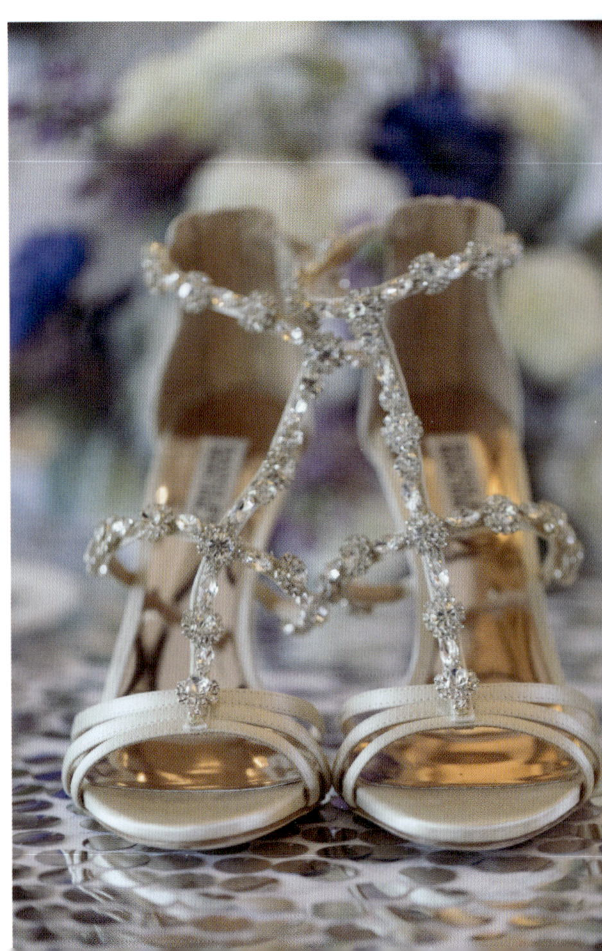

Our Wedding Day Gear

This is a good time to talk about gear. Let me make one key point to anyone starting out who has only one good camera body. Please do not embark on photographing a wedding with just one camera, no matter the brand, how new it is, or how reliable it has been. You cannot photograph a wedding without a backup body of like quality.

I made this point at a workshop many years ago, and one participant took my words to heart. With a wedding to photograph two weeks later, she borrowed money from family to immediately purchase a second (used) camera body just like her other one. Immediately following the wedding, I received an email from her, written with (happy) tears flowing, thanking me for saving her photo career. As it turns out, the mirror in her original camera body fell out and rendered her camera useless, just a few minutes

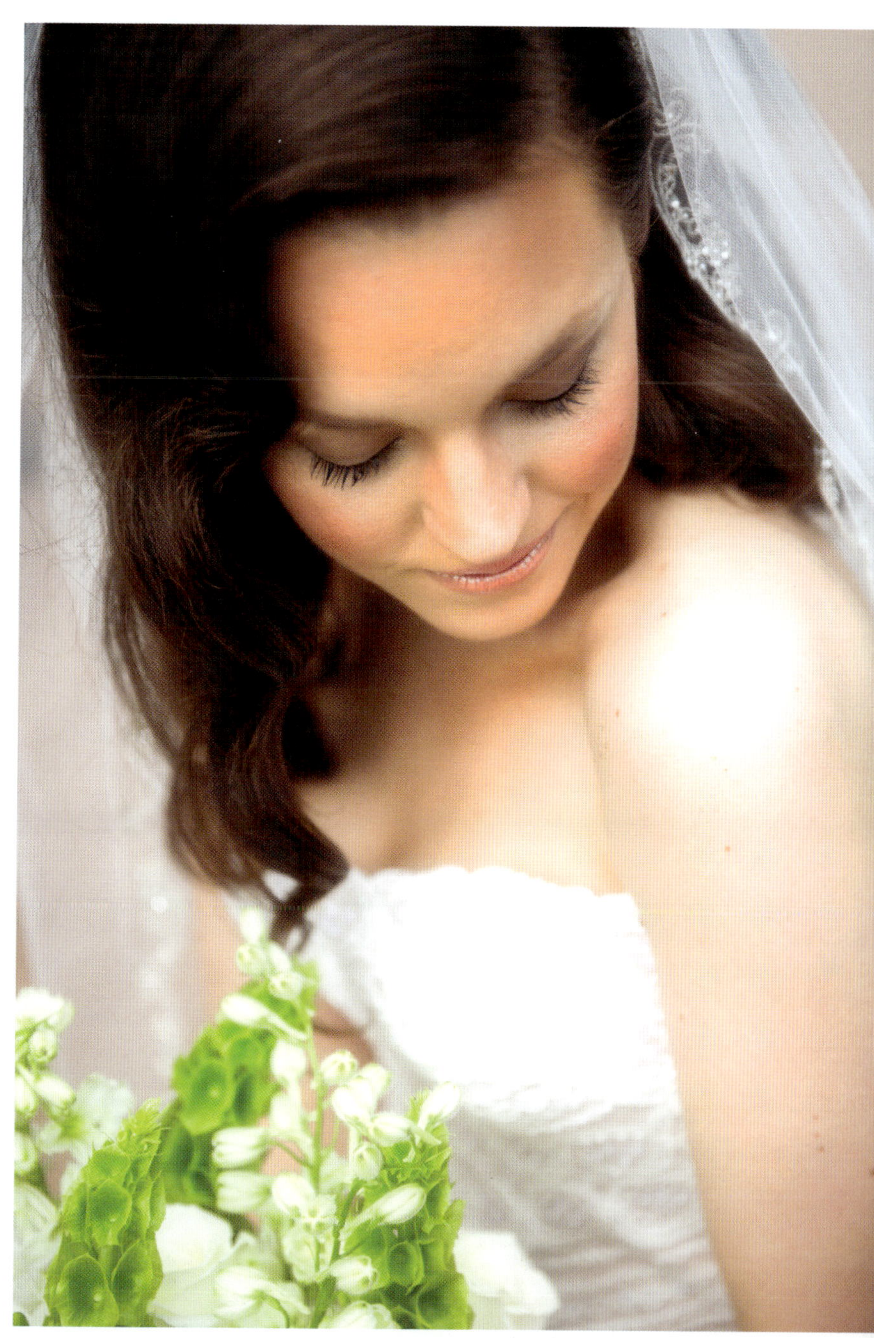

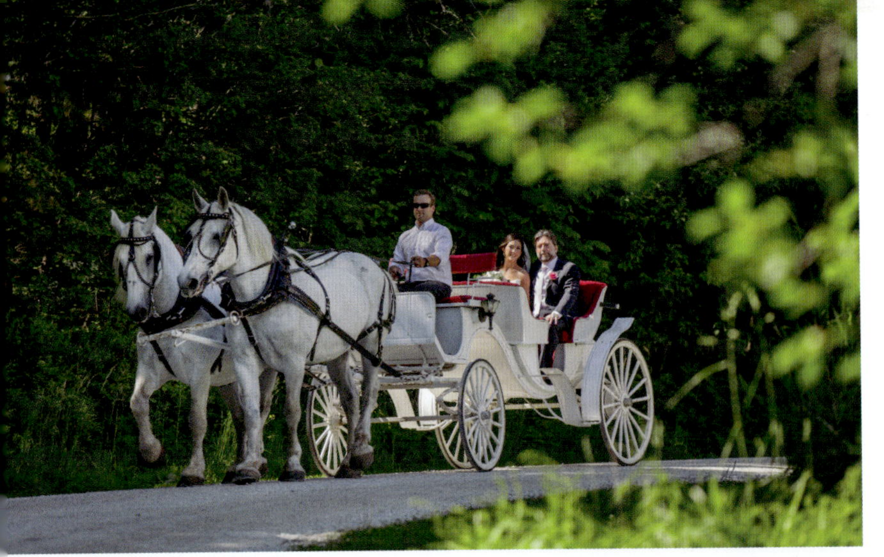

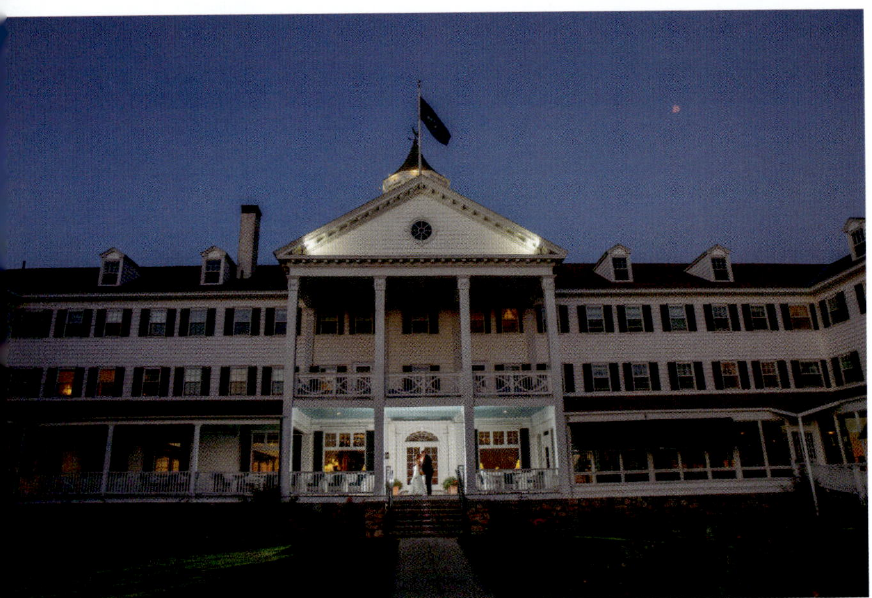

into photographing that wedding. That second body she bought and had at the ready saved her that day. I love sharing happy-ending stories, especially ones where I was somehow a participant.

Here's a list of what's in our bag and why it has worked well for us. We're Canon shooters, but the specifics and ideas here readily apply to Nikon, Sony, and other brands, too.

Cameras

Each of us carries two Canon 5D Mark IV bodies. Russ' are equipped with the Canon battery grips, which allow day-long shooting with plenty of reserve power.

We also have a drone camera that we love. We'll talk more about it later.

Dual Memory Card Slots are a Must. Our cameras are equipped with dual memory card slots. This isn't a "nice to have" feature. It's one that is vital for wedding photographers and anyone else who photographs anything that can't be repeated. Having the two slots isn't the full story. Setting the camera to write to both cards at the same time is key.

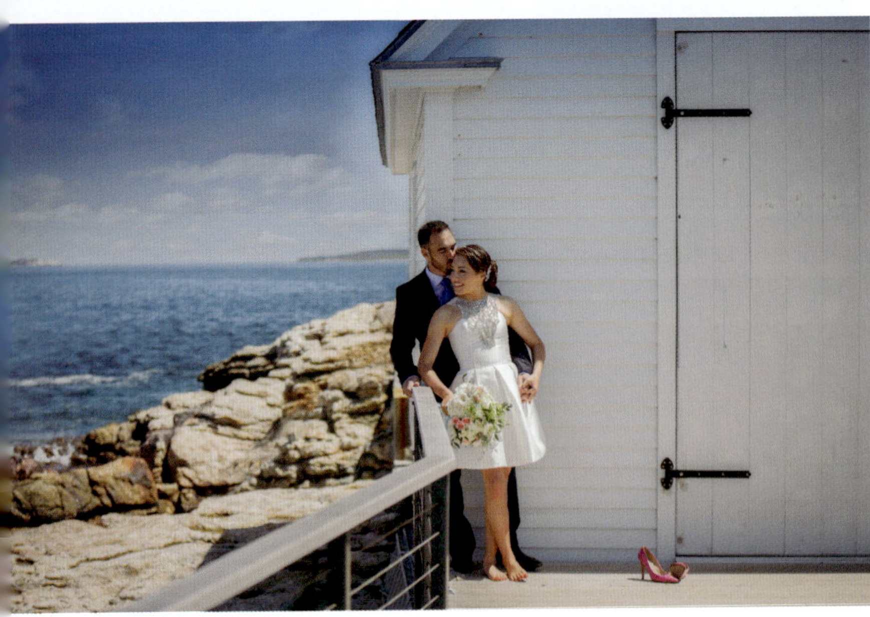

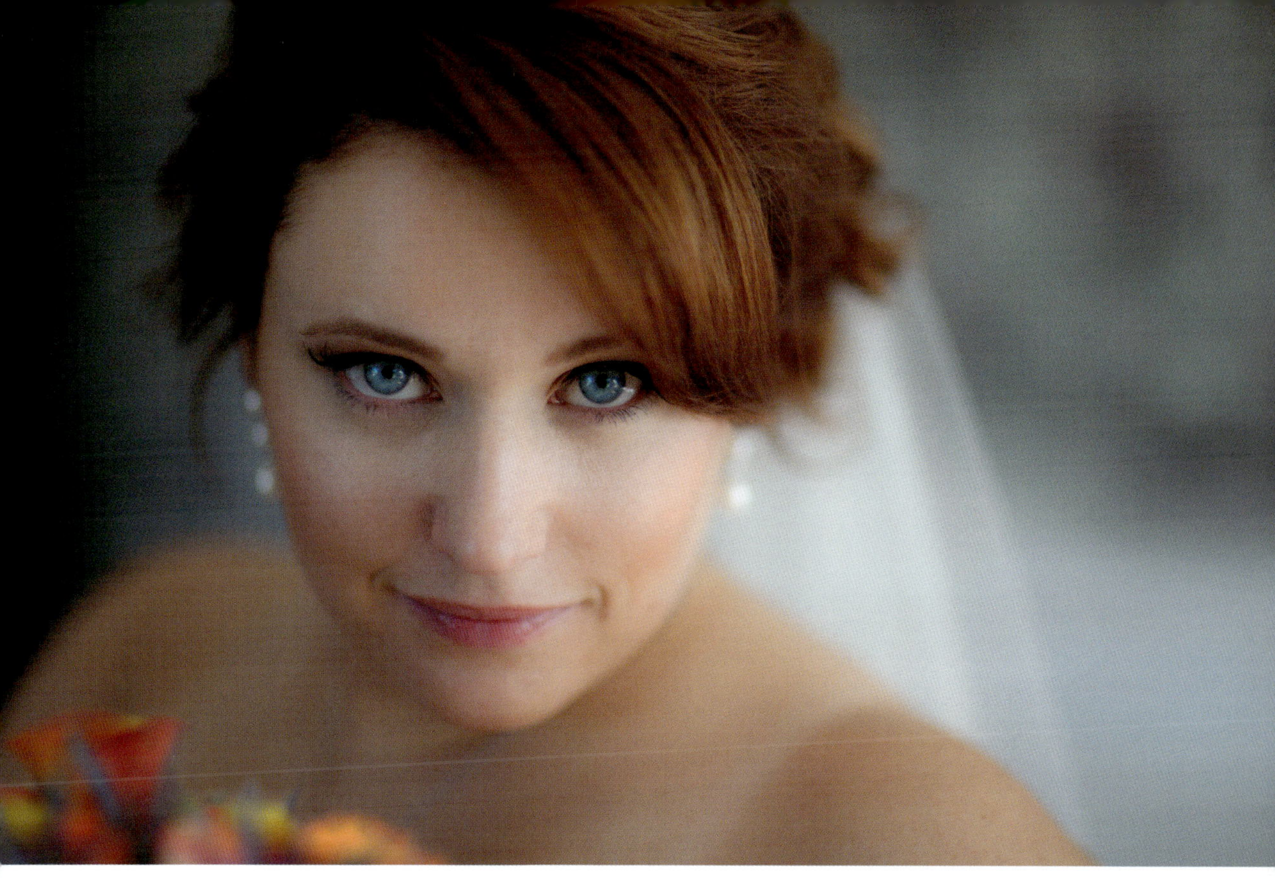

We recommend that you choose cards with a fast write speed. We use 128GB cards and thus never need to change them the whole day. 64GB and 32GB cards work fine, too. Just have spares with you. There is profound comfort in knowing that every shot is instantly backed up. Card failures are rare these days, especially when using top-end, brand-name cards, but there's so much at stake that nothing should be left to chance.

Shoot in RAW Format. Raw files, as opposed to JPEG files, have a far greater ability to record detail in shadows and retain detail in highlights at the same time. Using Adobe Lightroom at the post-processing stage makes using Raw files totally transparent and affords you the greatest quality in your images. As large memory cards and huge hard drives are very affordable, there's simply no reason not to shoot in Raw format. There's no reason to shoot one in Raw and the other in JPEG. Unless your camera has a mega-megapixel sensor (>30 megapixels), shoot in large Raw format as opposed to medium or small, and save the files to both the main and backup cards. Use the same large 128GB card size in both the main and backup slots, and you'll be good to go, all day long.

Lenses

We're big fans of Canon-brand lenses. We each carry a short zoom (e.g., 24–70mm L Series II f/2.8) and a long zoom (e.g., 70–200mm IS L Series II f/2.8). While we do have several fixed-focal-length lenses, the current-generation Canon zooms we use are amazingly sharp, even wide open, and the enormous advantages these zooms afford (having so many varying

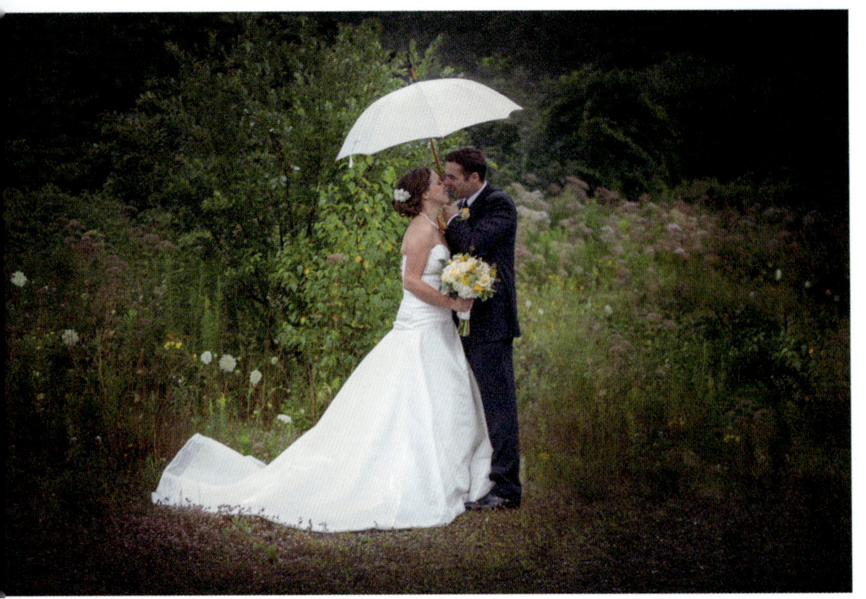

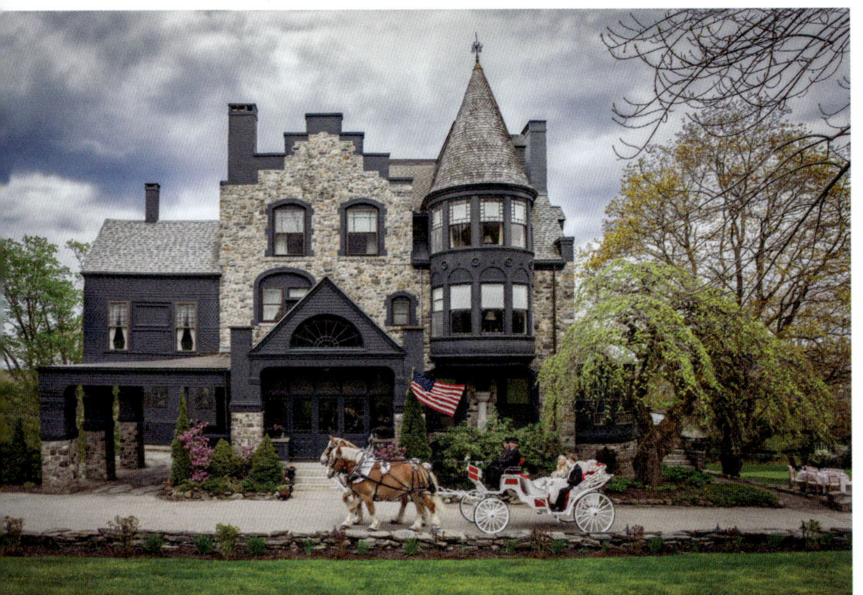

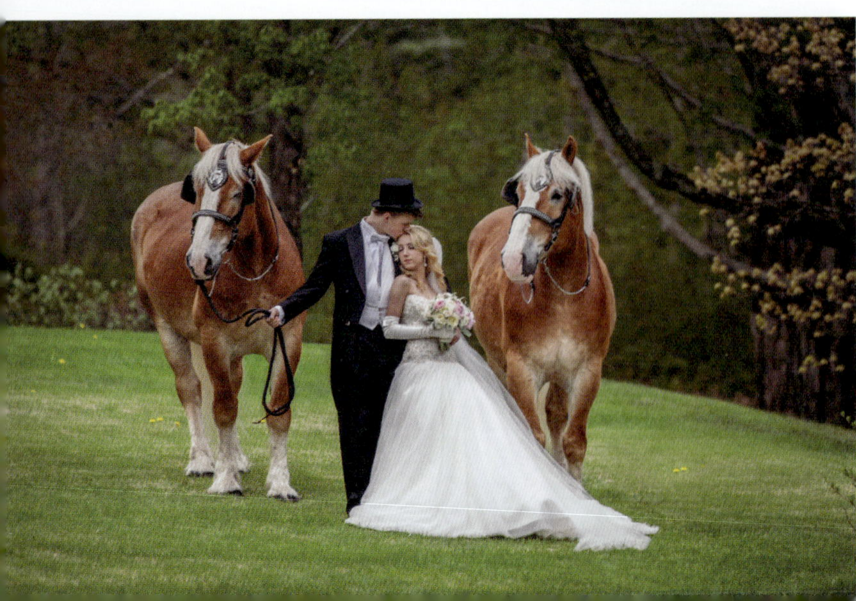

focal lengths in hand at all times) far outweigh any advantages of using fixed-focal-length (prime) lenses. With the Mark IV body's high ISO capability, the prime's advantage of larger maximum apertures is largely moot, too. When we set our apertures to f/2.8, this works both for low light and for generating a nice out-of-focus background (the "bokeh").

We also get lots of use from our two Canon 16–35mm f/2.8 II L lenses. Our 100mm f/2.8 Canon L macro is used for ring and detail shots. The Canon 85mm f/1.4 is most often used for bridal portraits and first-dance shots. We have a 15mm Canon f/2.8 fisheye lens that is a good choice at certain times, such as on a crowded dance floor with the camera held high overhead, and pointing back down.

Aperture Priority is Your Friend. By the way, we shoot in aperture priority mode anytime we're not using flash. We adjust the aperture for the desired depth of field and set the ISO for the relative light level we're in. Our trusted camera bodies set the exact shutter

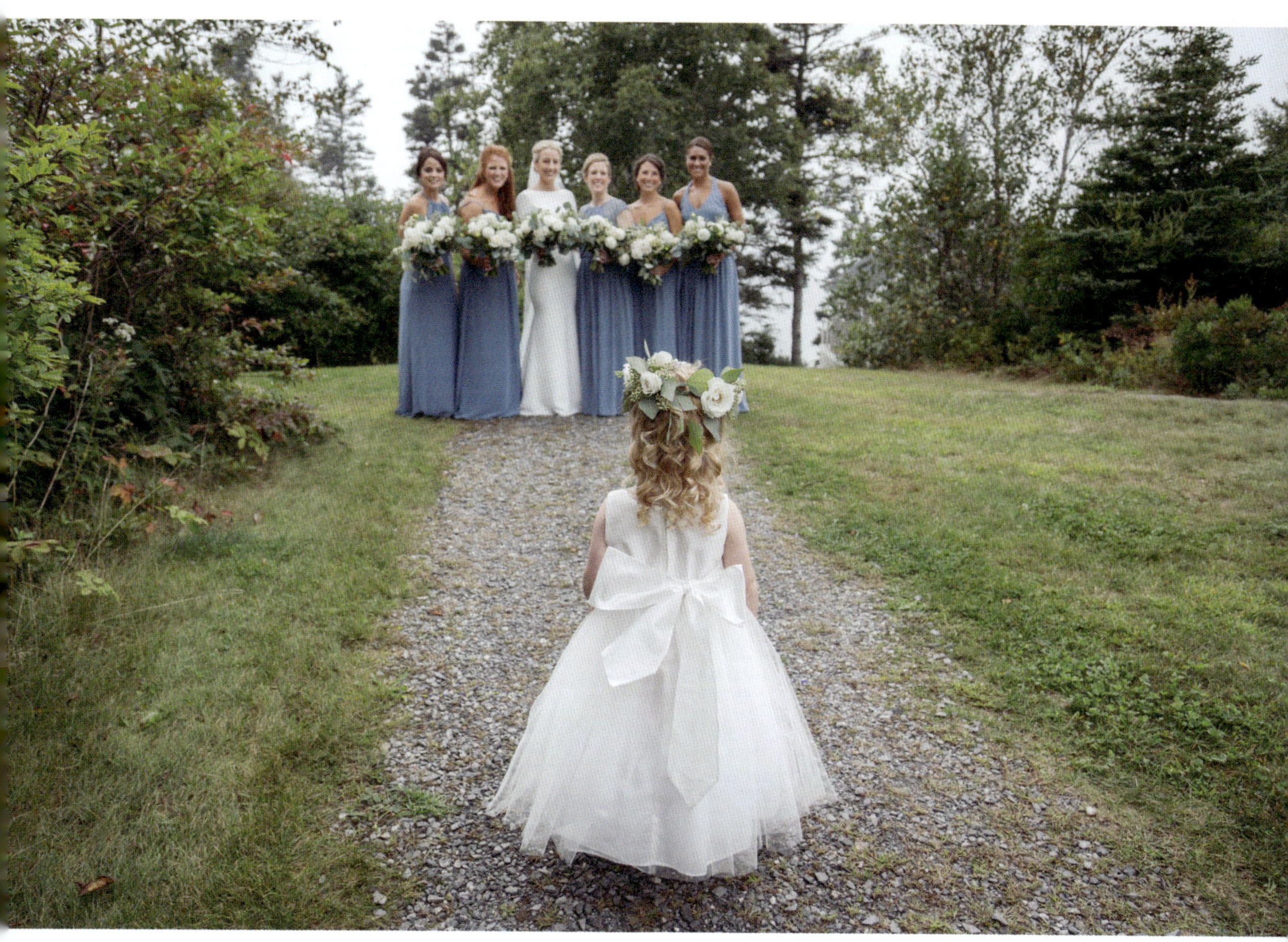

speed. We keep our thumbs on our camera's backside "jog dial" to manually dial-in exposure compensation to make up for backlight or dark areas that can fool the camera's built-in metering system.

Flash

When we do use flash, we switch our cameras to full manual mode and set the shutter speed (usually $^1/_{250}$ second, the "sync speed") and ISO, typically with the flashes on automatic—that's ETTL for Canon users or TTL for Nikon users. A great thing about today's cameras is the smart inter-communication between devices. Even if we have not changed the shutter speed, as soon as an attached flash is turned on, the camera brings the shutter speed down to the correct sync speed.

When we do use flash, we switch our cameras to full manual mode and set the shutter speed . . .

We do sometimes "drag the shutter" when using flash, by bringing the shutter speed to, say, $^1/_{30}$ second. This allows the existing light to provide mood and ambiance in the image when that's what we're looking for. Dragging the shutter can also allow for some motion blur on highlighted portions of the frame not covered by the flash.

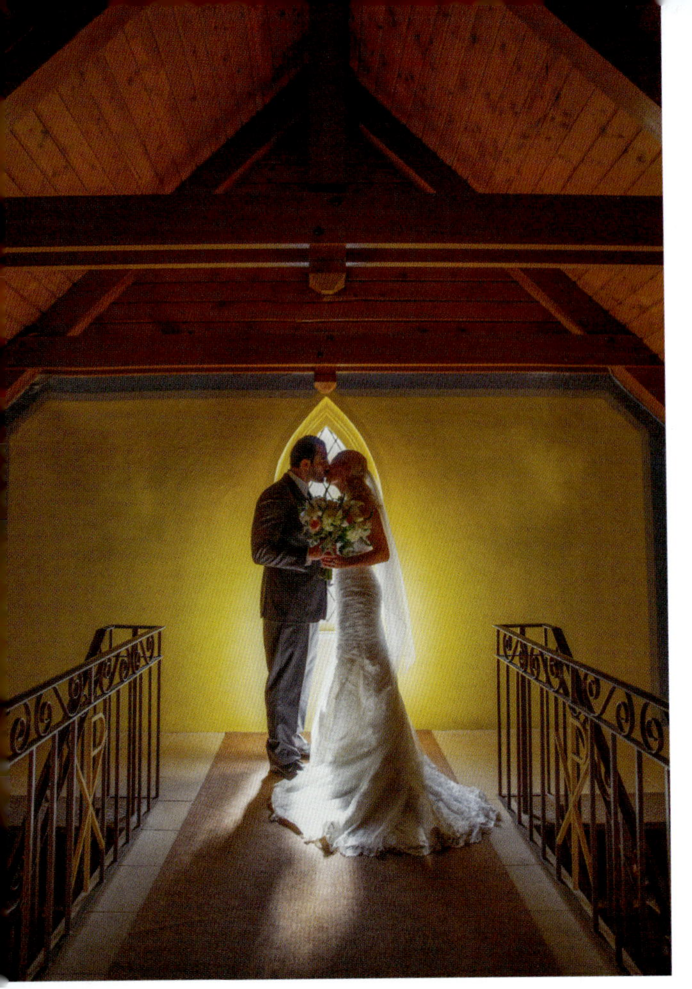

Off-Camera Flash. We have the option to set up off-camera flash for certain venues and particular needs. Off-camera flash works really well in tented receptions, as the generally white tent material works superbly to bounce the light from our flashes. Our Canon 600EX-RTs have a very reliable built-in radio network, and we can change all the settings directly from the master flash or transmitter mounted to our cameras.

Mastering off-camera flash takes a lot of practice and requires that you have access to the reception area earlier in the day for setup and testing. Don't try to do this setup during the wedding!

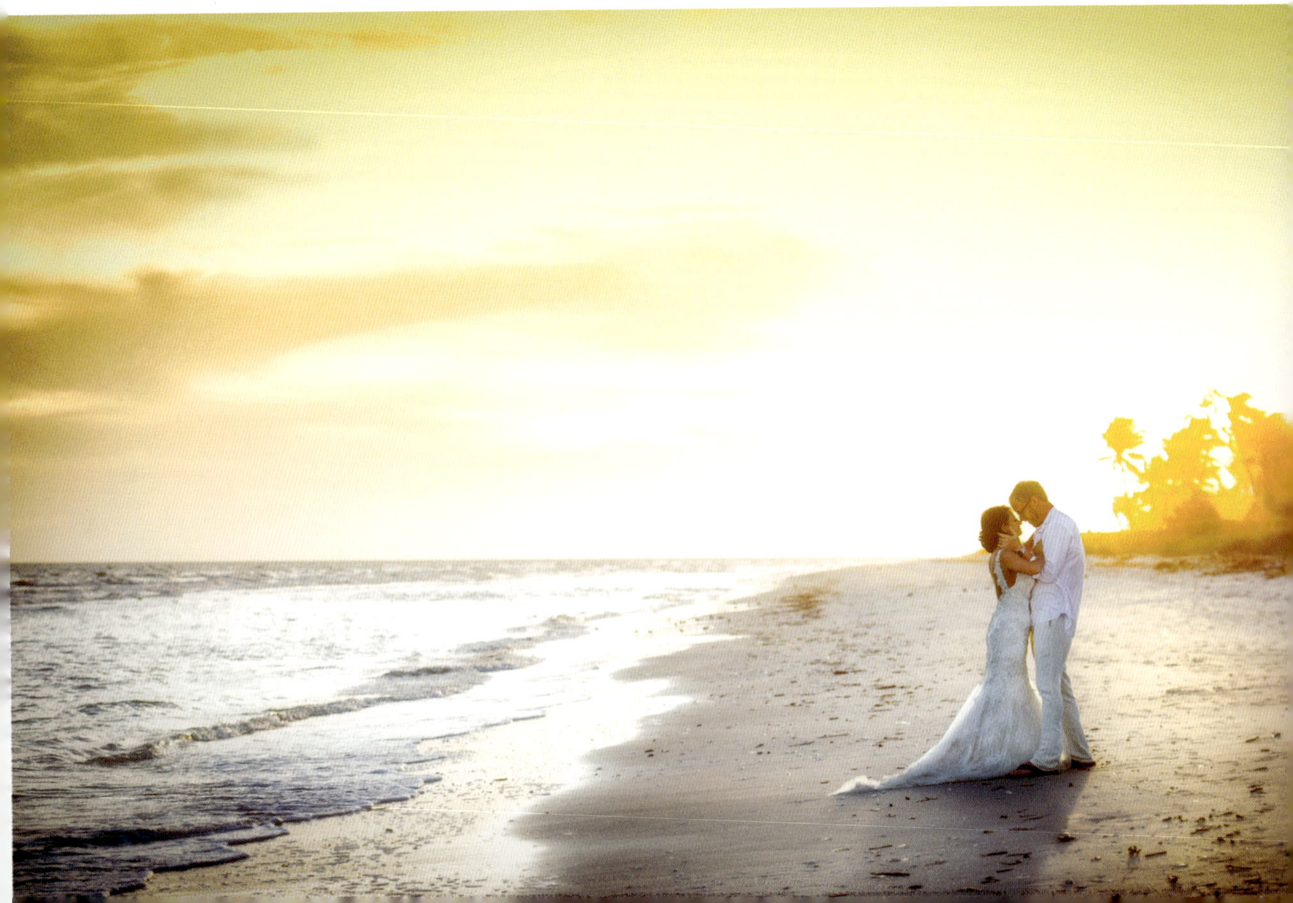

Flash use is a potentially complex topic. While we do know our way around flash, both on-camera and off, we tend to use the most simple, effective solution possible. We have six Canon 600EX-RT flashes and two Canon ST E-3 RT flash transmitters. We try to wait

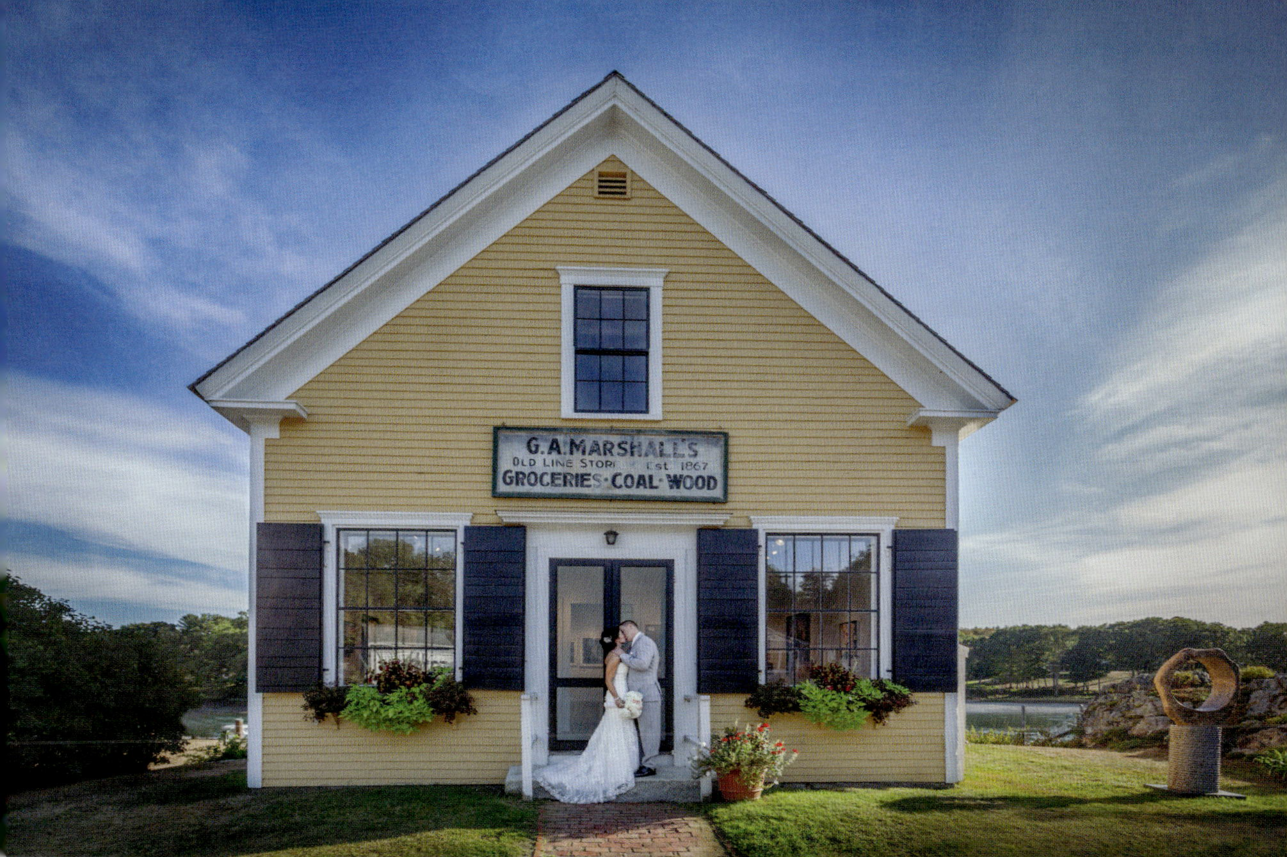

until absolutely necessary before starting to use flash. When we do, we assess what the room dynamics call for, and we sometimes choose an off-camera-flash setup. If, however, on-camera flashes with some type of modifier will work fine, that's what we use.

When it comes to modifiers, we like the lightweight, simple, and effective "bounce card" type, such as the line manufactured by Demb. We've changed the mounting system to heavy-duty plastic self-adhesive hook-and-lock fasteners that make it quick and easy to attach and remove the units from our flashes. If it weren't quick, it would be cumbersome, and cumbersome doesn't cut it on wedding days.

Batteries

Oh, how important are the batteries? We've found that Powerex Professional 2700 mAh rechargeable NiMH batteries have a rather long life in our flash systems. We can usually shoot all night long at a wedding reception and never need to change them. Yet, we carry about ten dozen freshly charged AAs with us, as running out of battery power when working professionally simply isn't an option.

We also have spare Canon camera batteries with us, though I can say we've never had to swap one out, even after 12-plus-hours shooting with two in the camera grip.

Ensure that all batteries are fully charged before packing and heading off to a wedding.

Accessories and an Emergency Kit

In the car are various stands, a small softbox, reflectors, Manfrotto Justin clamps (look these up; they are extraordinarily versatile), bungee cords, miscellaneous spare parts, and essentials

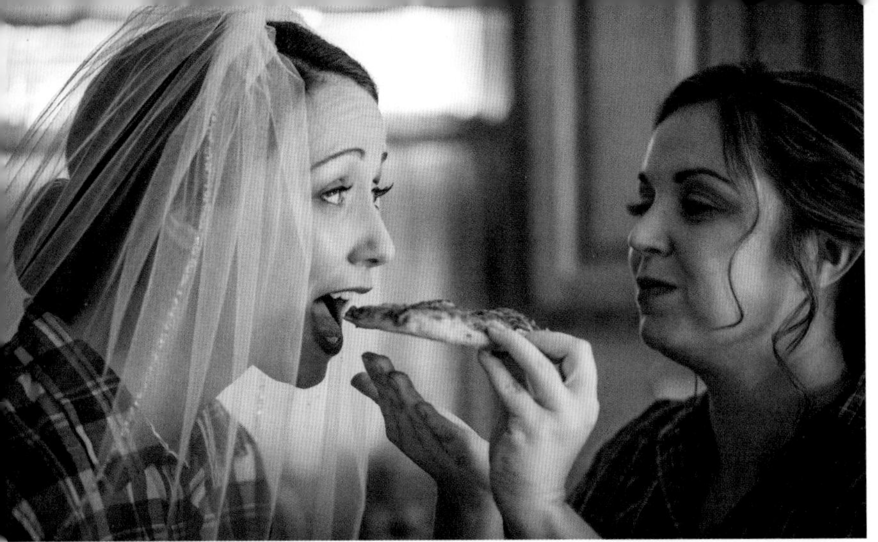

like a first-aid kit, safety pins, hairpins, sunscreen, lots of water, and nonperishable snacks. We also have a small container of hydrogen peroxide and cotton swabs with us. We've saved the day on more than one occasion with these last items. We remember a time when a groomsman cut himself and bled badly on the white collar of his dress shirt. Once we had him leave the stain to dry up, we gently kept dabbing at it with the swab and watched it vanish before our eyes.

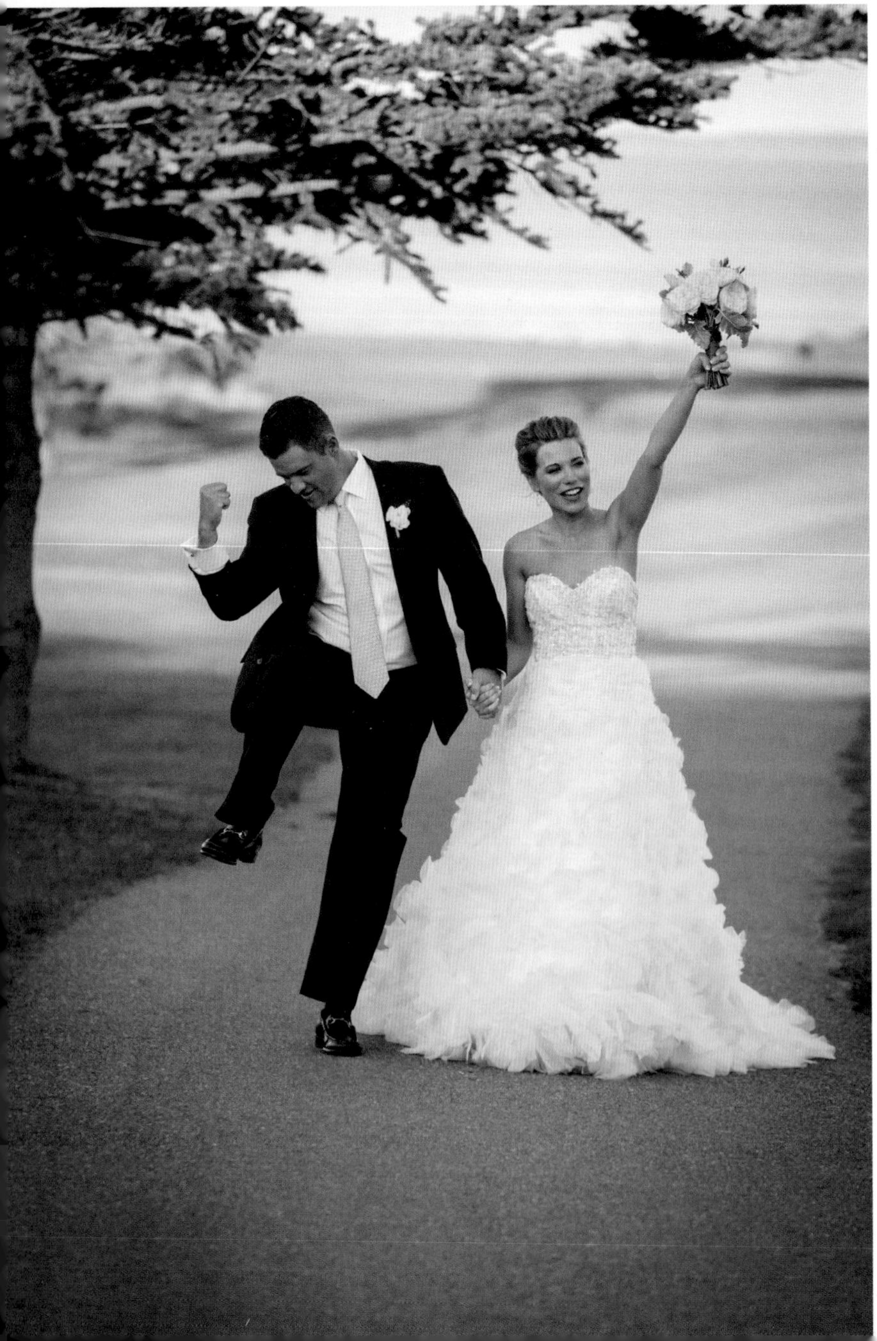

Memory Cards

We carry spare memory cards, but never need to change them because we shoot on fast 128GB Lexar Pro cards in both of the slots in each camera. Buy the fastest, best-reviewed memory cards you can, and obtain them only from reputable sources. There are countless inferior imitators out there, and you don't need a card failure mid-wedding!

Spare Shoes and Clothing

Bring a change of shoes. This is huge. You can almost instantly "recharge" yourself by slipping into a pair of comfortable shoes at the halfway point of your shooting day. Oh, and pack spare clothing, too.

Bags

We carry all of our things in ThinkTank rolling bags. We both have an Airport International bag for each of our two cameras and their main lenses. Then we add a smaller rolling ThinkTank bag for the remaining lenses, and another small rolling bag for the 100–400mm lens mounted to a fifth camera body that's with us as yet another backup. The flashes and accessories for them are carried in a separate bag so that, when needed, we can bring one bag in and start setting them up and using them. This bag also contains our six flash modifiers and some spare batteries.

ThinkTank bags are rugged, smart, and highly recommended. This company was founded by creatives who know the needs of photographers. Use the link below for free shipping and a free gift:

https://www.thinktankphoto.com/pages/ workshop?rfsn=219964.b6749

Straps

We each carry two cameras for most of the wedding day, so a dual-camera strap is essential. We've had good luck in the past with the SpiderBelt holster system, though our current favorite solution is the Moneymaker strap from Holdfast. These high-quality straps simply work better than anything else we've tried. The weight of our heavy cameras is distributed nicely across our shoulders.

Storage

We have an organized system of storing our cameras and lenses outside of their cases. There are two reasons for this: One, upon returning to our office after a wedding shoot, with everything having a designated place, it is obvious if we're left something behind. Likewise, when packing to leave, we know we're not forgetting anything when its place on the rack is empty. Even when we come in from a wedding one night and have to leave early the next morning for another, we unpack, gently wipe down our gear, and put it on the shelf before repacking. It sounds excessive, but this system has never failed us.

Canon Professional Services

We're members of Canon Professional Services (CPS). The program provides pro photographers lightning-fast turnaround of gear needing repair. When we've had to send something in for repair, it's almost always because we've dropped it. With the platinum-level membership, an item that fell victim to a Saturday mishap, when shipped out on Monday morning, is back in our hands by Wednesday at 10:30am—*of the same week!* Canon even sends a prepaid FedEx label to cover the outbound shipping. How's that for service? Oh, and with the various membership levels comes proportionately greater discounts on repair—and free loaner equipment if the item can't be immediately returned for any reason. Nikon and Sony have similar programs in place, too.

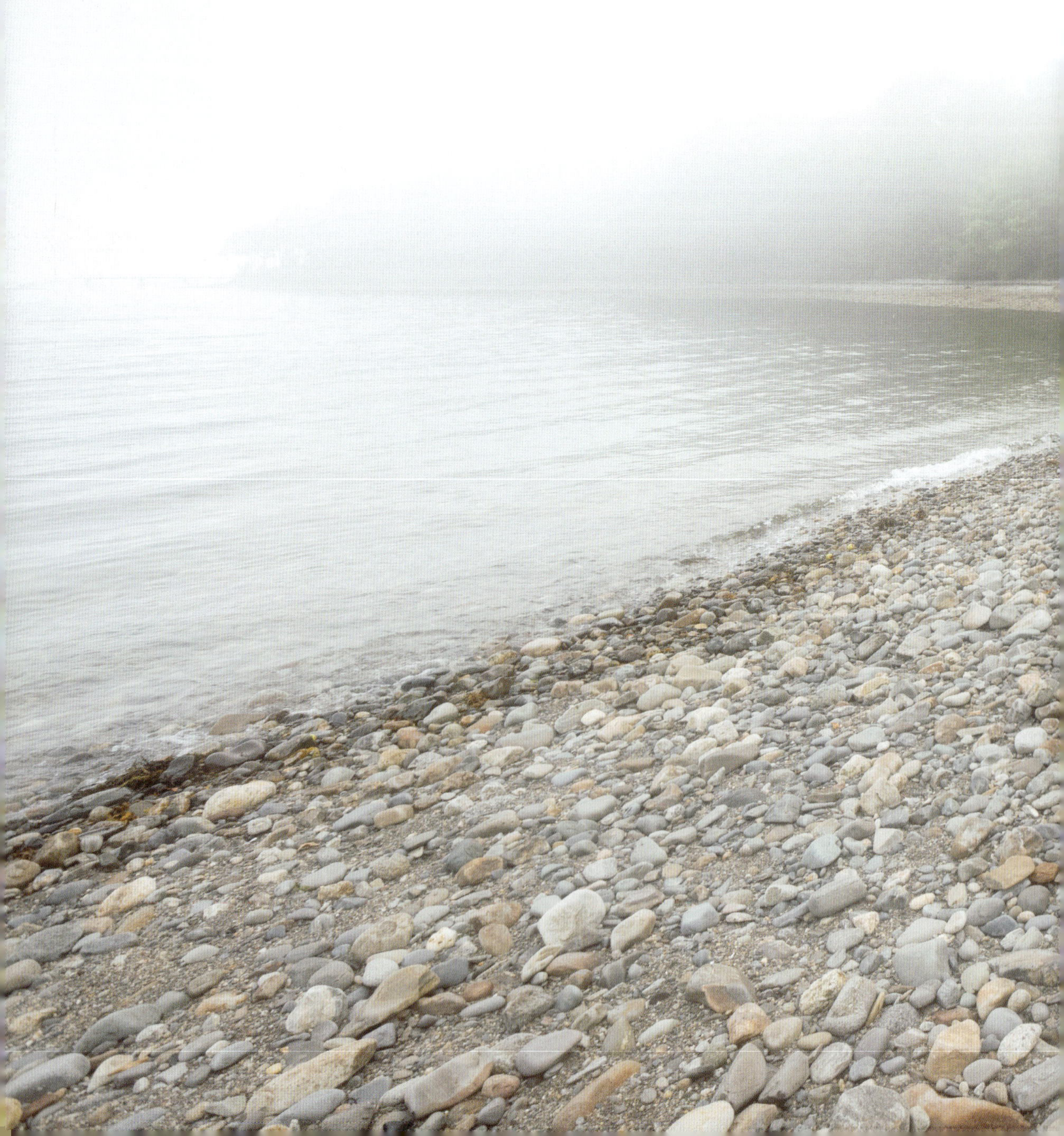

The Wedding Day

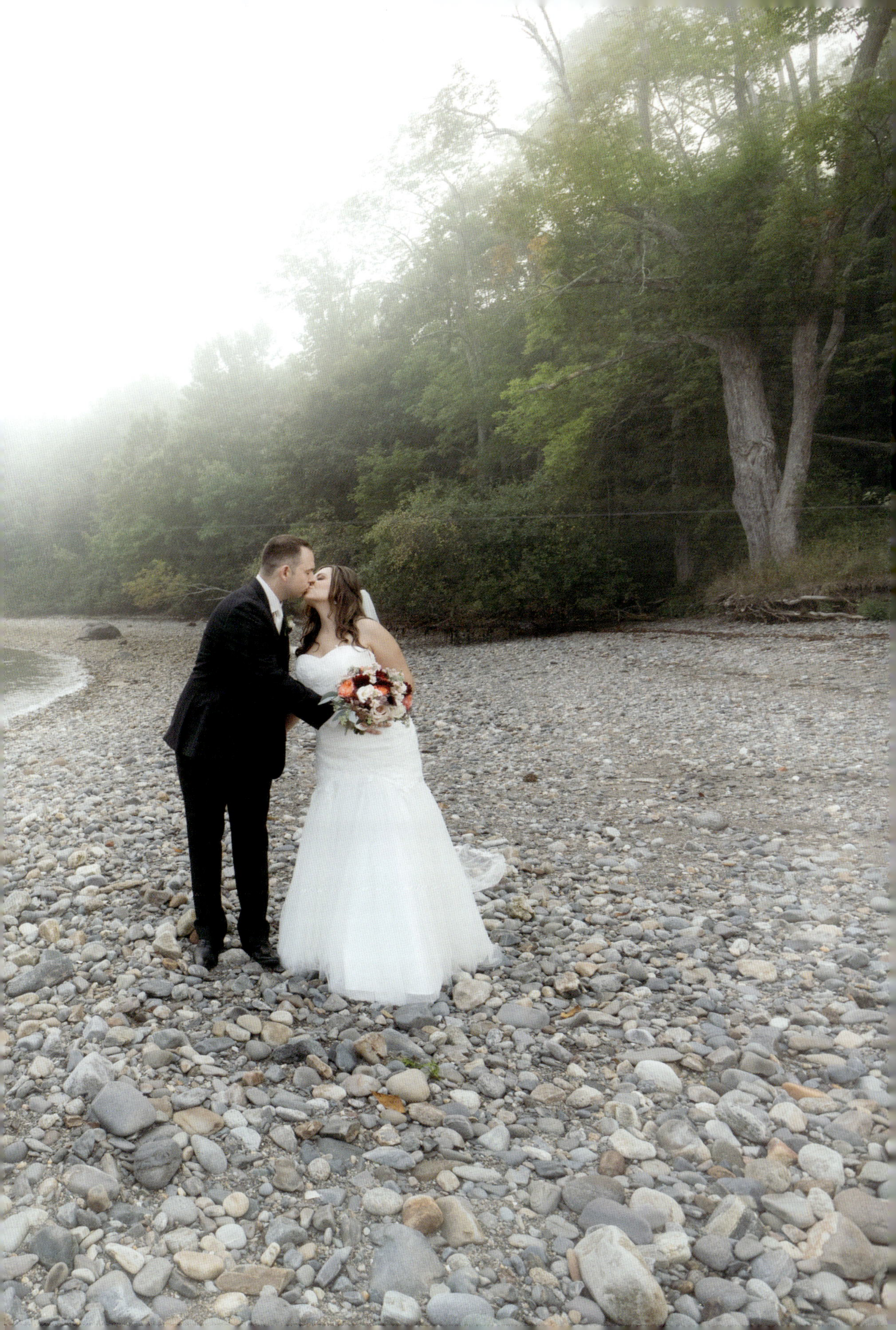

It's the Wedding Day

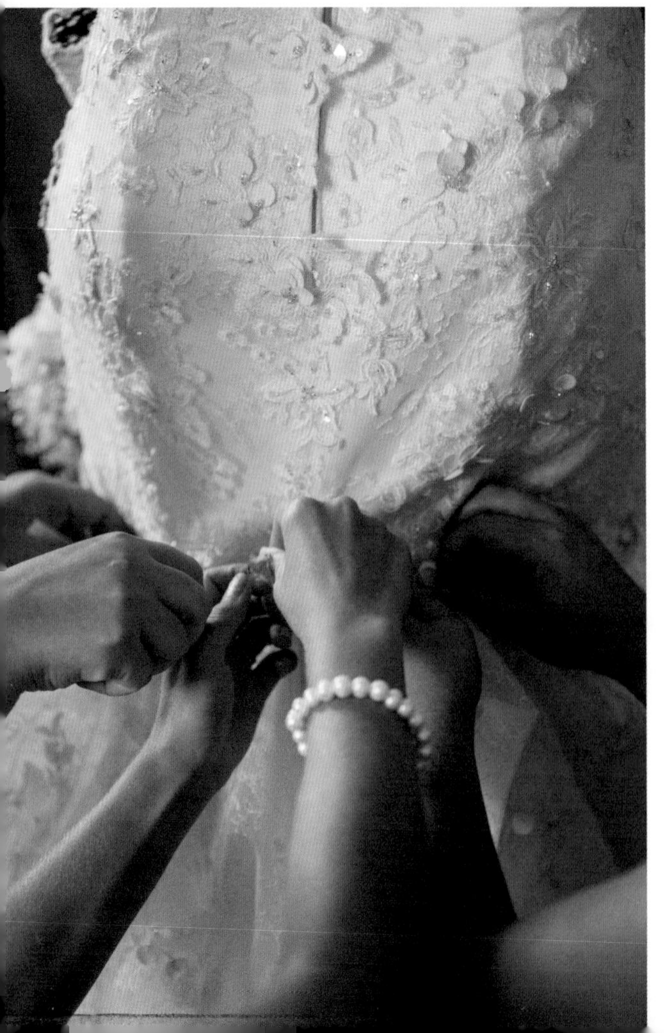

So, you're packed, your batteries are charged, and it's the day of the wedding. You know where you're going; you've been there many times before. Let's say it's 90 minutes away. The schedule you've created has you starting at 11:00AM. So, head out at 9:30AM, right? No! You need to allow for the unexpected: closed roads, heavy traffic, construction, a flat tire, etc., not to mention coffee and bathroom stops. An extra hour is the bare minimum in our book. Bring something to read, or something to do, when you do arrive with plenty of time to spare. That quiet hour is so worth having compared to the stress of a delay en route or, heaven forbid, being late to arrive.

We usually meet first with the bride on the wedding day, so that's how we'll describe our process here.

Don't show up with an army of camera gear around your neck. It can be intimidating. Rather, arrive five to ten minutes early, chat with everyone there in a really friendly way, then find a convenient yet out-of-everyone's-way place to set your gear. Then, get your gear on and start photographing an awesome wedding!

Capture the Details

Photograph the bride's gown on its own if there's someplace nearby worthy to hang it. Get the bride's approval before doing this, and ask her to have someone carry it for you if it needs to be moved. If there is no viable place to take a photo of the gown, don't do it. Assure the bride that it will look much better on her once she's wearing it, anyhow.

Two Photographers

When there are two photographers, each is typically in a different place. There are times, though, when we find maximum benefit in working together for certain segments of shooting. One example is doing the bridal portraits, when Liz spends more time helping the bride to relax than she does photographing. Our

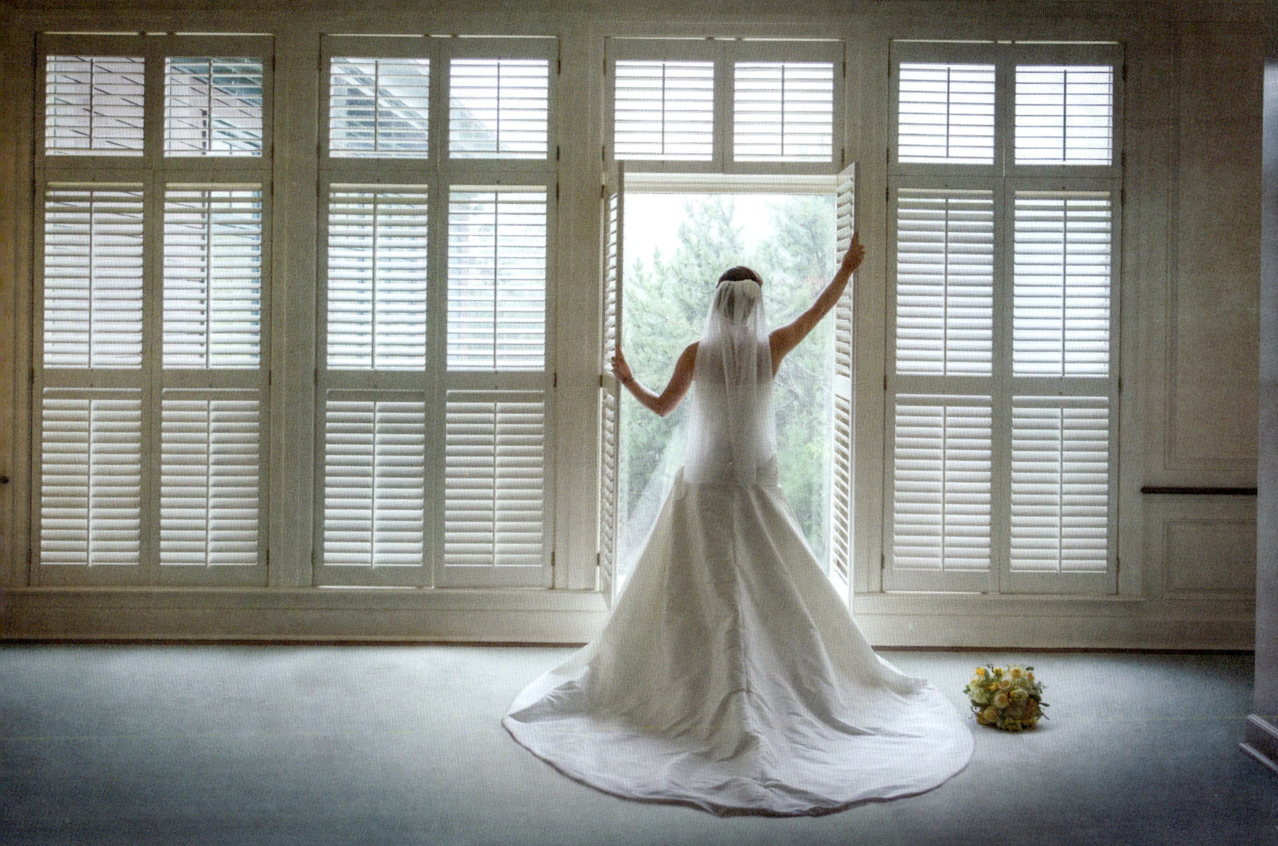

workflow has us working together as a team 100 percent of the time. It works great for us.

Our workflow has us working together as a team 100 percent of the time.

Events Before the Ceremony

What happens between now and the ceremony will depend on whether or not there's a first look. Keep a close eye on the timeline you've created. For the sake of this overview, we'll assume there will be a first look. This being the case, as we're doing our work in the time leading up to the first look, we're looking for the right location to do it. The couple has already been told that we first need to find good light along with a suitably private location. These are the first two considerations by a significant

margin. This particular part of the day isn't about the most stunning backgrounds—it's about the emotion on the couple's faces.

Before the first look, the bride has completed her hair and makeup, and we've photographed her getting into her gown.

Sometimes brides want to do a first look with their dad once they're fully dressed, and this would be a good time to squeeze in five minutes to accomplish that.

Bridal Portraits

It is also important that we find the best place to take the bride to do her formal bridal portraits. We look for a clean, light-colored background (as close to white as possible) with natural light that will fall onto our subject. We try to avoid using flash and often use a portable white reflector to help add fill light on

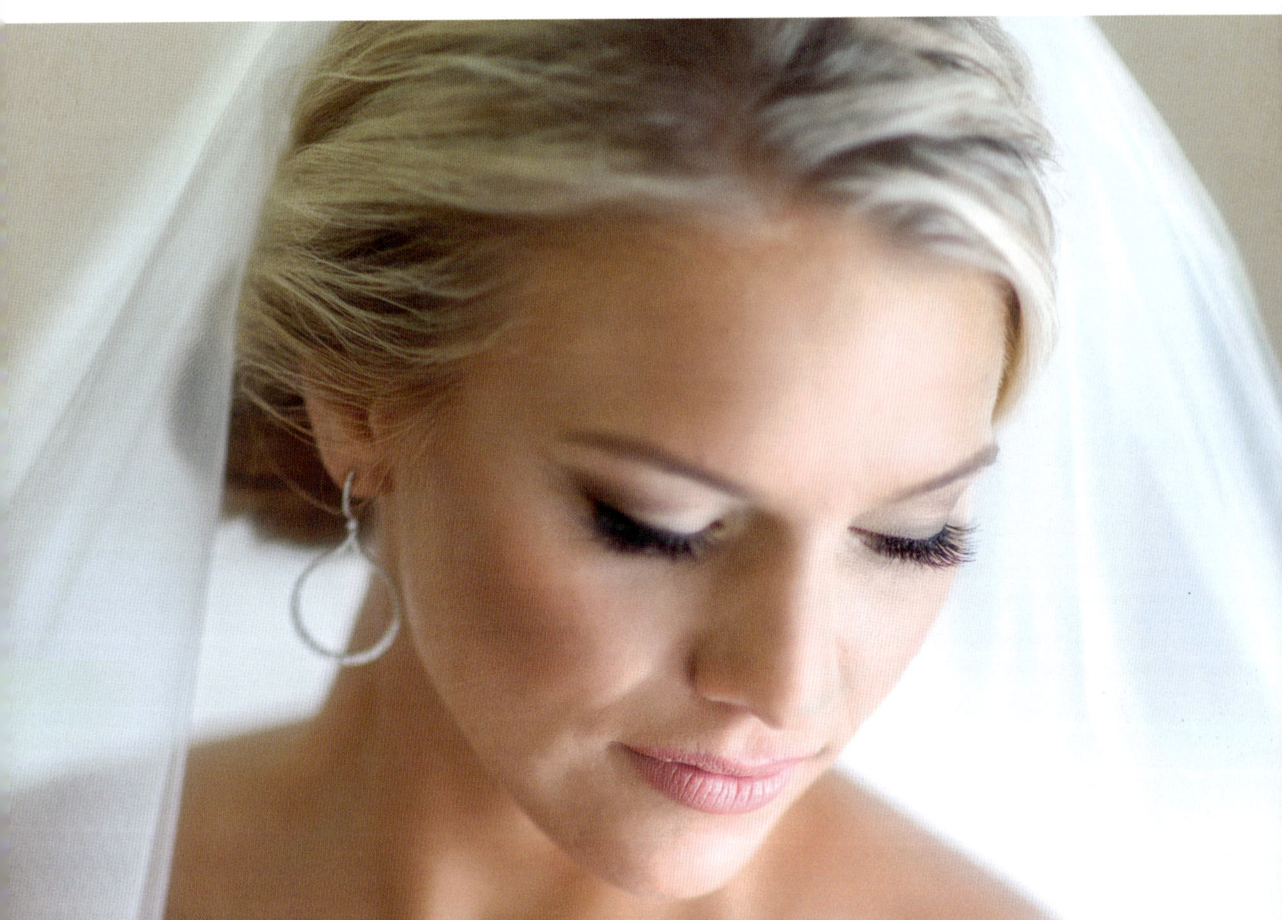

the shadow side of her face. We generally use an 85mm f/1.4 lens for these portraits, at or near wide-open. This requires careful focus on the pupil of the near eye. A word to the wise: Don't use a lens like this without first committing to a lot of practice with it before the actual wedding day. A 50mm will actually do quite well, too, as will shooting at a somewhat more forgiving f/2.8 aperture.

We ask everyone to leave the room where we're doing the bridal portraits. It's a very important, special, quiet time. Well-meaning bystanders often feel compelled to suggest poses to the bride, or tell her to smile, which turns into a huge distraction and can cause confusion for the bride.

We do a variety of eyes closed, looking down-left (or right) images, then have her look through our lenses. Telling the bride to look "though" us rather than "at" us helps to achieve beautiful, pensive expressions. Then we ask her for her best smile. Throughout the process, Liz makes sure the bride is taking deep breaths, doesn't have a wrinkled or worried-looking brow, is bending a knee and putting her weight on the other leg, and that her shoulders are down and she looks relaxed. Quiet words of encouragement will help set a perfect and happy tone. We don't do this often, and we say so, but we provide a "sneak peek" of a favorite shot from the series. Doing so can provide a big boost to the bride's confidence.

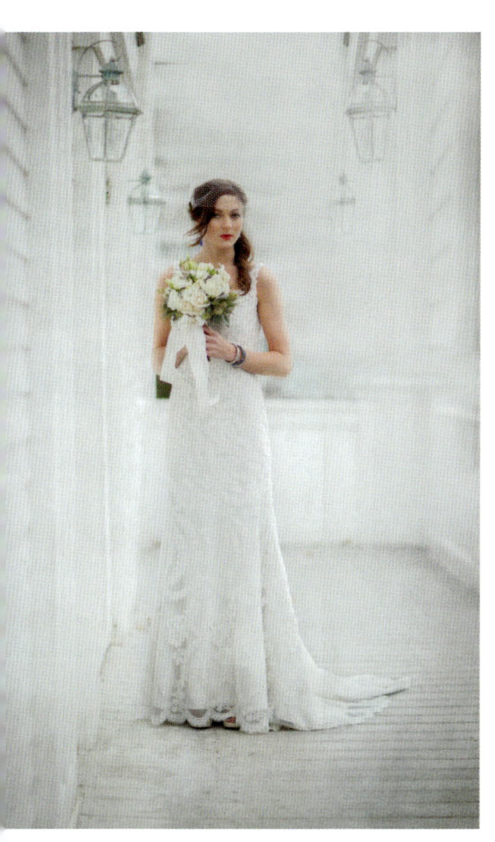
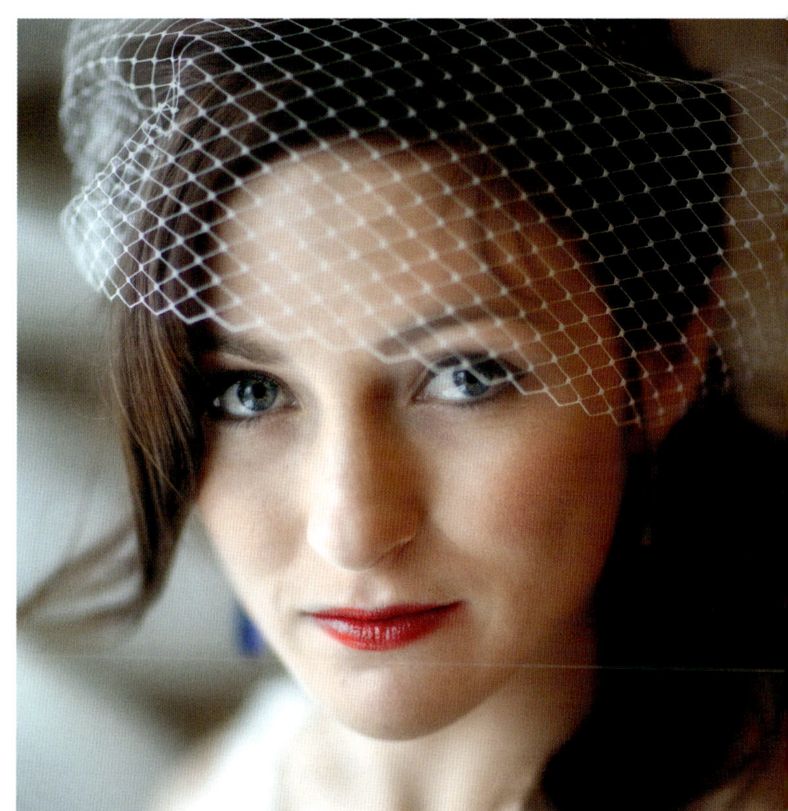

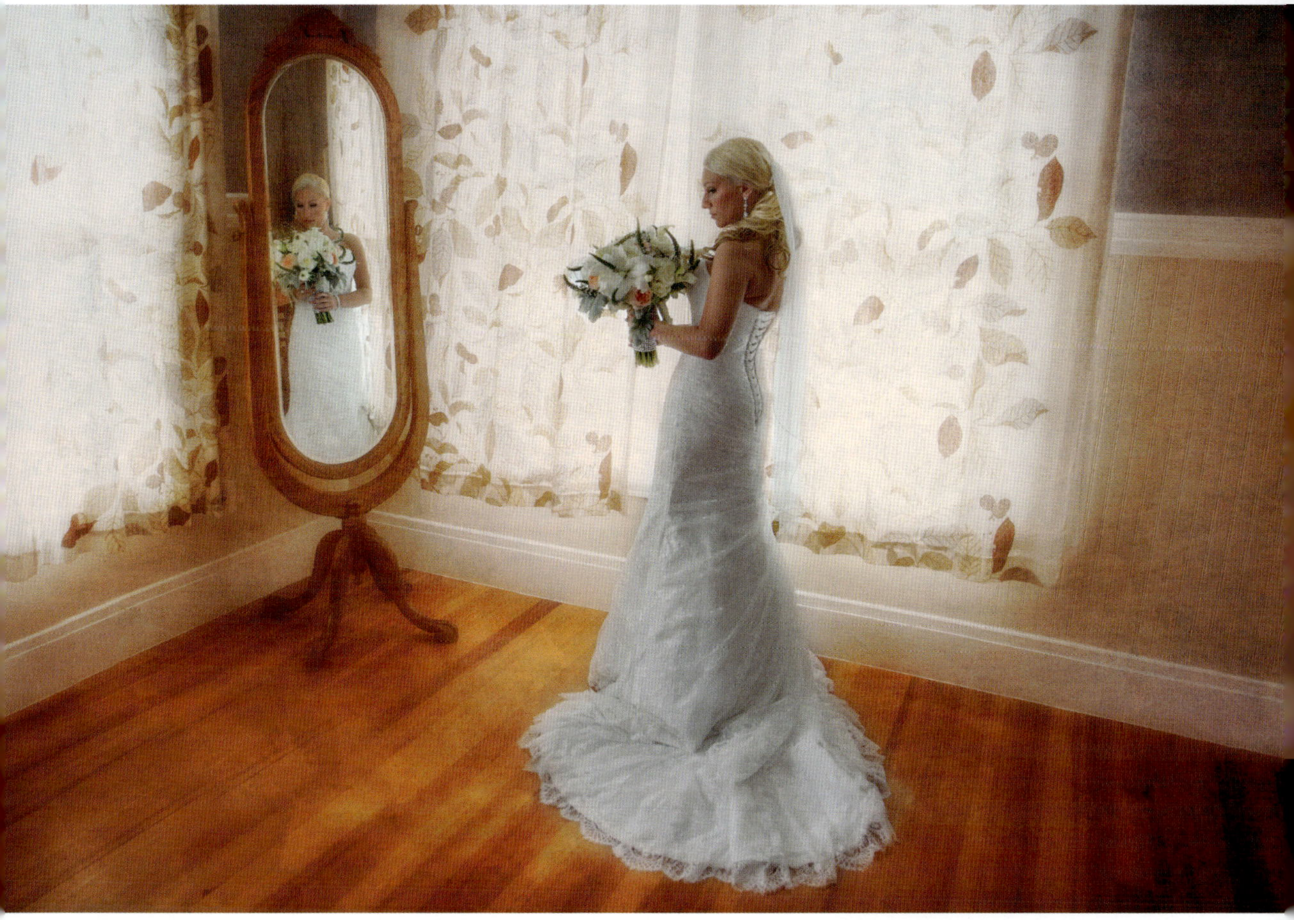

Saying, "You look incredible!" with genuine emotion pays big dividends, too—but don't overdo it.

First Look

When it's time to stage the first look, have your second shooter meet the groom and place him in his spot. Then have him turn away, back-to, so he won't see the lead photographer getting the bride in place a few moments later.

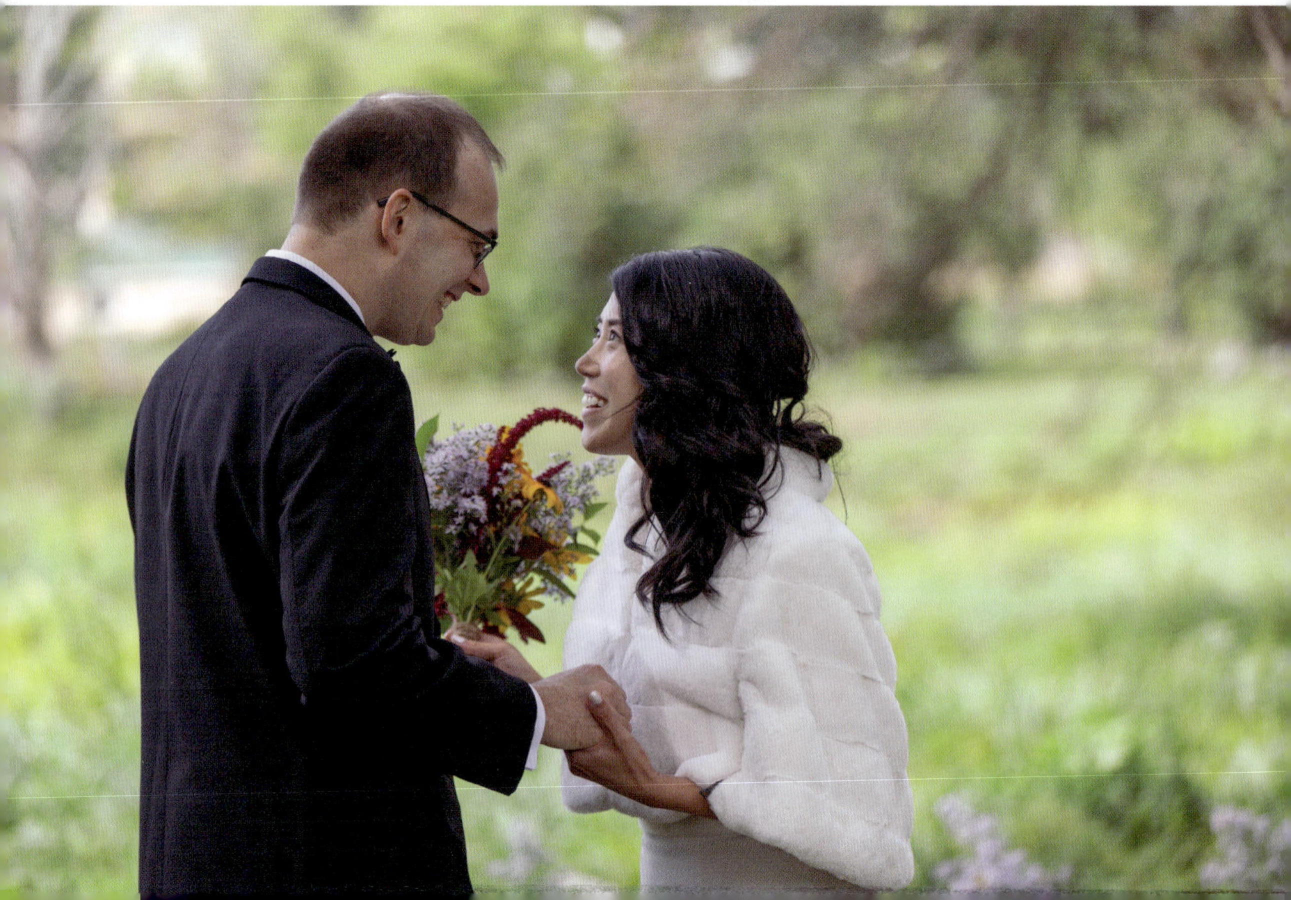

First looks are private for the bride and groom, and their photographers. The only exception we make is to also coordinate with videographers, when applicable, to be there, mirroring what we're doing. No matter how well-meaning they may be, bridesmaids, moms, sisters, brothers, etc., are a distraction at this time. We want to do what we can to make this a private and special moment for the couple. We've also coached, ahead of time, that it's

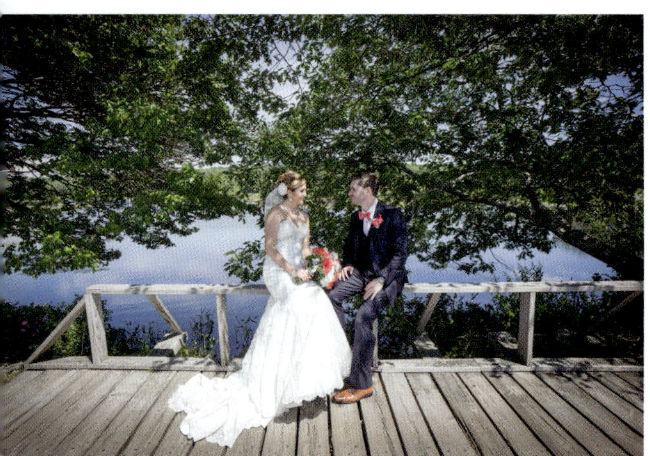

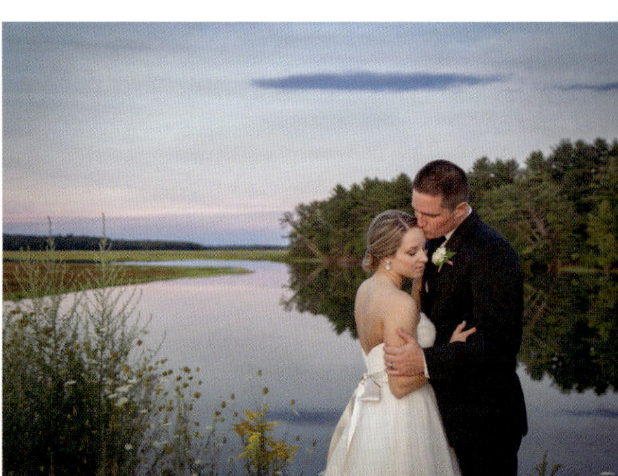

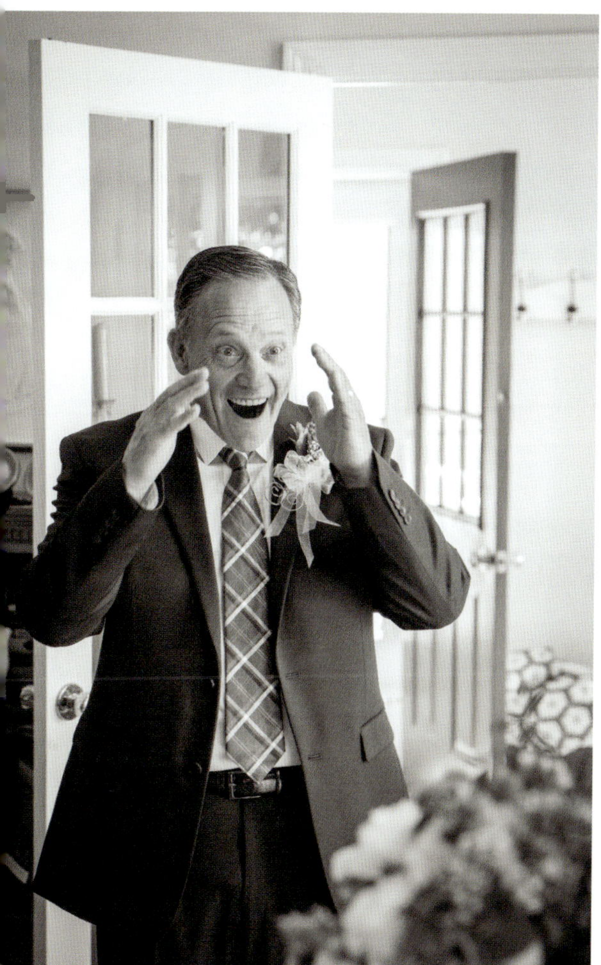

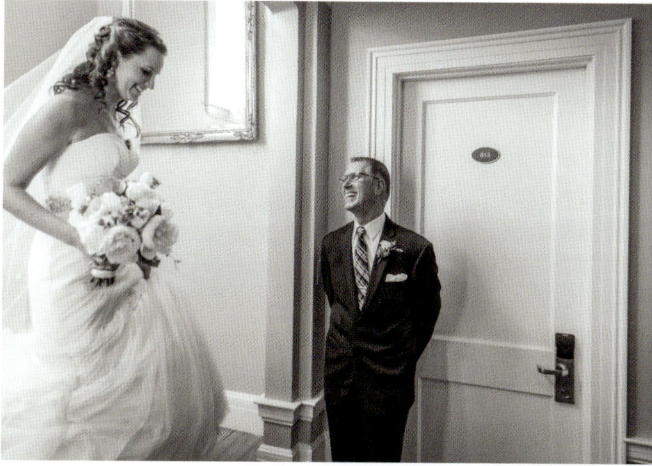

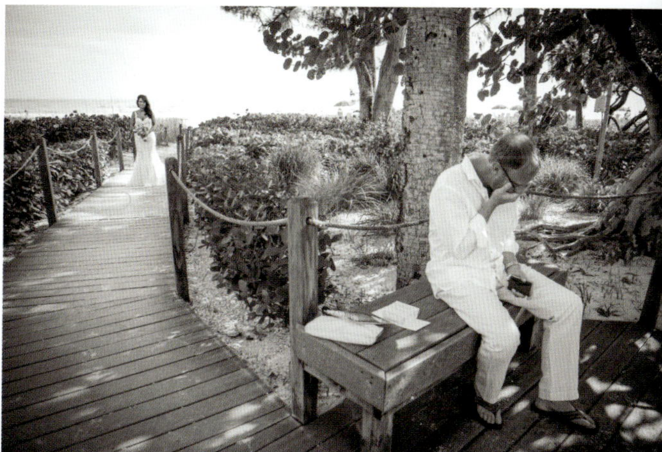

more than okay to let tears and emotions run freely. We've captured some of the sweetest moments of the day with especially emotional first looks. We still get choked up doing first looks much of the time.

When the groom is in place (back still turned), we position the bride about 20 feet away, facing him. We then move to the side of each of them and shoot diagonally so we stay out of each other's field of view. The person photographing the groom selects a focus mode

The first look is all about the couple's emotion.

that will be optimal for capturing a subject moving into the camera's direction. When both photographers are prepared, we gently tell the bride that if she is ready, to call for the groom to turn around and walk to her. She stays put; this helps keep her gown clean. We use our long lenses for the initial phase of the first look and crop in closely on their faces. Remember, this is not about the scenery and background. That will come soon enough. The first look is all about the couple's emotion.

We gradually work back away from the bride to give the couple privacy, then move with wider lenses to a side view of the couple. At this point, we give the pair a few minutes of

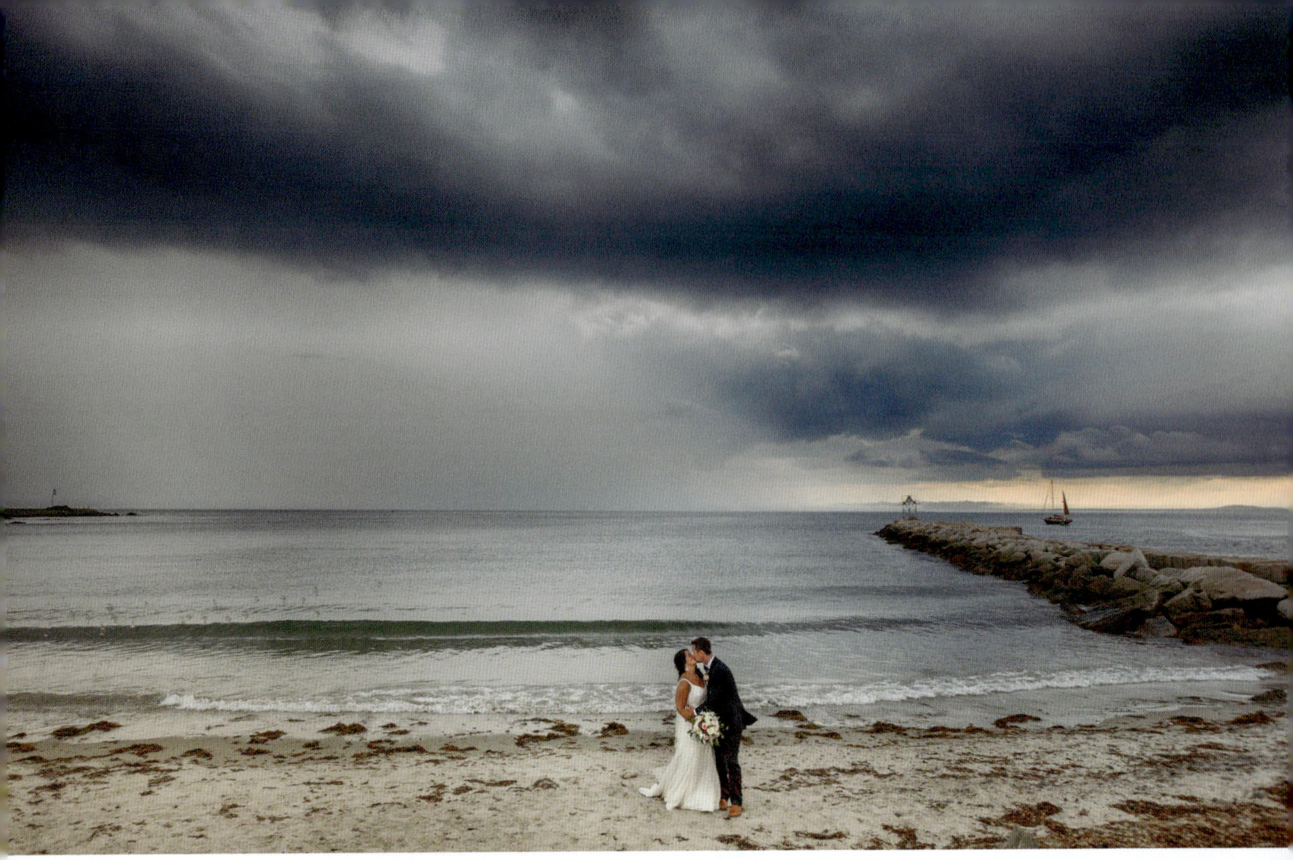

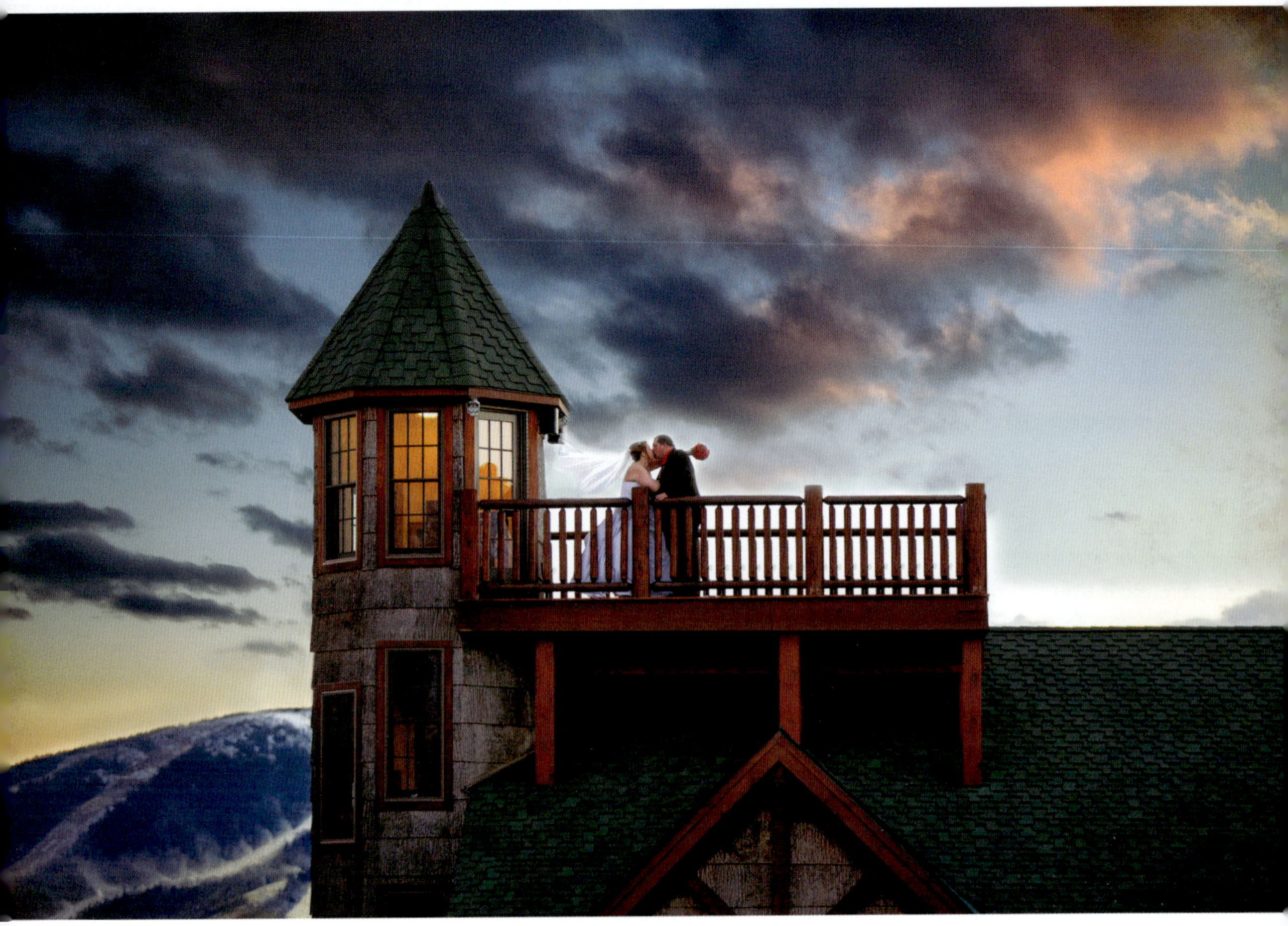

quiet time. We then bring our car over to the first-look location so that the couple can jump in with us for the allotted time for their artistic set.

The Artistic Set

We're based in Maine, and there are many great locations that we love to take our couples to for their artistic set.

We're known for our "environmental portraits," in which couples are photographed at stunning natural vistas, beaches, oceanfronts, jetties, and other natural landscapes. We typically shoot these images wide, with the couple comprising a small percentage of the frame. In the rare event we're photographing in a new location, we'll scope it out using Google Earth or visit the location before the wedding day.

Most, but not all, of our time spent with the bride and groom is devoted to the artistic set.

We love to have our couple ride with us to some nearby places for the variety this provides. We'll stop where we have an uncluttered background and good light and do the formal bride-and-groom pose. This is one of the rare shots for which we have the couple look into our lenses. It's a fairly close-cropped, mid-chest-up, classic view.

No matter what you may choose, defining a style to call your own when photographing the

We typically shoot these images wide, with the couple comprising a small percentage of the frame.

artistic set can be a real plus for your business.

As we wrap up our time with the bride and groom and return to the wedding venue, we'll already have ensured that the women and men of the wedding party are awaiting our return at the designated time. It's not an option to

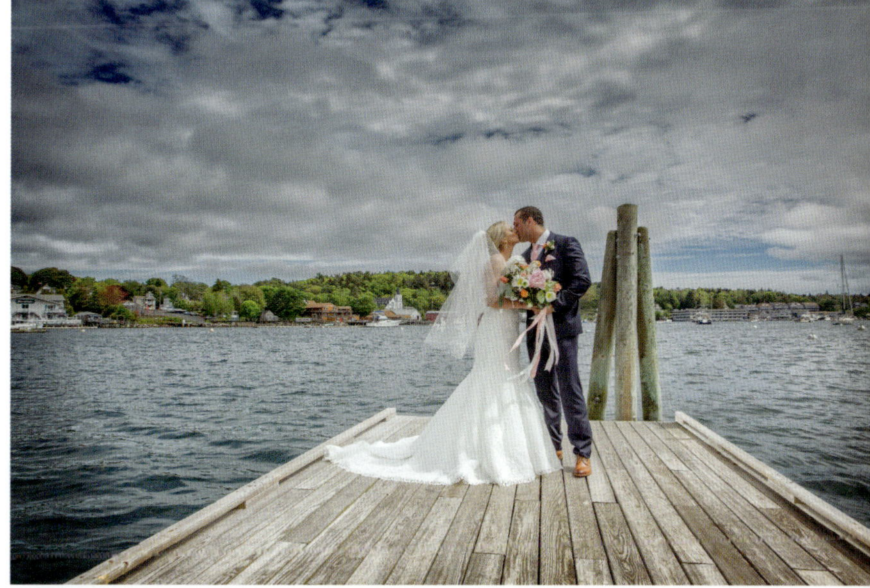

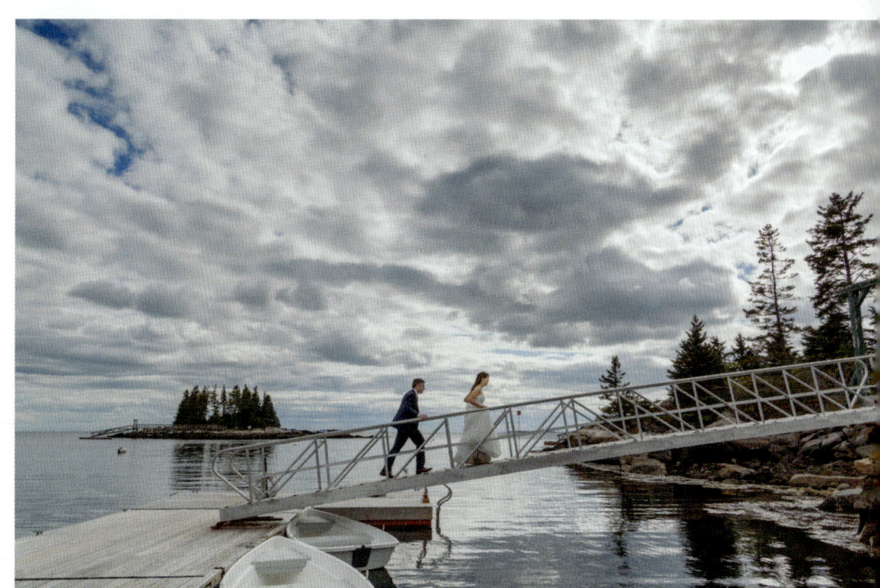

overrun this time. This is why we're loved by all the wedding coordinators wherever we shoot.

Drone

This is also the time, conditions permitting, that we'll do a creative and artistic photo of the couple using our Mavic 2 Pro drone with its high-resolution Hasselblad camera. It's a fairly complicated process—one, in fact, we'll be writing a separate book about in the near future. Until then, here are the most pertinent facts about how we use our drone: (a) We're FAA certified for this type of commercial use. This is required! You cannot provide shots taken with a drone to anyone else in the betterment of your business, whether or not there was any money exchanged, without the proper FAA Part 107 certification for commercial use of small unmanned aerial vehicles; (b) We don't fly over other people; (c) We endeavor to never cause a distraction with our drone; and (d) We don't fly at times or in conditions and locations not allowed by the FAA Part 107 certification.

The Wedding Party

Next, we'll photograph the bride with her bridesmaids, the groom and his groomsmen, and the entire wedding party. For each of these combinations, we like to grab a formal, posed shot, then quickly grab a more "loose," fun style. When we photograph the entire wedding

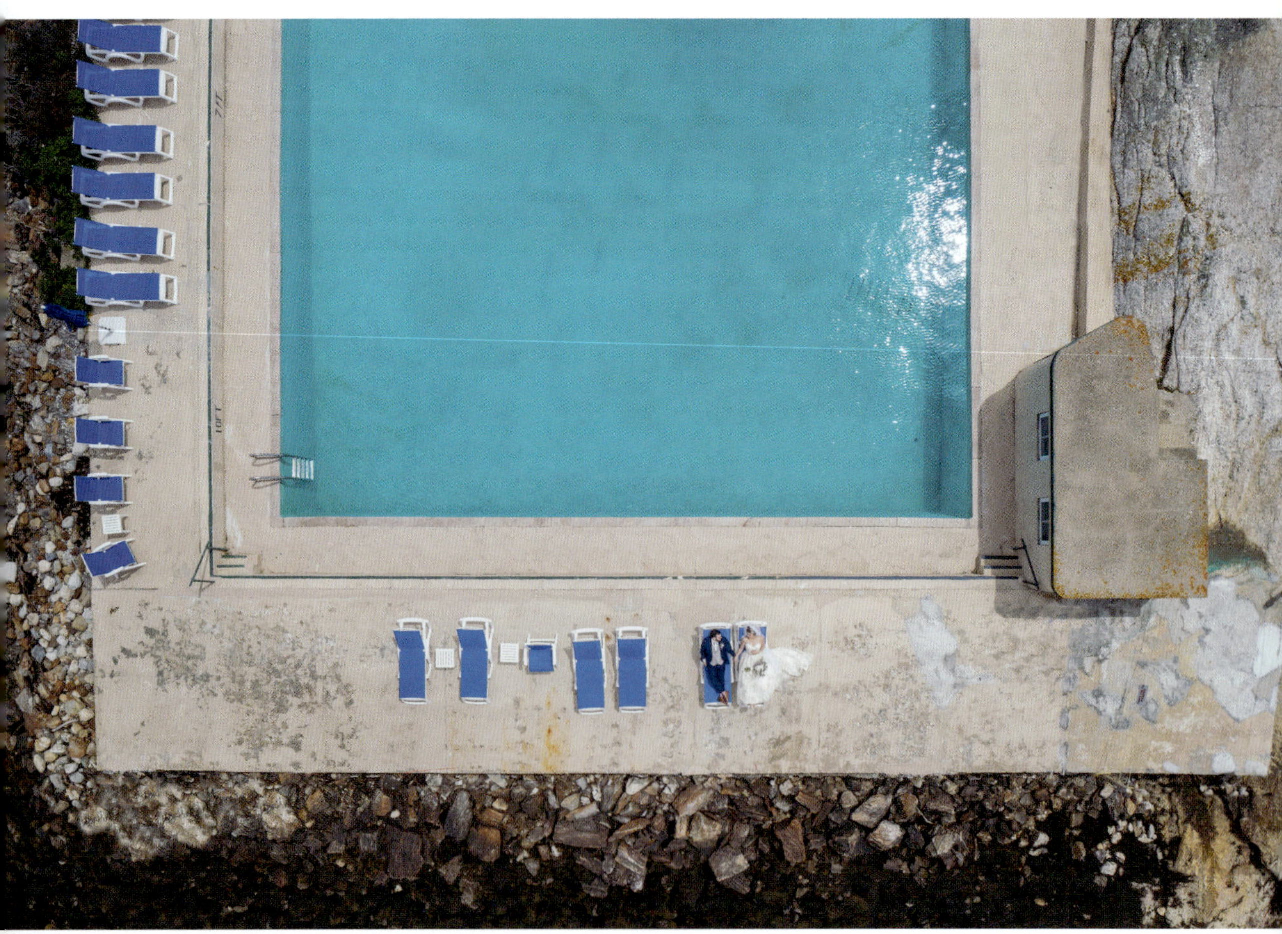

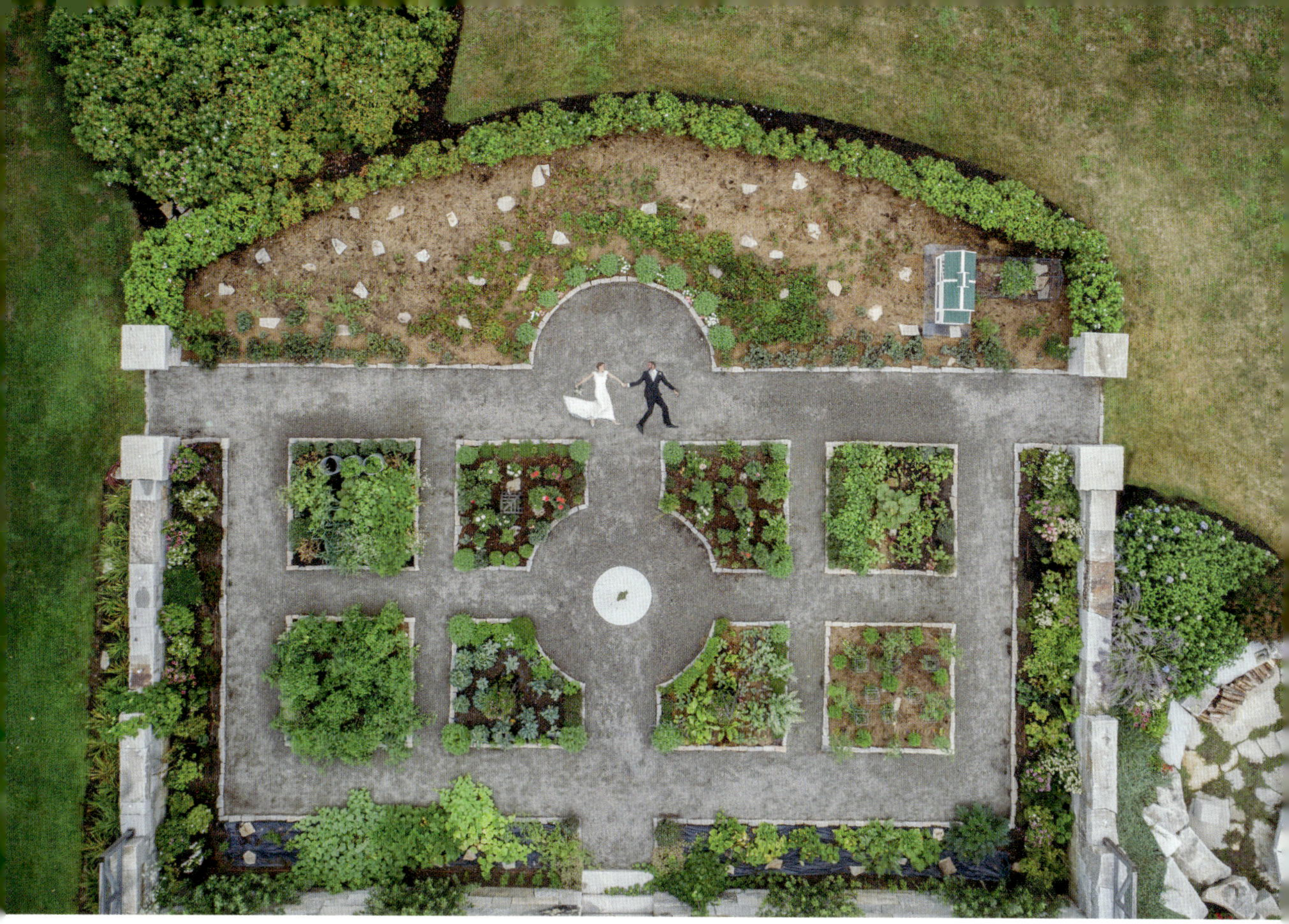

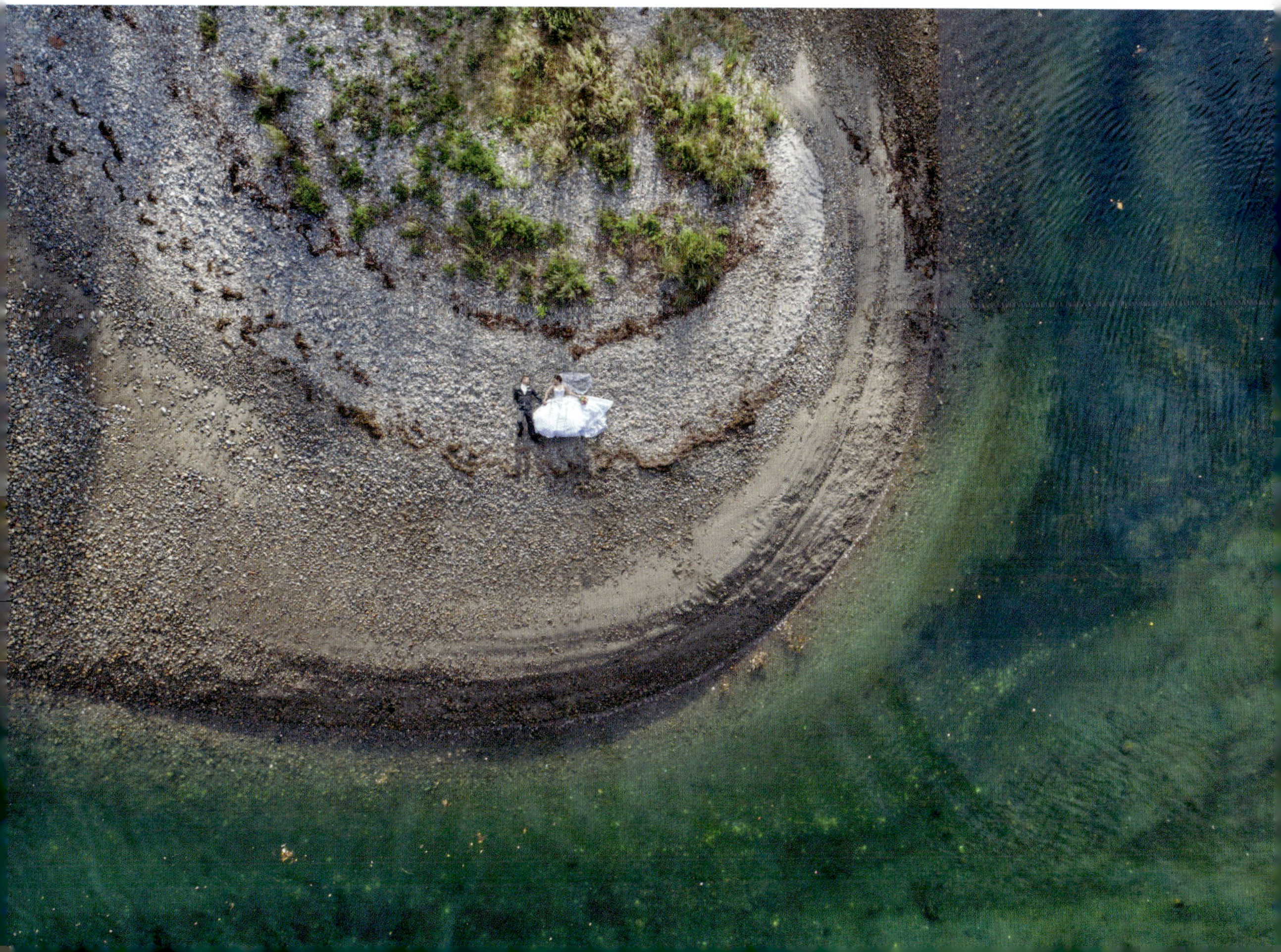

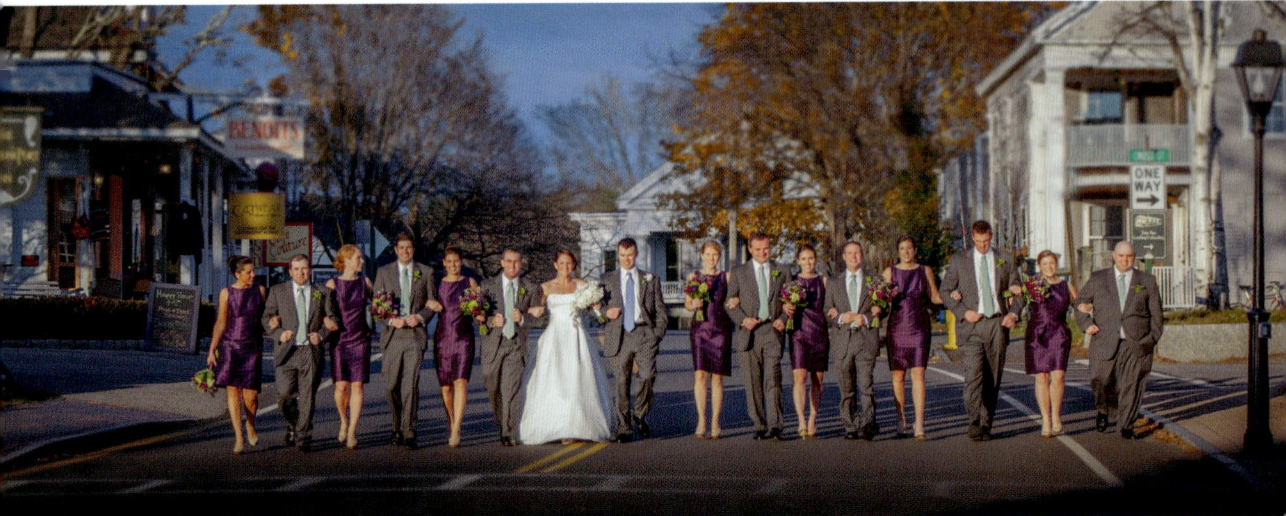

party, after a shot with the bride's attendants on one side and the groom's men on the other, we have everyone mingle as couples (typically with the person whom they'll be walking with for the recessional). We also photograph the bride with each of her bridesmaids/men individually, along with the groom individually with each of his groomsmen/women.

If we've not yet done so, we will then move on to take the groom's solo portraits.

Family Photos

As we're wrapping up with the wedding party, we have the right people gathering for family photos.

Family photo time can be very hectic, but it's possible to make it flow seamlessly. So, we do what we can ahead of time to help ensure things run smoothly. Here's the process:

First, we let the couple know that family photos are typically best limited to parents, grandparents, and siblings. We have both the bride and the groom create a list of everyone to be included. We see a good number of photographers ask for this list. We prefer to

ask the couple to appoint a "helper" or "photo captain" on each family side—someone who knows most everyone. This person will see the list ahead of time, speak to each person, and tell them the time and place to meet to be in the family photos. Then, when it's time, it's up to this helper to round up the crowd and send them up when called. Meanwhile, they have the next group on deck. This system, for us, is far smoother than trying to manage the family photos ourselves.

This process may sound complicated, but it's amazing how well it works. As the photographers, we can concentrate on good composition and great light, and when everyone's in place, we raise our hand, and with a clear and commanding but friendly voice, we have them look at us, and we take three to five shots. We thank them and promptly ask for the next group to be brought up.

During this process, there will be folks lined up behind you with their smartphones and cameras trying to grab these group shots. We don't try to stop them; this isn't the same thing to us as it would be if people were trying to steal posed creative shots. However, we do not allow the group we've just photographed to stay put while everyone grabs their smart-phone photos of the family. There simply isn't enough time! If you had 15 different groups to photograph, and it took just two minutes for each, with this alone you'd need 30 minutes. If that turned into even just five minutes for each group to allow bystanders the chance to shoot, this 20-minute segment of the day would turn into an hour and a quarter! This simply isn't

. . . it's up to this helper to round up the crowd and send them up when called.

an option. The bride and groom will be your advocates. Just ignore what may be going on behind you with others trying to photograph, and promptly have the helper move the next group in. People will start to realize that maybe this isn't the best time to try to take photos. Again, this is all done in a friendly manner. We're do not advocate any rudeness whatso-ever. Ultimately, you have a job to do, and it would be your fault (even if it really wasn't) if things went awry with anything having to do with the photographs.

Downtime

Before the ceremony, we build some downtime into the schedule so the bride and groom, wed-ding party, and family involved with the photos thus far can hydrate, relax for a few moments, and refresh before the ceremony. At this time, we transition to the ceremony site and prepare for the wedding ceremony.

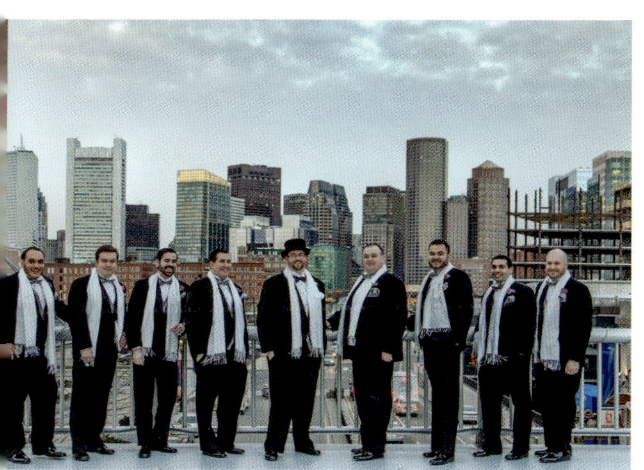

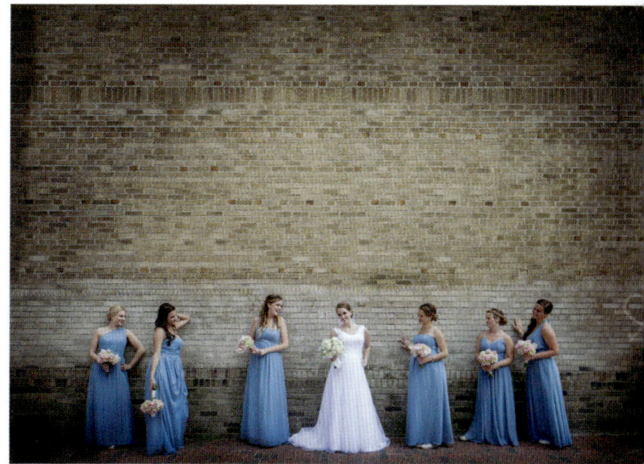

The Ceremony

As a two-photographer team that works together at every wedding, we operate silently and in full synchronization with each other. It's something that organically occurs once you and your second shooter have worked together enough times. Until such a time, have a plan in place as to where the lead photographer will be and where the second photographer will be—but don't over-plan, since it's impossible to do an effective job with too much predetermined location planning. The lead has to be able to move freely to suit what's happening and must be able to react to the unexpected. The same holds true for the second shooter. Just have a plan in place for who'll cover what key segments of the day and from what vantage point.

Before the ceremony begins, be sure to have introduced yourself to the officiant. Assure them that you'll abide by any rules of the clergy or house of worship. Civil officiants will likely have fewer or perhaps no rules. In all cases, be as discreet and professional as possible.

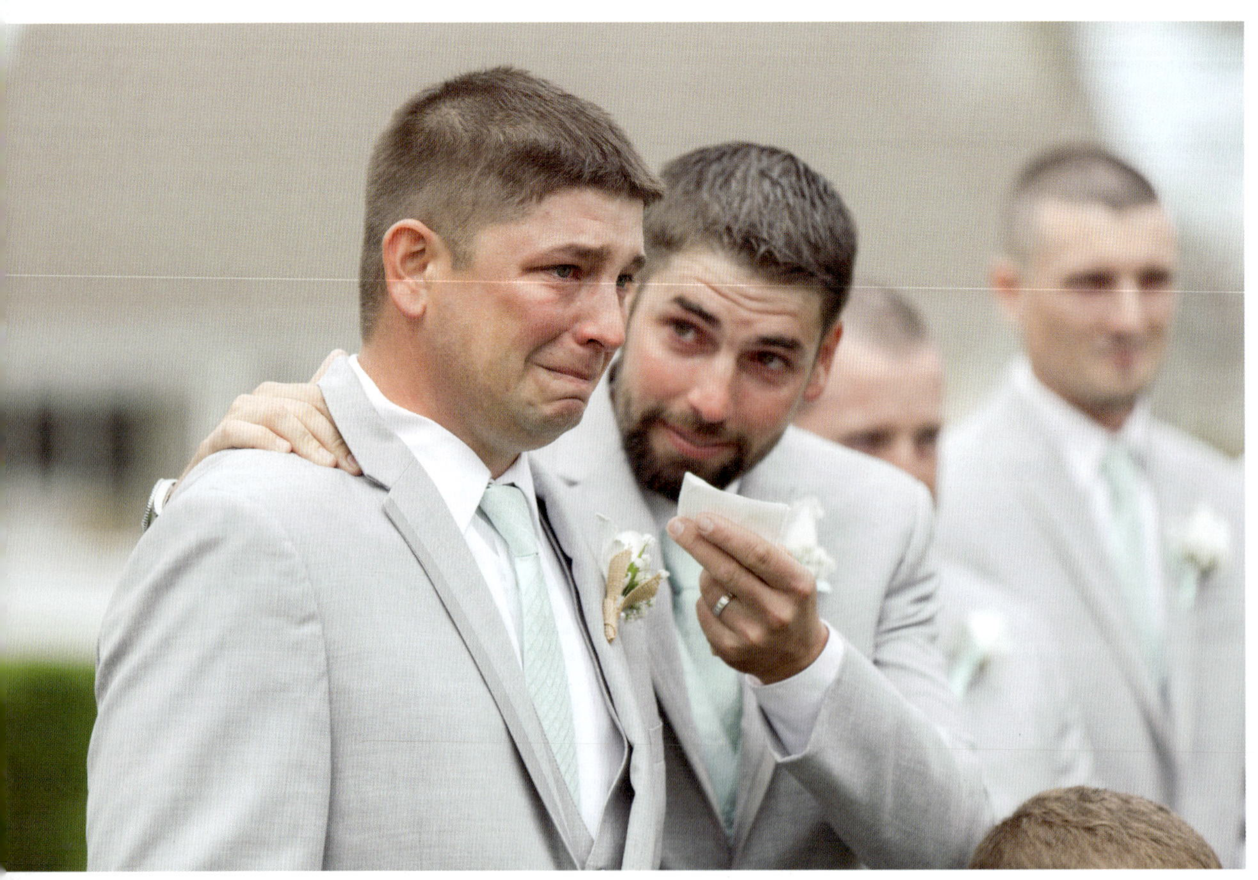

Find out how long the ceremony is expected to last. Estimates given for in-church weddings are typically more accurate than those for less formal outdoor services. We're often told a number of minutes of expected length, then find it look half the time we expected.

You'll need to be ready for the vows and first kiss, and that means being where you need to be ahead of time.

Wherever the ceremony is happening, try as best you can to get some scene-setting shots of the location.

The Processional

For the processional, there's just one right place for the lead photographer to be—the center aisle, and truly centered—for the entrances of the wedding party, but mostly for the bride and (usually) her dad walking her up the aisle.

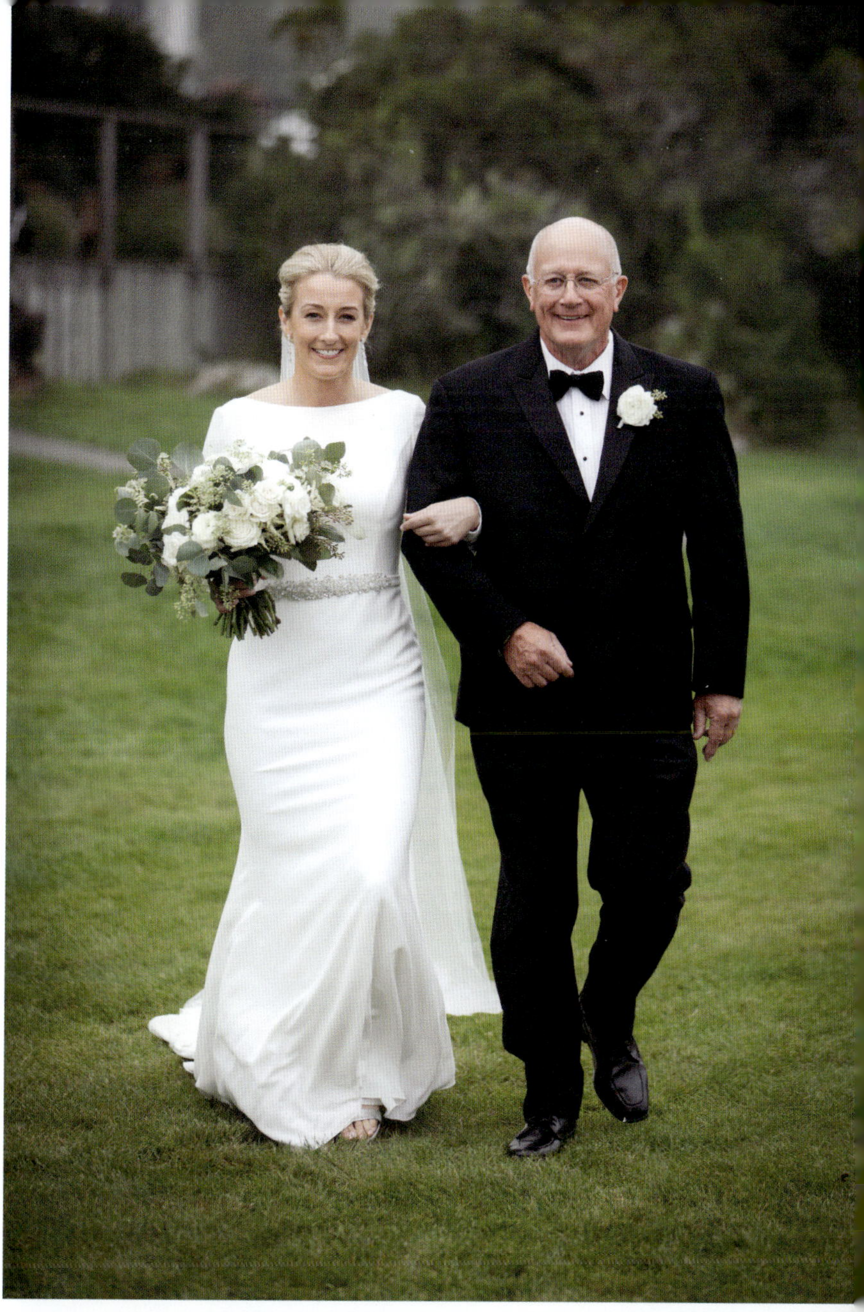

For indoor ceremonies in churches, lighting can be tricky. This is particularly true for the processional, as the doors leading from outside are often not only aligned with the church's center aisle but are left open, creating a strong backlight

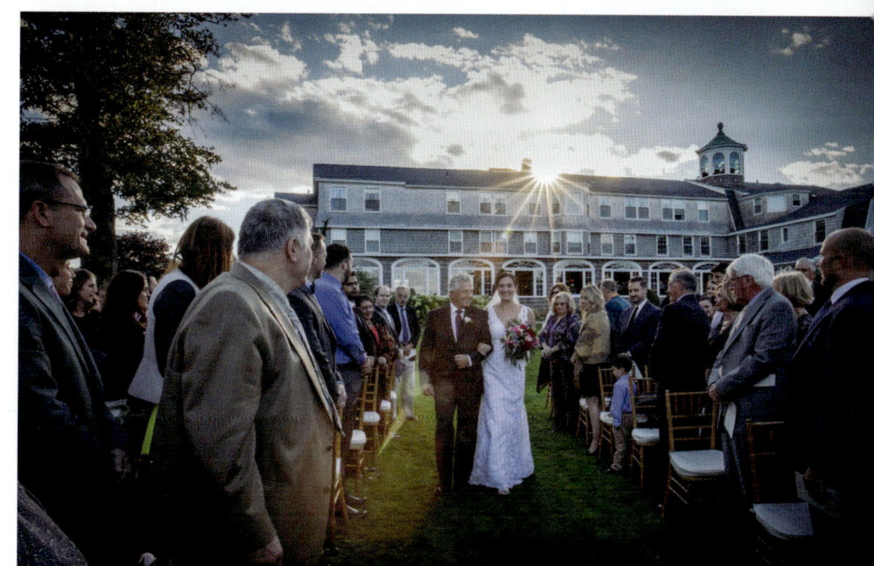

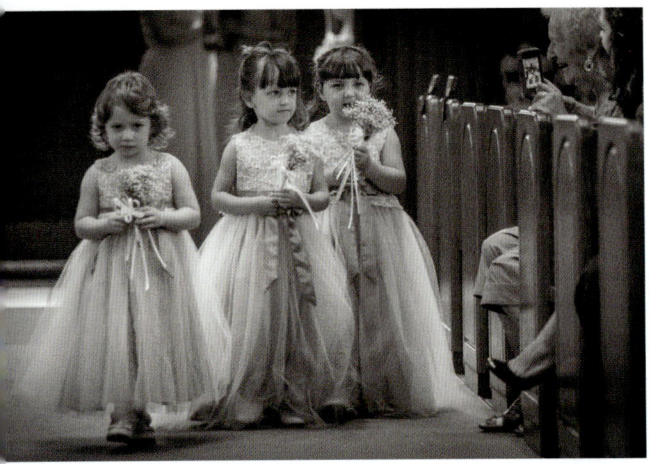

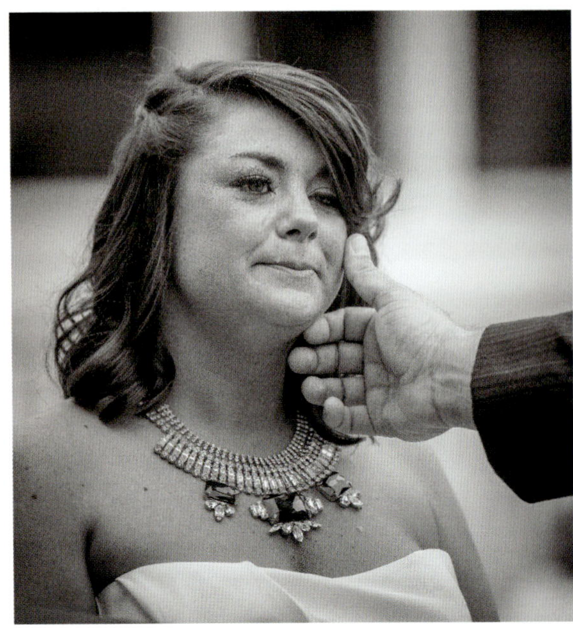

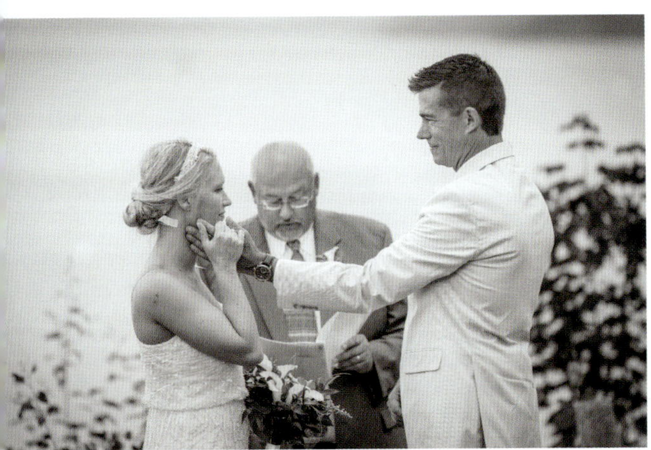

bride is inside. If closing the doors isn't an option, you may try setting your exposure for the light that will be falling on her face, rather than the overall scene, including all that backlight. The third option, maybe the simplest and technically "safest," is to use flash. On-camera flash with a bounce card will often work well, and it is quick and easy to set up. Rarely is there time, unless you have a dedicated helper, to set up off-camera flash and reflectors in a church, and if you did, it would not be discreet.

So, you're centered in the aisle for the bride's processional. Of course, you'll need to step out of her way well before she comes close to you. It's a good idea to use a long zoom lens so you can be most of the way up the aisle and still get some great close-ups as the bride and her dad enter. After you step aside to let them pass, carefully come back out into the main aisle, being careful not to step on a long train. Switch to a wide-angle view of the bride being handed off to the groom. Your second photographer would be well advised to shoot

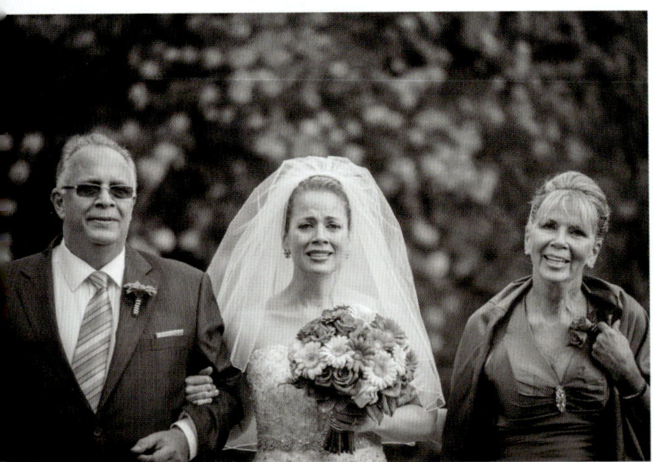

situation, especially when they open to the outdoors. There are some solutions, of course. If you're striving to shoot with available light, try to arrange for the doors to be closed once the

this segment from the front for a better view of the facial expressions and then focus his or her attention on the groom. Even in cases when there is a first look, the walk up the aisle is like a "second first look," and it provides a great opportunity to capture genuine emotion.

Once everyone is in place, the lead photographer can go down the main aisle and circle back to the front sides for close-ups of the bride, opposite the second photographer, who's doing the same with the groom. Just know, especially in churches and synagogues, where you can and cannot be.

The Ceremony

During the ceremony, be discrete. Do not call attention to yourself. Move fluidly and in sync with your second photographer. Have we mentioned that it's a good idea to wear "quiet soled" shoes?

For the key parts of the ceremony, the lead photographer is usually positioned in the center aisle, halfway or all the way back, using a 70–200mm lens. Ideal placement will depend on the length of the aisle and the distance you need in order to be able to fill the frame with the couple.

The second photographer can often get great close-ups of the ring exchange from the front/side.

Always remember, in houses of worship, to determine in advance where you are and are not allowed to be.

Recessional

We use zoom lenses, so we can stay at the back and, for the recessional, zoom in on the couple and back off when they approach us. If your camera has a "servo focus" mode, in which the

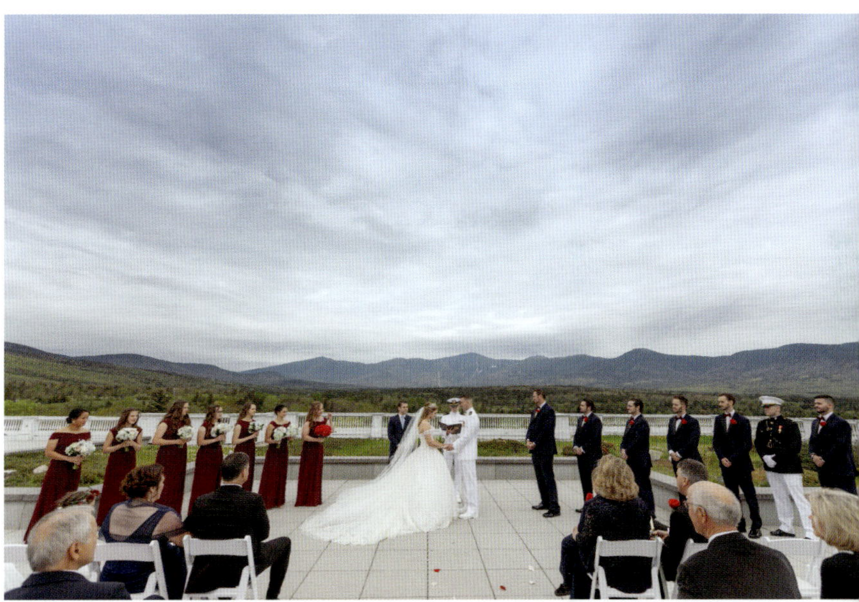

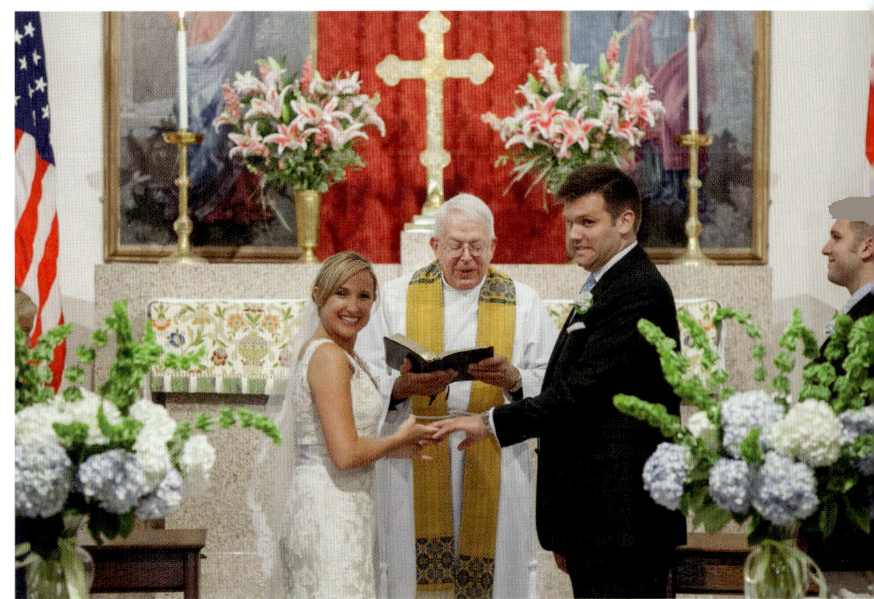

system is optimized to focus as your subject moves straight toward the camera, activate it for the recessional, providing you plan to stand still and let the couple approach you.

An alternative way to photograph the recessional is to walk up the aisle to about 20 feet from the couple, use a very wide angle lens, and then walk backward, shooting as fast as possible. If you're inside a church, you may need to use an on-camera flash. To help ensure your flash can keep up with this rapid shooting, we suggest using a high ISO (it'll lighten the load on your flash), fresh batteries, and an external/auxiliary battery pack, if your flash supports one. There'll be a lot of high fives, smiles, and activity, so be prepared for

some great shots here. The downside to this approach is that the couple could feel a little intimidated with you facing them, at a short distance, as they walk down the aisle. They're so caught up in the emotion of the moment, though, that this isn't usually an issue.

If you are photographing a church wedding, and you used the walking-backward-with-the-couple approach, duck into a pew before you reach the doorway, let the couple pass, and then grab some really awesome shots as they

There'll be a lot of high fives, smiles, and activity, so be prepared for some great shots here.

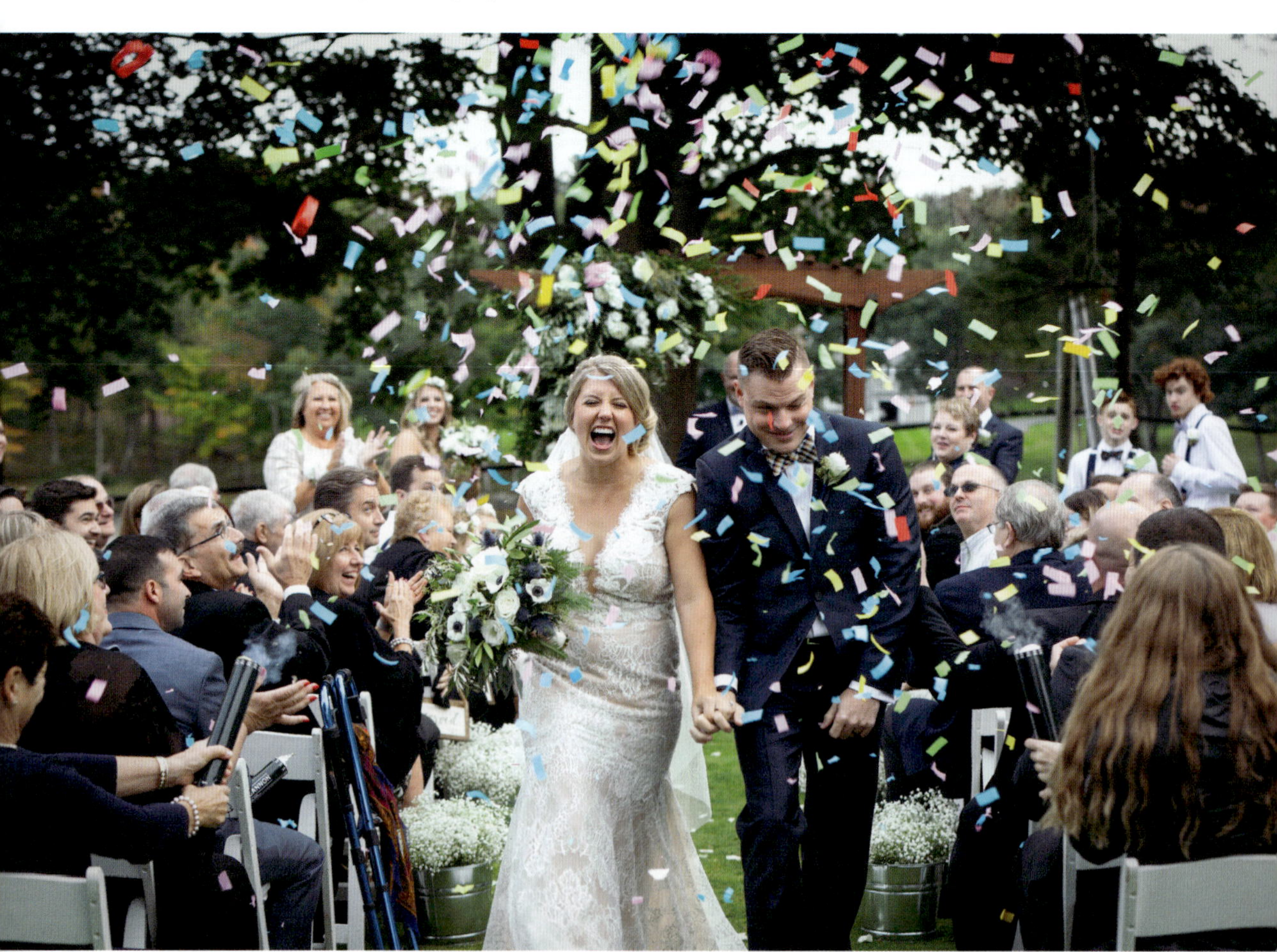

walk through the first doors, to the vestibule, then outdoors. Don't hesitate to say "Kiss!" as they pass through the doors. You could actually chat with the couple before the wedding and ask them to do this. It's amazing how often they remember to stop to kiss.

If your clients' wedding is in a church with a balcony or choir loft, send your second photographer up there and have them align true center with a wide or fisheye lens to photograph the recessional. It makes for a fantastic photo op. We feel that if you can't be centered, the shot will be so compromised that it may not be worth the effort. Sometimes the balconies are locked, so planning ahead can make all the difference between getting and missing an award-worthy image.

Don't underestimate the richness of the photo opportunities the recessional provides. There is no other point in the day when the bride and groom are beaming as radiantly and naturally!

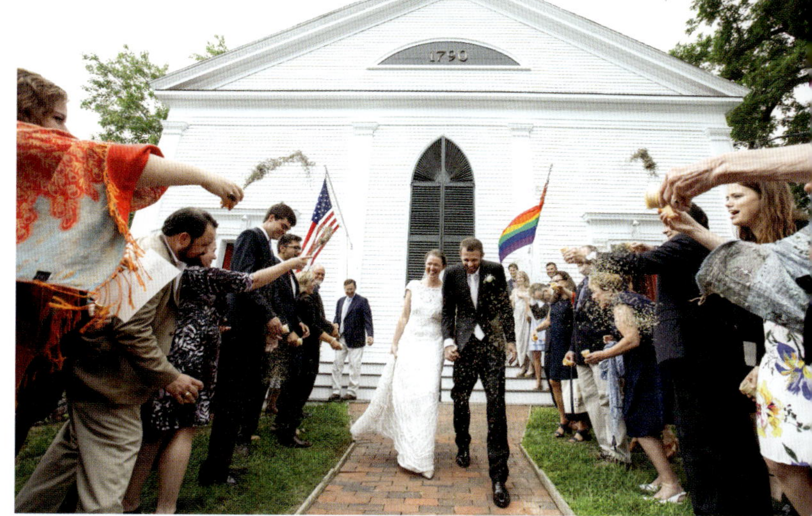

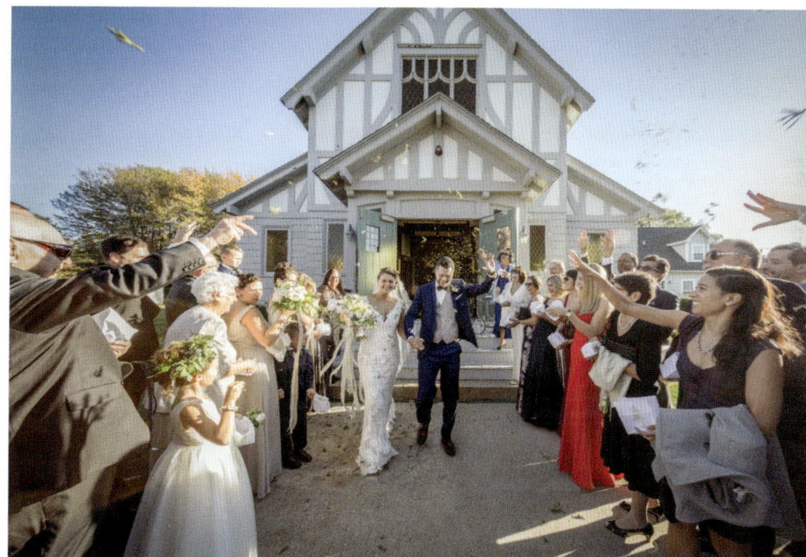

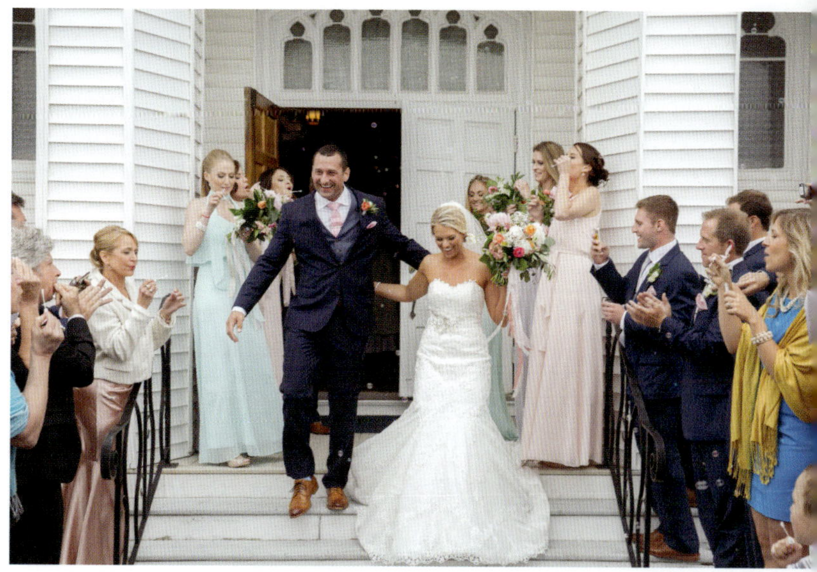

Following the Ceremony

If you've done a first look with your couple, you're now at the point of the day when you're virtually done directing anything; everything else will happen organically. Starting with the cocktail hour (which can run more than an hour), things are pretty much in the hands of the coordinator at the venue.

If you have had the benefit of doing the first look, it's likely that all of your off-site, wedding party, and family photos were done early, and the couple can attend the cocktail hour. They can use this opportunity to mingle with guests whom they've yet to greet, giving them more time to party during the reception. This fact alone can be enough to compel your couples to opt for choosing to do the first look. It's a win–win!

Remember when we were talking about what to pack, and we brought up the subject of spare shoes? If it's anywhere near the halfway mark of your day, now would be a good time to change into the second pair!

Cocktail Hour

If you've done a first look, everyone, including the photographers, will head to the cocktail hour. We get photographs of details like trays of drinks and hors d'oeuvres (when the trays are fresh and full, when possible!). Action shots of people's hands reaching in for a food item are fun to get. Anticipating when a person in a conversation is going to laugh is a great way to grab some candid photos. Just avoid shots of people eating.

Toward the end of the cocktail hour, we typically move into the reception room ahead of the guests for table, cake, detail, and overall scene-setting shots.

What if There Wasn't a First Look?

When the couple does not choose to do a first look, the timeline is a little different.

First, the time leading up to the ceremony is dedicated to the details, candid shots of the

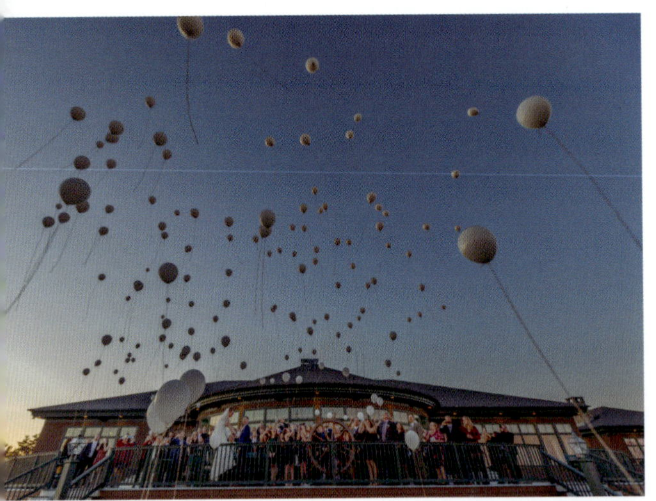

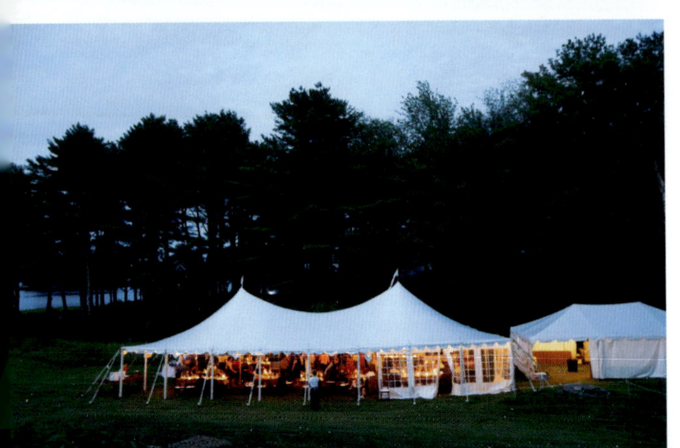

bride's preps, bridal portraits, and the women of the bridal party together in groups and individually with the bride. When the men are close by, we'll do the groom's solo portraits. We'll also capture shots of him and the men of the wedding party, plus individual shots of the groom and each of the men. There may be a first look with the bride's dad to photograph, too. We want to be sure to allow for a little downtime before the ceremony, as well.

After the ceremony, we're in rapid-fire mode. We gather the family members who are to be included in the family photos. We can't afford to wait for anyone who's strayed off, so the role of the designated helper of each family is huge here. We cannot afford to take more than 15 to 20 minutes to get this whole segment done.

Next, we complete whatever is missing from the wedding party shots. Most of the time, we'll have already completed the bride's side of things, and hopefully the groom's side, too. If not, we do them now. We've learned never to rely on someone saying, "We'll just do it later!"

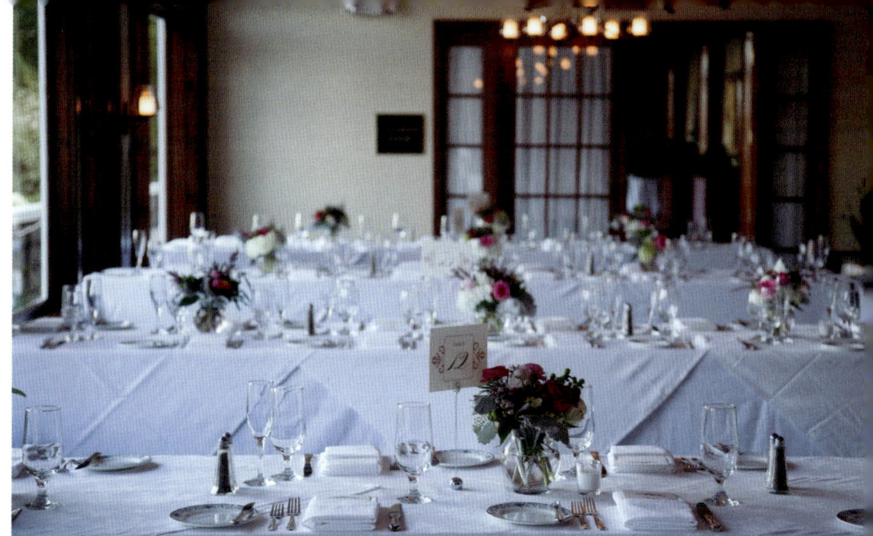

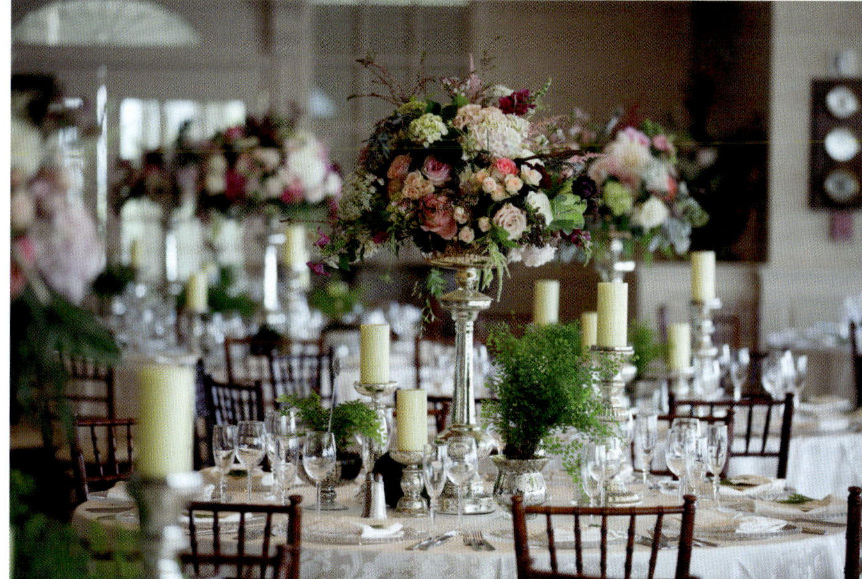

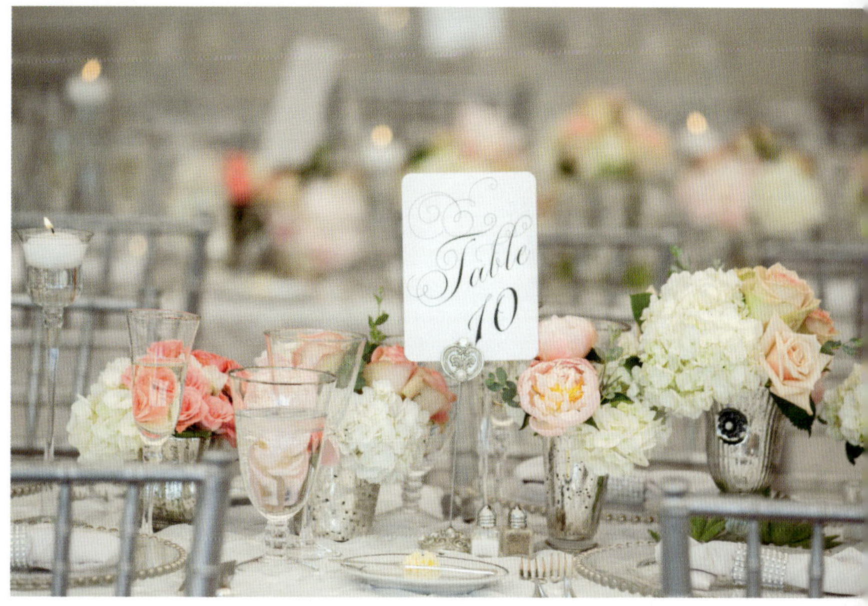

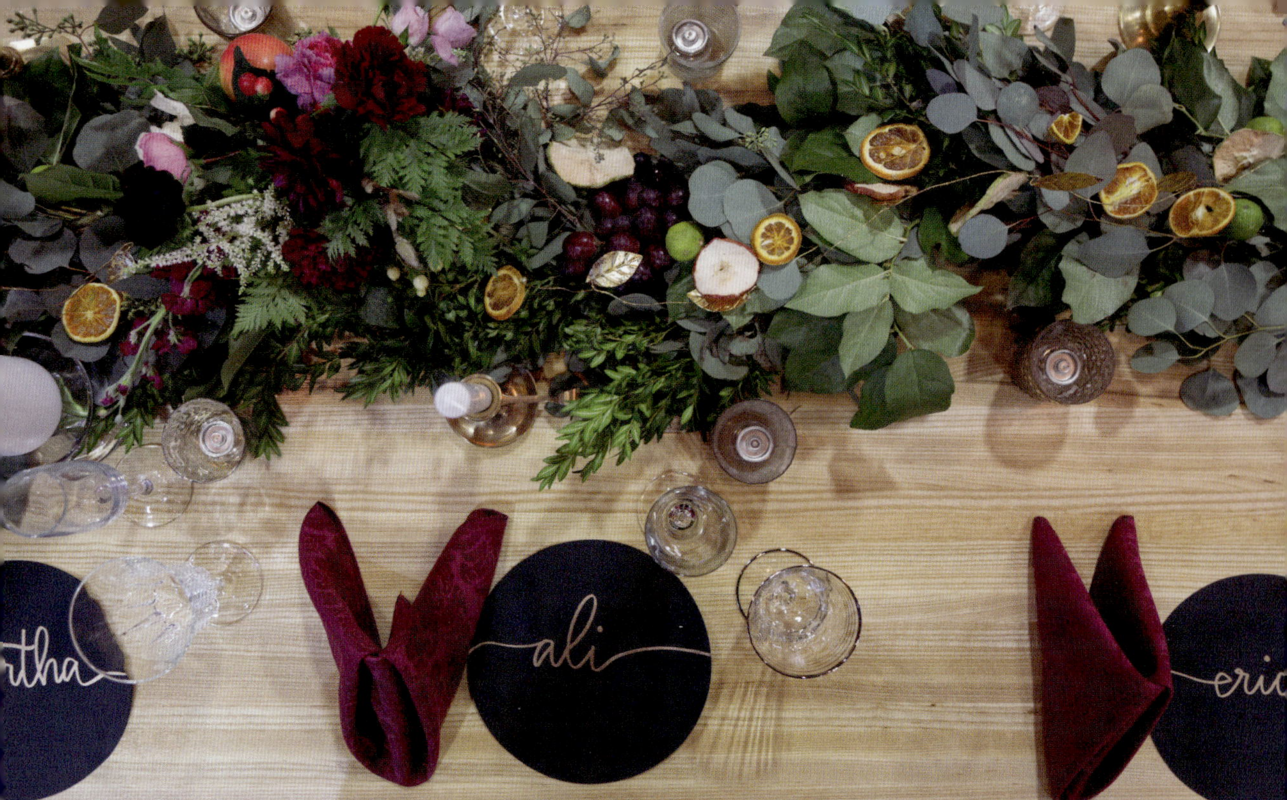

Experience has taught us that "later" seldom, if ever, happens at a wedding.

Next, we get the men and women of the bridal party together. First, we position the women on one side (customarily the left side as you're looking at them), the couple in the center, and the men on the other (right) side. Capturing one quick camera-aware formal shot is the first goal. We then have them loosen up, perhaps posed as couples, and ask them to laugh, reminding them to look at each other or at the couple, not at the camera. After maybe ten minutes, we deliver the good news that the wedding party rocked it and can head to the cocktail hour.

While cocktail hour is underway, and until it's time to return to the venue, we photograph the couple's artistic set. We tend to go off-site with our couples, but this may not be necessary at certain venues.

We make sure to get the couple back to the venue on time for the introductions at the reception, per our notes on the timeline. We double-check with the venue coordinator to ensure there have been no changes to the timeline. Schedules can and do change on the wedding day, for a variety of reasons! We like to have the couple there five minutes before they're needed. Getting back a bit early shows we respect the need to keep everything else on track.

As you can see, a wedding without a first look results in more "crunch time." That can lead to a great deal of stress for both the photographer and the couple. This is in no small part why we strongly encourage every couple to do a first look.

The Reception

Often, right after the couple is introduced, there may be a first dance, toasts, and perhaps a blessing before the salad and meal courses. We try to get photos of plated meals without interfering with the staff serving them. As soon as the wedding party is eating, it's your time to eat, too. It generally takes some help from the couple to ensure that this happens. It's important that you're fed and hydrated so you'll be at your best to finish the day's shooting.

The rest of the night, you'll adhere to the schedule set by the venue. The timeline you developed with your couple will have emphasized the need to ensure that all the key events held during the reception will be complete by the time your coverage ends. You'll want to be sure to get at least some of the dance party photographed, but there's rarely any need to stay for the entire reception, unless there's a special event like fireworks or a sparkler send-off at the end that couldn't otherwise have occurred earlier during the reception.

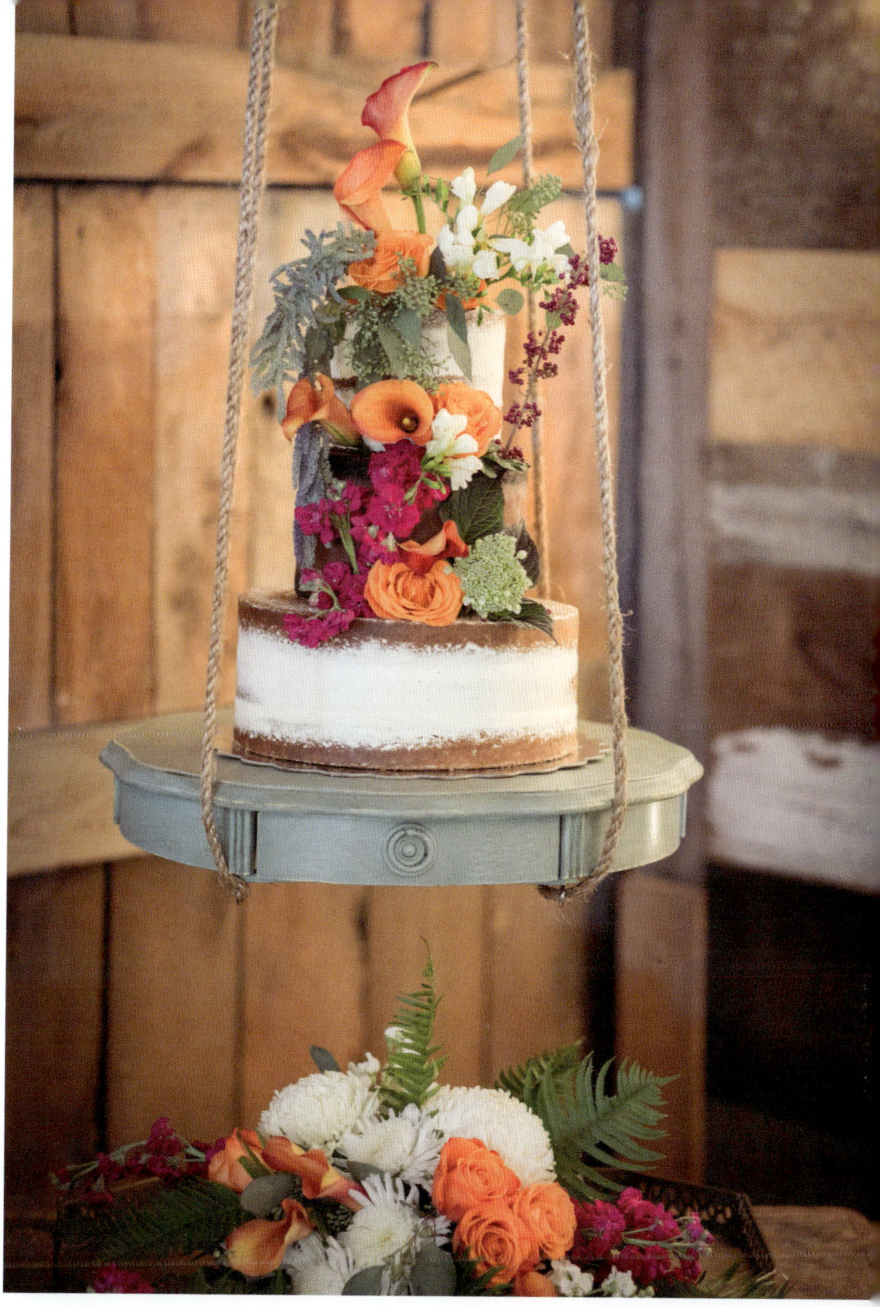

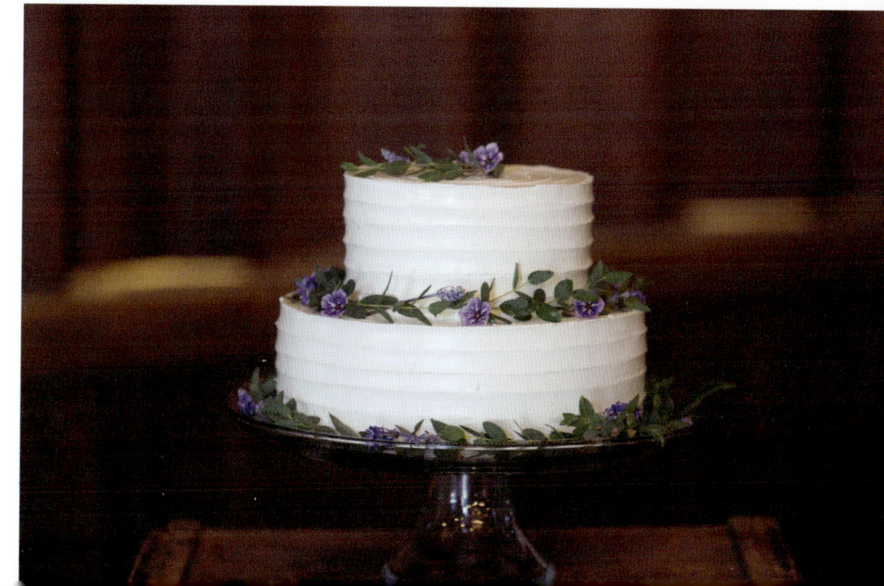

A high ISO and a fast (f/2.8 or better) and really wide lens (we love our 16–35mm f/2.8 for this, with or without flash depending on the light in the dance area) and the camera held high and pointed downward makes for fun images.

At Jewish weddings, the Hora, generally played to the *Hava Nagila,* is one of the most fun and photo-rich opportunities. For this, use your super-wide lens and dial in the highest ISO setting your camera will allow without excessive noise, as you'll be shooting a lot! There's so much moving around in circles that we recommend on-camera flash, set to ETTL,

with a bounce card. Off-camera flash may or may not work well for this fast-paced shooting, so use it only if you're experienced and aware that bad light can happen if you inadvertently shoot into a flash. Results will be more consistent, and the light just fine, with on-camera flash, done right. If you have an external battery pack for your flash/flashes, as we talked about earlier, use it.

You'll know it's time for the Hora when you see two chairs being set up to hoist the couple into the air. This is a wild, fast-moving time, and it's critical that you work your way to the center of the dance floor immediately. Be next to the couple as much as you can. Practice shooting blindly, holding your camera high and pointing downward. Photographing the first few seconds when the couple is in their chairs is critical. This is when they (often the bride) will have eyes popping wide open and mouths gaping with joy—and fear of falling out of the chair, though we've never seen this happen. Just stay with the couple, and be ready when they're set down and the action is repeated

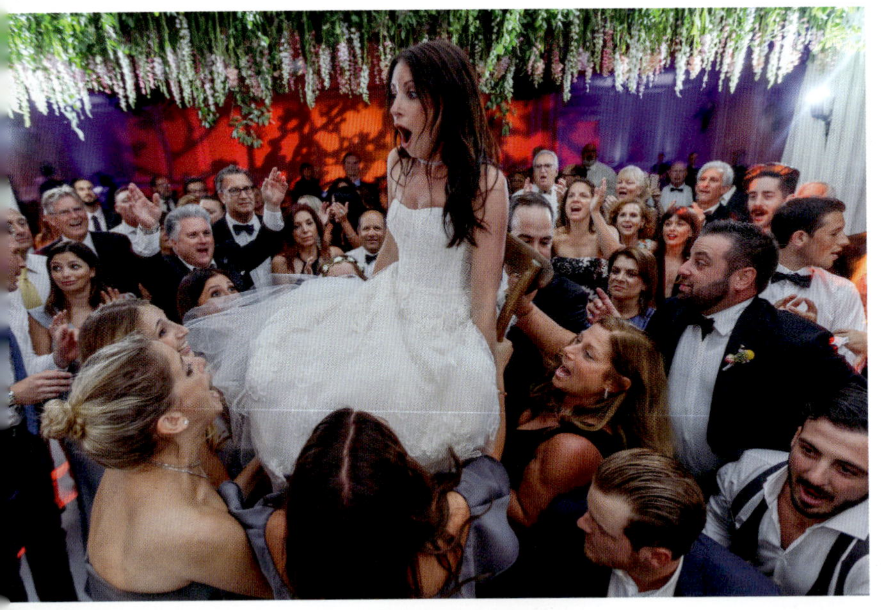

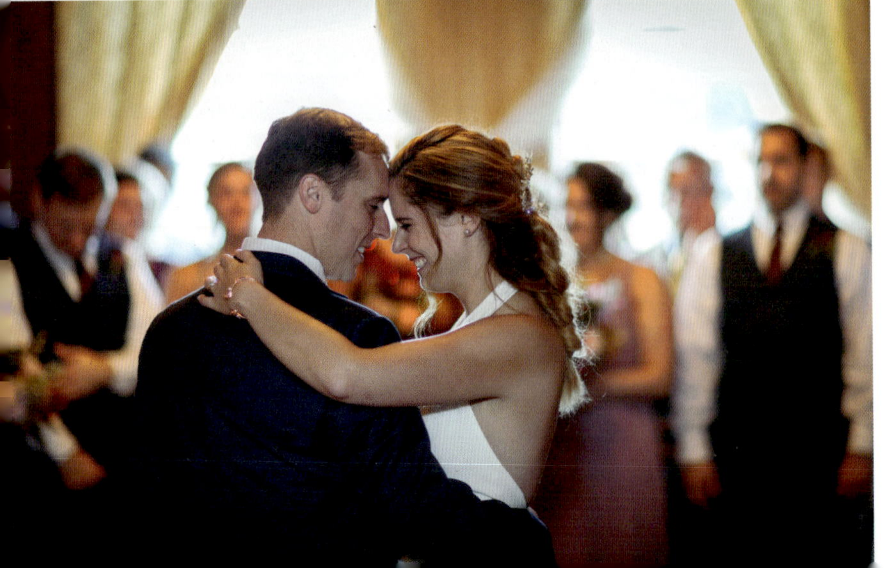

with the parents. That said, it's the bride-and-groom shots that matter most, and because they're lifted first, you'll have just one chance to get things right. It's one heck of an awesome time. Have fun and shoot, shoot, shoot!

You Made It!

It's approaching the end of your coverage, and you're likely exhausted and exhilarated. Find an unobtrusive time before leaving to personally thank the couple for having you, briefly give them an idea of what will happen next, and ask them if there are any other photographs they want you to take.

Packing Up

As the night goes on, we generally consolidate our gear so that there isn't a lot to pack when it's time to leave. Once we have wrapped up the photography for the day, we begin to pack our gear into the car. We remove the main memory cards and place them in our memory card wallet. We love the Gepe Card Safe cases. We carry spare, unused cards in green Gepe cases, and we use red cases for our "exposed" memory cards. One Gepe case will hold all four (one from each camera) of our main CF cards.

We feel it's important to keep the exposed cards on your person until you get to your office. You can keep your backup cards in the cameras, as this makes for a second copy in a different place.

Packing neatly, with everything in its place, will help you know right away if you've left anything behind. If you put everything in the carry bags where things belong, anything that's missing should be obvious.

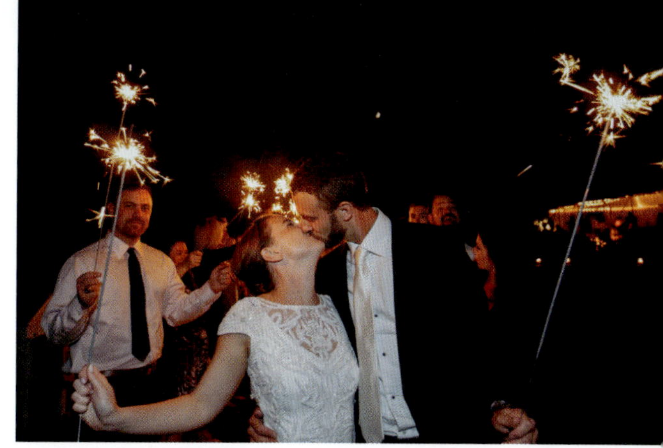

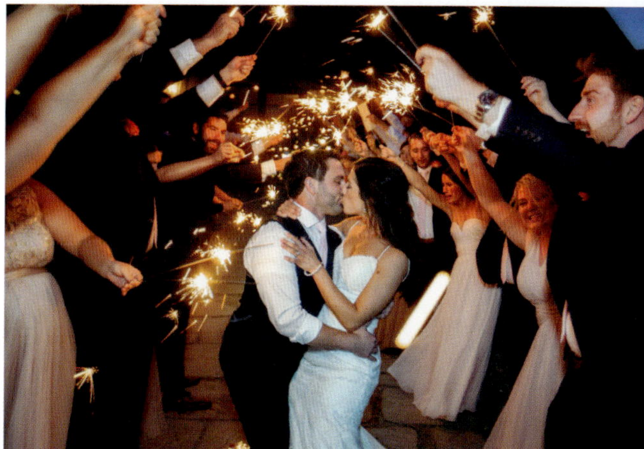

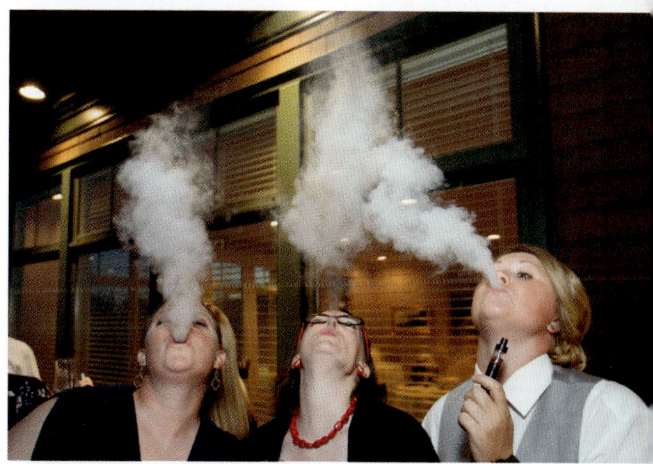

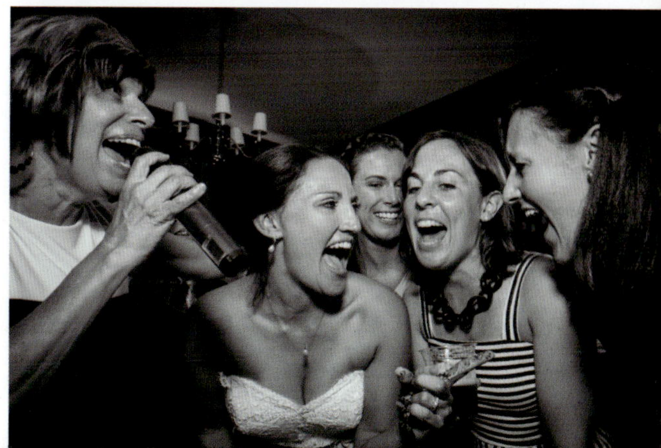

After the Wedding

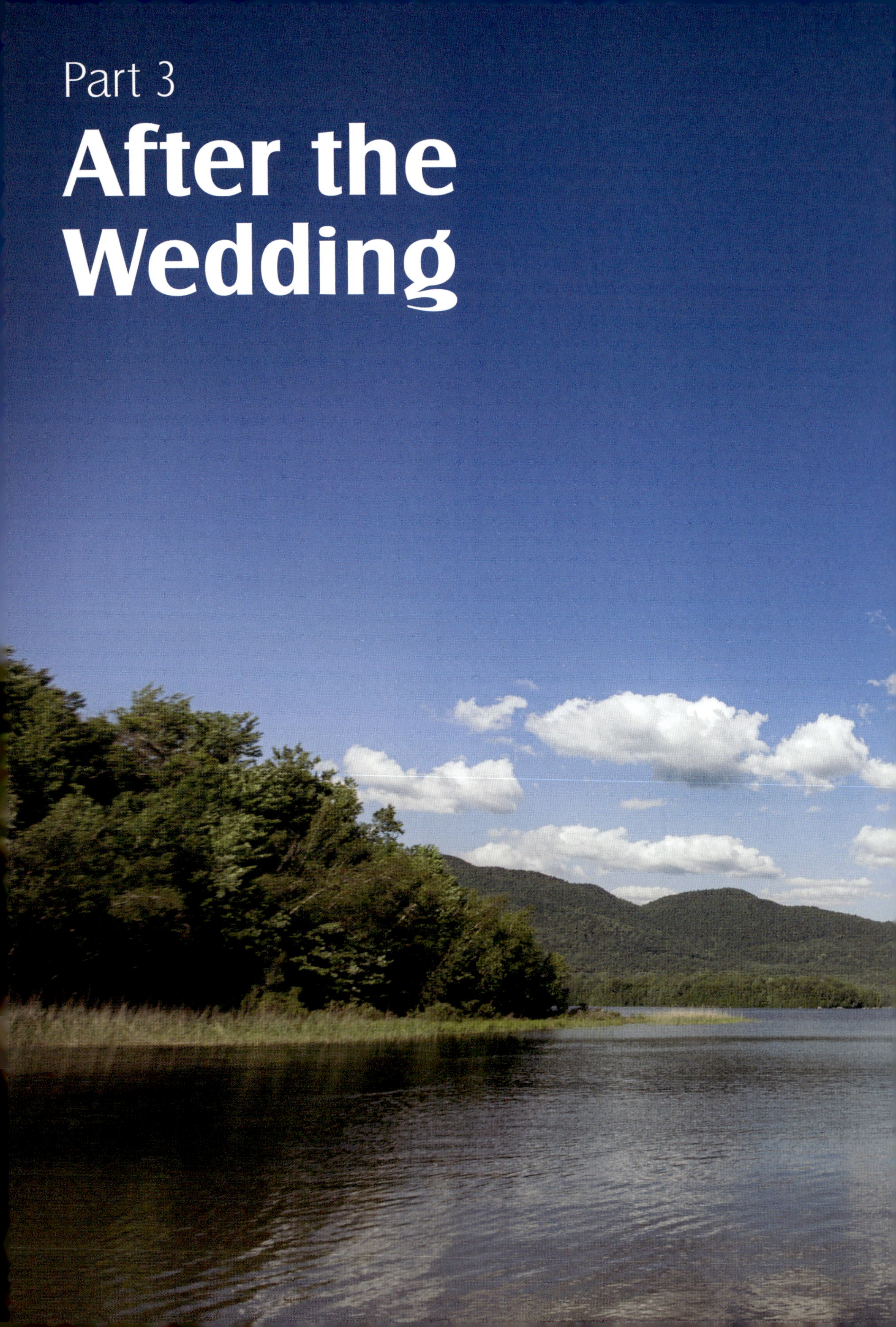

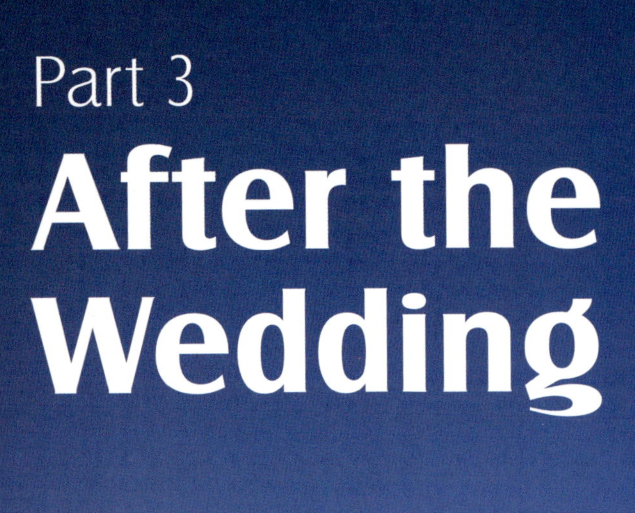

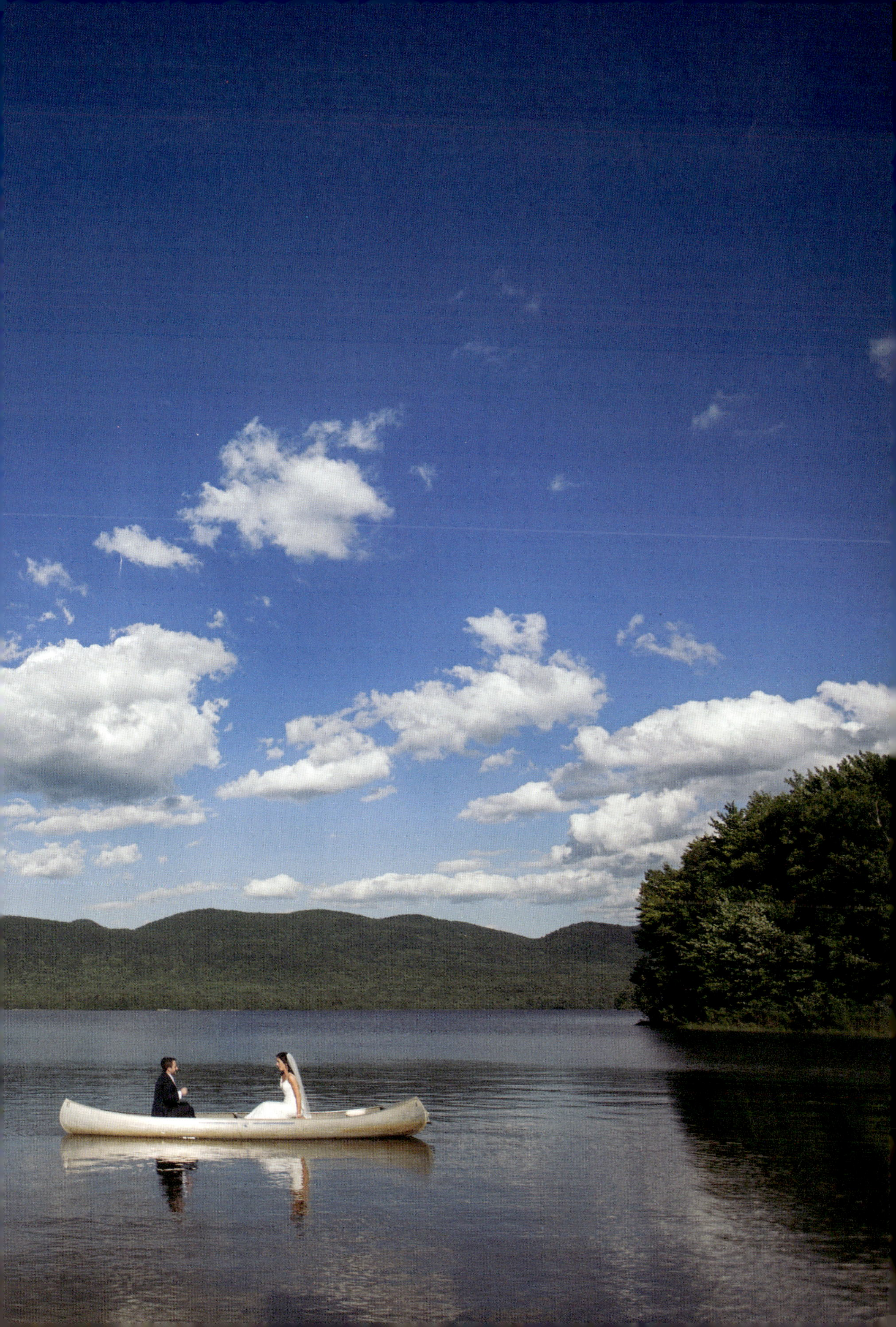

Critical Post-Wedding Activities

Unpacking, Downloading, and Backing up

Our office is located in our home. So, when we get in from a wedding, no matter how late, we bring everything inside (stands, clamps, reflectors, and minor items excluded). We remove all batteries and immediately start recharging them. We gently wipe down all the camera exterior surfaces with a microfiber cloth sprayed with a little bit of lens-cleaning fluid. We inventory our gear by putting every item back on our shelves and in its designated place.

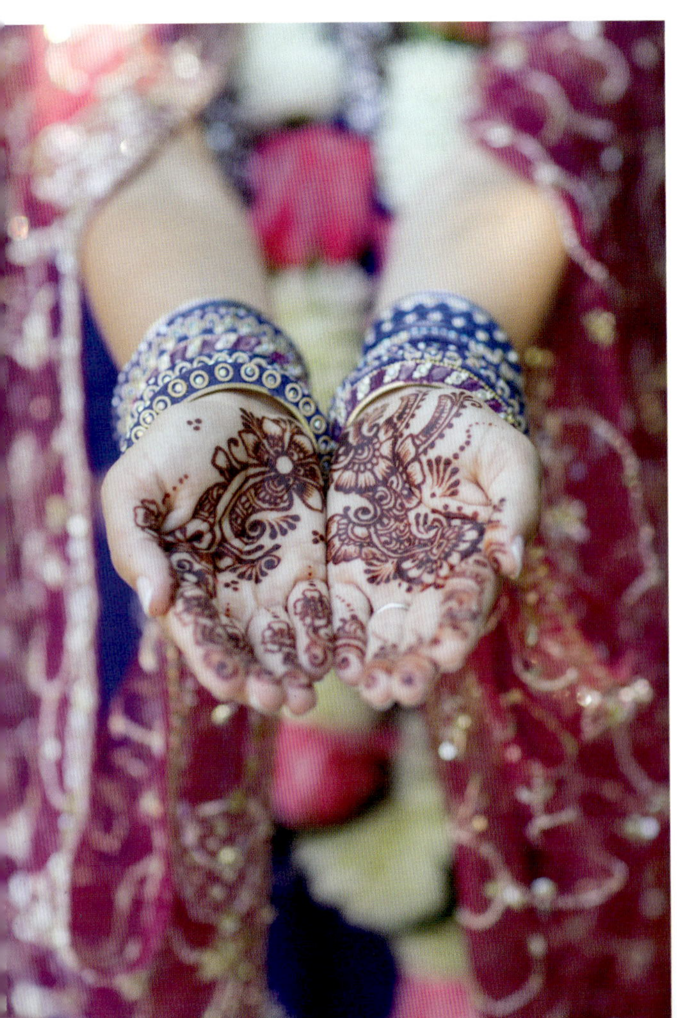

Four camera bodies, all lenses, six flashes, and everything else? Check. Everything we took with us has come back.

Simultaneously, we get to work at our photo processing computer. We use Apple Mac computers because they're rugged and dependable, and the Mac OS is intuitive and steady. Windows PC owners and fans may rightfully claim the same is true of their systems.

Downloading the Memory Cards

Notice that we haven't gone to sleep yet. Yes, we're tired, but there are some critical things that must be done.

We start by downloading the memory cards from the day. As mentioned, we used 128GB pro-grade Lexar cards, so we have just four cards to download (plus one from the drone camera if we've used it). Even with heavy shooting on a wedding day, these cards are generally at most half full; they're that large. For our card readers, we have two Lexar USB3 hubs. Each hub has four bays that we've set up for the variety of card types we use. No worries if you don't have a system like this. Individual card readers work fine, though you will have to swap out cards as each download is completed.

There are a lot of steps here, so bear with us. Each one is very important.

The Post-Processing Begins

With our four cards loaded from the day's photo-taking, we then use Adobe Lightroom (Lr). We make a new Lightroom catalog for every photo shoot we do. It keep things optimally organized, at least in my mind. We name the folder in a logical manner, such as "02 14 19 Hannah Sam wedding."

The above-mentioned folder is saved to a large (8TB) high-performance hard drive in a four-bay drive enclosure made by Other World Computing. We did extensive research and everything pointed to using hard drives made by HGST, whose failure rates were a fraction of that of other leading brands. The four-drive enclosure hooks up to our Macs using a fast Thunderbolt connection. There are so many great things about using Thunderbay hard-drive enclosures. Among them are that instead of four external drives and four power supplies and plugs, there's just one. Next up is the lower-cost-per-terabyte option: a bare, "uncased" hard drive, and the ability to choose so many sizes and performance specs. Then, they're "swappable," allowing us to keep a year's worth of data near at hand at all times. We actually have three four-bay enclosures, which keeps eight drives available for instant access. We have the main drive for the current year set up as a RAID 1, wherein a second physical hard drive mirrors the first for immediate redundancy. The latest model of the

Thunderbay enclosure is available with six slots—all the better! Typically, we add a new drive each year. By the time we run out of slots, we can quickly slide out the oldest drive, leaving it in its frame so it can be slid back into the enclosure at any time it's needed again. Otherwise, it's placed in a small box, labeled with the name of the drive year inside, and stored in a safe.

Fireproof/Waterproof Backup Drive

At the time of import, we also immediately prepare a backup folder on a different hard drive. We check the box in the Lightroom Import menu labeled Make a Second Copy to. For this second copy's location, we use (specifically) ioSafe hard drives, as they're fireproof and waterproof. It's like the backup copy is being written to a vault that's protected against the #2 peril, fire, and the #1 peril, water damage! We highly recommend adding this step to your workflow and backup plan.

Using Lightroom to Import from Multiple Cards at Once

Since Lightroom doesn't directly support importing from more than one memory card at a time, we have to use a slight bit of trickery to make this happen. In the Source panel, instead of using the memory cards listed under Devices, which does not allow multiple selections, we choose Multiple Cards from the Files section listed under Devices. Voilà! Multiple selections are allowed.

Following the panels in Lightroom from the left, where we were, along the top, we've taken care of the "From." Now be sure the word "Copy" is highlighted in white. Follow along to where it says "To." Be sure to change the destination to the folder you made at the beginning of this process. If you forget to do this, your files will write to the last place you imported to, not to the new folder you just made.

You're almost there, but there are a couple more things to do. Check the Don't Import Suspected Duplicates box. Then, in file renaming, check the Rename Files box. The primary reason for this is that after culling the images for the client, you don't want obvious large gaps in file numbers. If you deliver a set and the file naming jumps from 101.jpg to 189.jpg, your client may very well ask, "What happened to 102 through 188?" Now, I know lots of people rename their files at the end of the process, but to me, this is cause for potential confusion. If you only rename files upon export to the client's JPEG set or online gallery, your original raw files still exist with their original numbers. You'd later need to somehow convert the numbers the client has with yours anytime you need to reach back into the original set for reorders or album work.

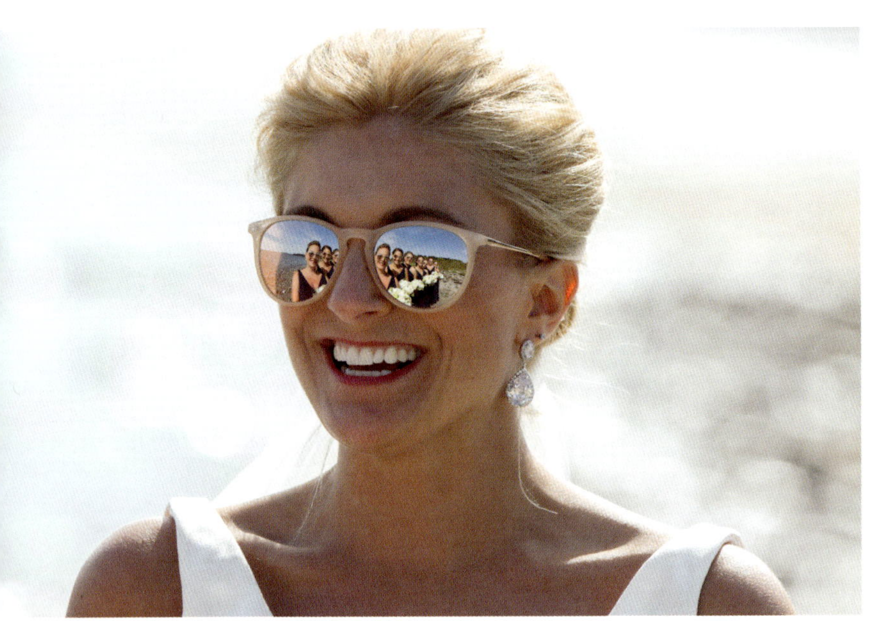

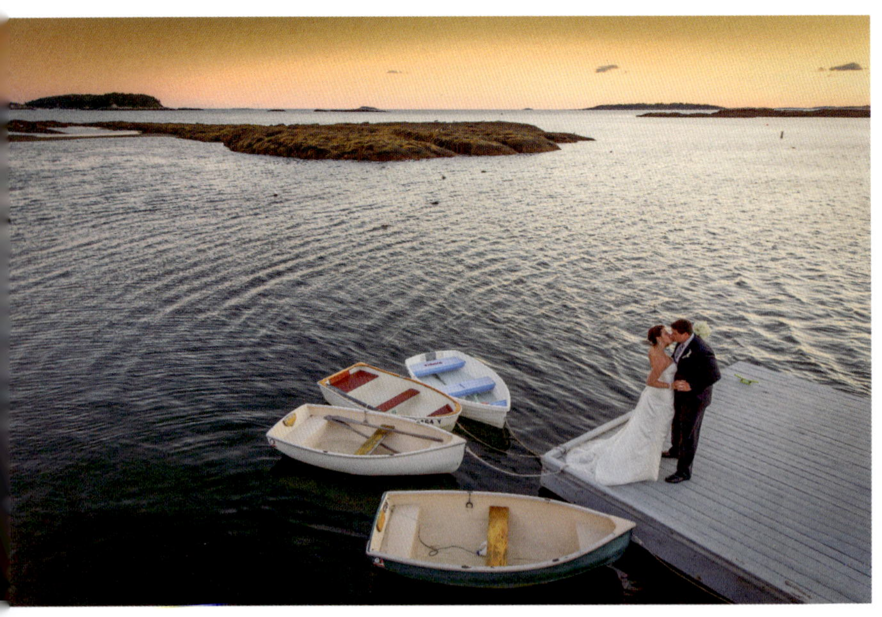

File Renumbering

Using the filename template editor tools built into the file renumbering system in Lightroom, it's easy to build a creative renumbering scheme that looks for all the world like some random number. We build a prefix that uses our clients' initials, such as "hbsl_," then use the settings to allow Lightroom to extract the hour, minute, and second from the original capture time of the image to generate a suffix. The resultant image number is something like "hbsl_113445." Clients won't realize, and won't care, that "113445" is actually the time the photo was taken. So, even if the next shot was nearly an hour later (of course that won't be the case), it would look like "hbsl_123341."

Again, there are huge cataloging benefits to doing this renaming now, not later. I can say we've never had any confusion with file numbering by taking this important step now.

Once the above steps are complete, press Import. Lightroom will proceed to copy every image from every loaded memory card to your main external drive, plus a second immediate copy to your specified backup drive.

Using Thunderbolt/USB 3 connections, even an import of ~3000 images takes just 15 to 20 minutes.

Still More Backups!

When the Import dialogue is finished, we do still one more additional backup. We use small external USB-C hard drives stored nearby yet off site. We then use our Finder (file manager) to copy the entire folder containing the Raw files and Lightroom files. Then, once put away, we can call it a night.

At this point, there are no fewer than *six* copies of the entire set of wedding images. There's (1) the main hard drive, (2) the RAID copy, (3) the ioSafe hard drive, and (4) the portable USB drives, (5) the original main memory cards, and (6) the in-camera backup cards. The memory cards aren't reformatted until we've ensured that all the other copies are in good order and work fine.

Hopefully, this will make it clear how important backups are for all photographs, but even more so for events, like weddings, that can't be repeated.

Once we start doing work on the image set, we occasionally update the copy on the ioSafe hard drive with the folder from the main drive, so the changes we've written to the updated Lightroom catalog get backed up, too.

There are other systems using RAID arrays that are even more sophisticated than what's described here. We recommend to do whatever you can to have a rugged, accessible, foolproof backup system in place at all times.

The Day After the Wedding

First thing the next day (assuming we don't have another wedding to go to, which is sometimes the case), we browse through the full set of images, looking for two specific things: Number one is to pick a set of favorite images, in at least a loose storytelling format, that we'll use to create our blog post for the wedding. Number two is to choose one image from within this set of favorites that we'll use for a social media preview.

First up is to use the Library module in Lightroom (in the clients' catalog) to apply filters to identify which images were taken by the second shooter. For no particular reason,

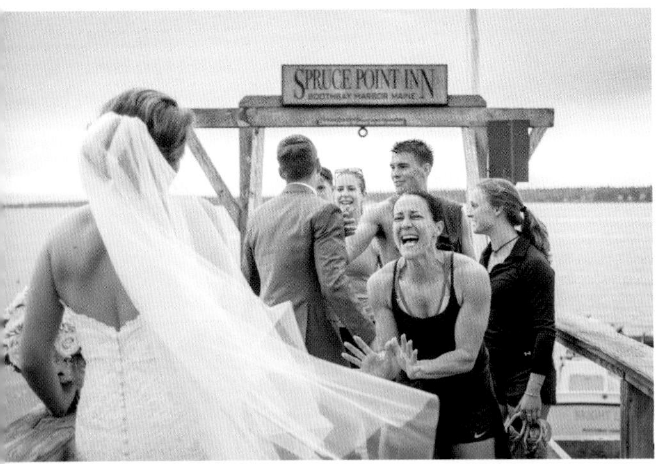

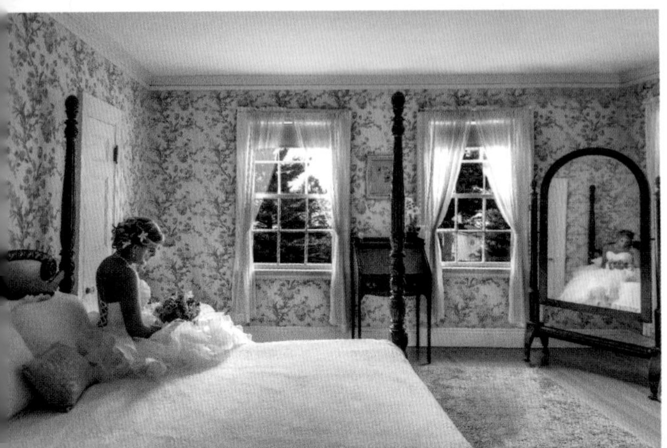

we mark these images in red. It's just helpful to know who took which images.

Rating the Images

We use the star-rating system to identify images, using the following convention:

- **1 star.** "Discard" images that won't be used/won't be part of the final set.
- **2 stars.** Shots that will be included in the client's final set.
- **3 stars.** One of our favorite images.
- **4 stars.** An exceptional shot to consider for future use in competition, etc.
- **5 stars.** Unused photo/reserved for specific use.

We'll do a run-through and select and tag the 3-star images. Again, we're looking for shots from the key segments of the day to present in a mini-story format. We typically include photos from the following categories: details, prep candids, bride getting ready, bridal portrait, first look, artistic (usually more than one) groom portrait, groom detail, women of the wedding party, men of the wedding party, the wedding party together, and a classic, more formal, camera-aware, bride-and-groom shot. Family photos are important, but we don't use them in the mini story. We try to ensure each image chosen is notably different than the others. This isn't intended to be the full gallery. Viewers quickly lose interest when looking at wedding blog posts when there's little variation from shot to shot. Wedding party images featured here are typically of the fun and casual variety, versus the more formal poses. Finally, we include photos from the first dance, maybe details from the reception dinner, perhaps a cake-cutting shot, and a few more images that show the fun of the party to round out the set.

One of our 3-star tagged images that includes the couple is selected as the preview photo for social media. We post this image to Facebook and Instagram in the evening (for better reach) of the day following the wedding. In the brief text, in addition to tagging the couple, we'll include something like, "If you want to see more, please like and follow Russell Caron Wedding Photography." In the description, we also tag every vendor involved in the wedding.

Next, we look though the 3-star image set and whittle it down to our ideal number of photos for our blog posts. That number is rarely under 50 and hardly ever over 90.

Editing the 3-Star Images

The 3-star images we'll feature in the blog receive what we call "advanced editing." In addition to basic processing that all our delivered images receive (which includes as-needed correction for exposure, shadows, highlights, cropping, horizon straightening, and the like, done in Lightroom), images slated for advanced editing receive additional work in Photoshop. This may include correcting skin imperfections, removing distracting elements, and more, as explained in the next section.

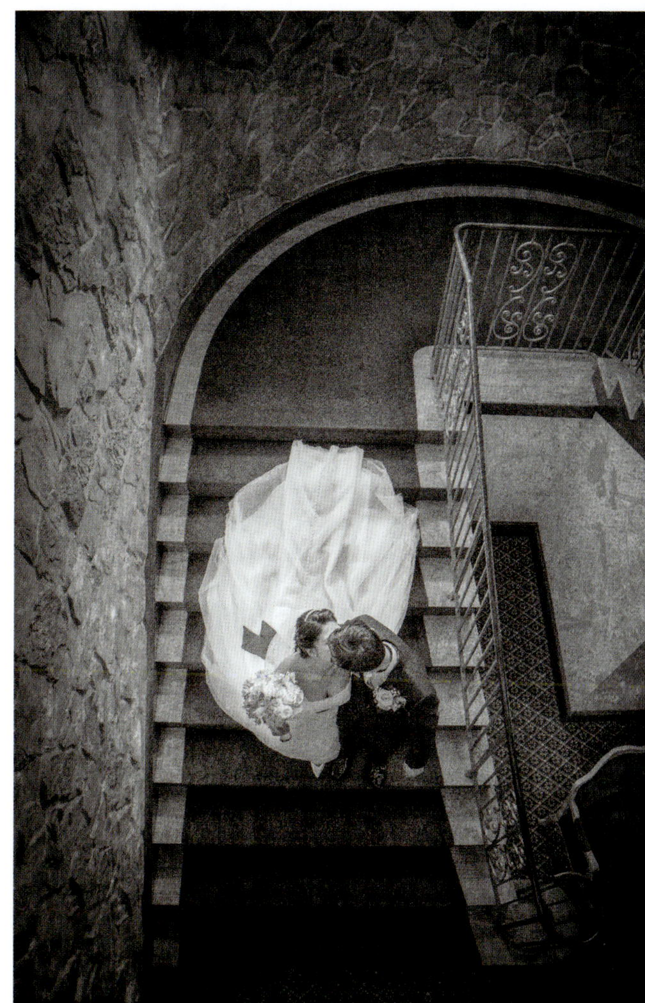

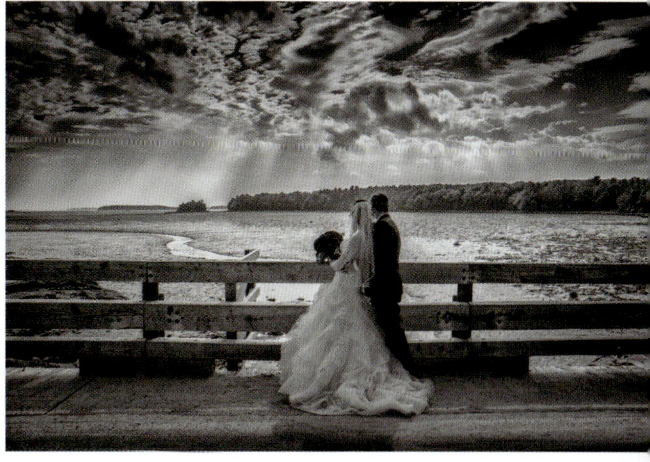

More Post-Processing Details

In Photoshop, we may do some vertical and horizontal straightening, de-skew architectural images, correct for lens distortion, edit out skin imperfections (especially in close-up bridal images), fix eye lines, and the like. In a group shot, let's say of the wedding party, we sometimes do a "head swap" from an image made in similar light where one of the subject's eyes is open versus closed in the main shot. We may edit out power lines in artistic photos and remove exit signs from the background of a first-dance image. While we don't have any hard rules, we generally take more liberty in what we feel comfortable editing out of images for our set-up/directed/posed artistic images than for candid or photojournalistic shots. We may dodge and burn to fix shadows on faces, and we sometimes apply a gentle texture for certain artistic images.

If you're not familiar with Photoshop, we recommend taking classes and practicing exhaustively . . .

If you're not familiar with Photoshop, we recommend taking classes and practicing exhaustively to become proficient in at least the fundamental functions that the program allows. It's a tool of the trade. Adobe's Creative Cloud for Photographers costs just $10 per month for the very latest versions of Lightroom and Photoshop, updated as they happen. Adobe Camera Raw, which provides new drivers for the latest camera models, is included, too. We feel that $10 per month for your core photography tools of the trade is a must.

Plug-Ins

There are two plug-ins for Photoshop that we love. Originally only for Mac, they're now available for Windows PCs as well. Made by Skylum, the first is Luminar, which includes a wide-ranging suite of filters that can streamline your post-processing. The skin-softening tool, in particular, can be useful and time-saving. The plug-in should be used with great care and restraint to maintain natural-looking images. Aurora, a type of HDR processor, is our other top pick. Wedding work won't see heavy use of an HDR editor, but certain shots, especially artistic photos from a drone, can see real enhancement from this tool.

When editing images in Photoshop, we always work on a duplicate layer. In this way, the work we do can be "dialed down" and brought to a believable and realistic level by reducing the opacity of the top, adjusted layer. For example, a bridal portrait can be easily corrected—*over*corrected, actually—for skin imperfections and under-eye lines. So while we may tune that top layer to "perfection," we like

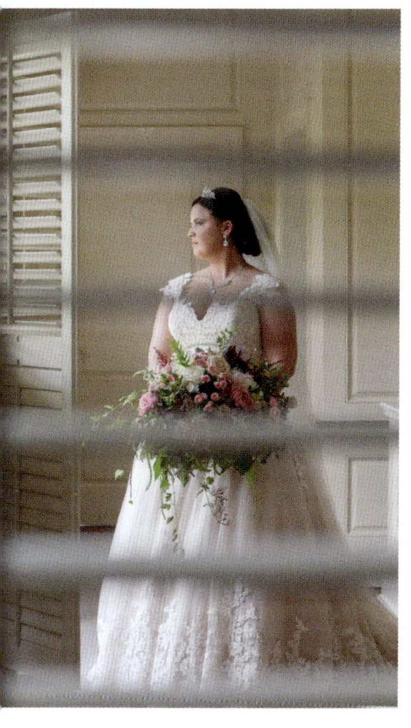 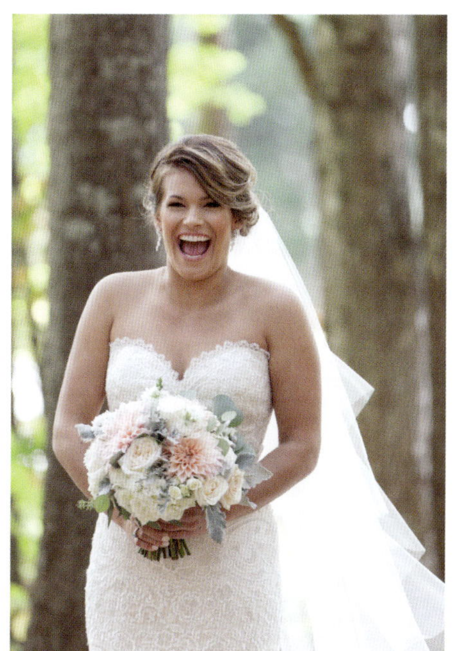 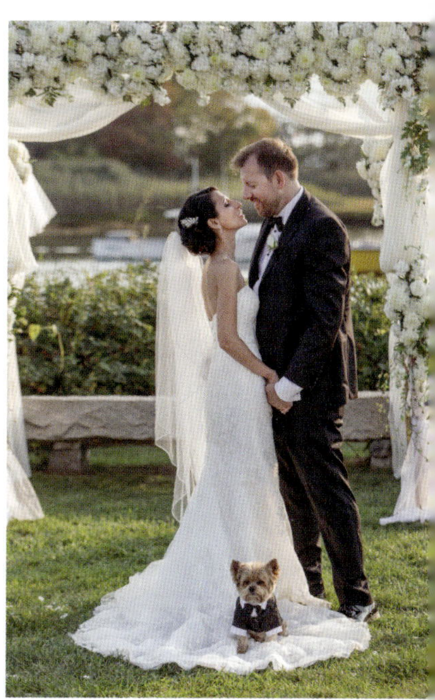

to dial in a more natural, believable look in the image by reducing the opacity. The amount varies, but the general rule is to bring the opacity down to the point that you can just begin to see, from the underlying layer, the imperfections you eliminated in the top layer.

Graphics Tablet

A big help to our detailed Photoshop work is our Intuous Wacom Medium graphics tablet. It replaces or at least supplements a conventional mouse or trackball and allows for a higher, more precise level of control. We've used tablets for years and can't live without them. We've heard that some people find them awkward. We're guessing that these folks simply didn't give using a tablet enough of a try. We believe you can acclimate to using a pen tablet quickly. Sure, the first hour will be awkward. Over the next two to three hours, you'll begin to get the hang of it. By the next day, you'll like it, and the day after that, you'll love it and never want to work in graphic design apps using a mouse again.

Exporting Blog Images

Once we have our set of, say, seventy 3-star, blog-worthy images, we export them as high-resolution JPEG files to a folder in Lightroom.

Collage Panels for Blogging

Next, we build collage panels in the correct size for our website using Blog Stomp. Blog Stomp can arrange images into pleasing-looking panels containing one or more images. We have it set up so that our logo appears in the bottom border area of the collage. Our preference is to use the one-image format, as this works best with sites like Pinterest. We have the image size settings in Blog Stomp set to output images to 1000 pixels in width, which is what our Word-

Dedicated Keyboard for Lightroom

A recent addition to our photo processing computer is a separate keyboard dedicated to streamlining our work in Lightroom. The Loupedeck + keyboard helps us cut several seconds out of the editing and review of each image. This can add up to several hours when editing a large set of images. In addition to time savings, it can help relieve repetitive motion injuries from too much mouse or pen work.

Press website deems optimal. Using the output settings, Blog Stomp also makes it easy to embed alternative text into the image. This can be a big advantage for search engine optimization (SEO).

Before we build the shell of our blog post, we choose two images that will be attached to the post. One is a featured photo that will be on the index page of our site. Like the Facebook preview image, we tend to ensure that this featured image includes both the bride and the groom. The same is true of the photo that will be automatically embedded as the banner image when the blog post URL link is pasted into Facebook. Word Press has these options; your website dashboard may differ.

Search Engine Optimization

In the blog post, we include a minimum of 300 words for SEO purposes. It's beyond the scope of this book to delve into SEO, so we recommend that you find a recent book on the topic or, better yet, reach out to local experts who can help you create blog posts and web content that will improve your organic search engine results for the most-used search terms that apply to you.

Building strong relationships with our peers in the wedding industry is important, so every wedding blog post includes a thorough list of all the vendor partners. This includes the venue, officiant, planner, florist, music (both ceremony and reception), paper suite provider, hairstylist, makeup artist, photo booth, videographers, cake baker, caterer, transportation service, and everyone else. Don't forget to specifically list the photographers, too, even though you'd think it's glaringly obvious. This keeps the list intact and avoids us being left out if someone were to copy and paste this from the site to another place. Not only are these partners listed, but their websites are all active links. It takes a bit of work, but it's valuable to you as an often-referred vendor partner.

It's our goal to post this blog within 48 to 72 hours of the wedding. Often, at that point, our couples are leaving for their honeymoon, and it's a great time for them to see the first samples of the wedding day images. It really helps build and keep the buzz going. It's not unusual to receive an inquiry for our wedding photography services from someone who has just seen the mutual friend's wedding blog.

So, at this point, there are about 70 finished images from the wedding. But we came in with 3,000 images. So, what happens next?

Well, we send our couple an email (from a signature template) that informs them of the date we expect (but can't guarantee) to have the full edited set of wedding images ready. The date we provide is "padded" a bit so that we under-promise and over-deliver. For example, if our office schedule is to finish Hannah and Sam's editing on March 15, we'll tell the couple March 22. We try or best to meet the March 15 date, so they get their set "early," in their minds. Unless there are extreme circumstances, we don't schedule the completion of more than one wedding per week. Things will start to back up in the office when there has been more than one wedding during a week. That's simply the way things happen while trying to keep everything in balance.

We Don't Outsource Our Editing

We don't outsource our editing. Why? There are several reasons: First, most outsourcing services still require the photographer to cull the set of images. This means selecting the "keepers." For us, this takes the most time in post-processing; it's even more time-intensive than finishing the images that are being kept. Second, we don't want to give up control over how the images are processed. Third, we want to save the time and complexity of uploading and transferring, then downloading and reviewing the work done by someone else. We contend that an efficient post-processing session can be very streamlined and may actually take less time. Plus, we'd rather pay ourselves to do this work than pay someone else.

Culling

We start in our Lightroom catalog of the wedding images to be edited. Step one is to assign a 2-star rating to all images that are to be kept. Keep in mind that there are already (in this example) ~70 images assigned 3 stars. In the process, we went through to get the initial set of images marked with 3 stars down to ~70,

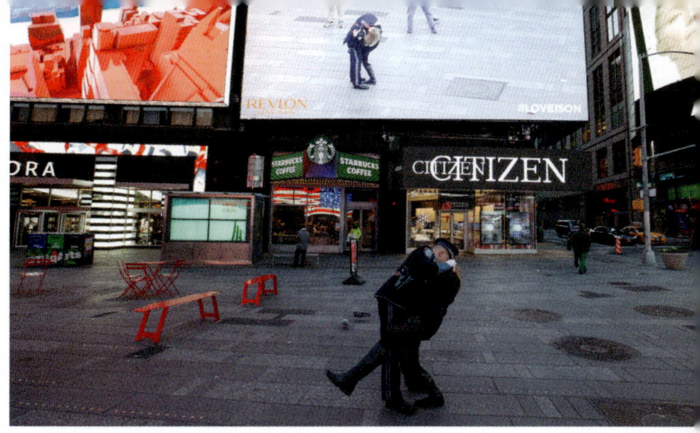

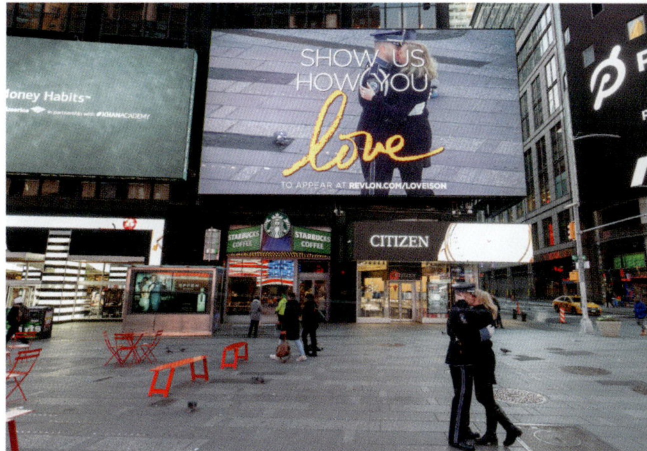

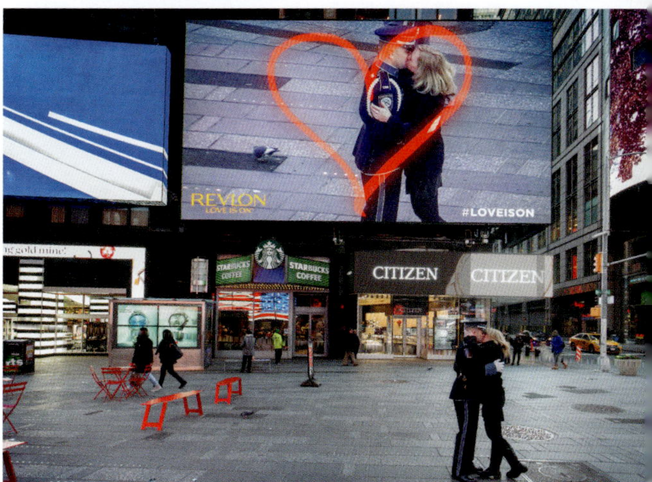

we also downgraded some images from 3, so as to keep them from being part of the blog, but in almost all cases, if an image was a 3, it deserves to be no lower than a 2. Therefore, the catalog already has some 3s and some 2s. You can have Lightroom show you only images that are equal to 1 and under (i.e., no star) so you can breeze through the images to be rated, though there's something to be said for seeing the preselected 2s and 3s for reference and to ensure no near-duplicate images are included.

Our goal, as we touched upon earlier, is to end up with 50 to 60 images per hour of coverage. That includes images by the lead photographer and second photographer. So, for our most popular package, which is ten hours with the lead photographer and seven with the second, we'll know we're in a comfortable range with 500 to 600 final images. In no way should the image selection be limited by the guideline. If there are legitimately, without near duplicates, more like 900 (or whatever!) great images from this wedding, include them. Similarly, if the number is a little under 50, that's fine.

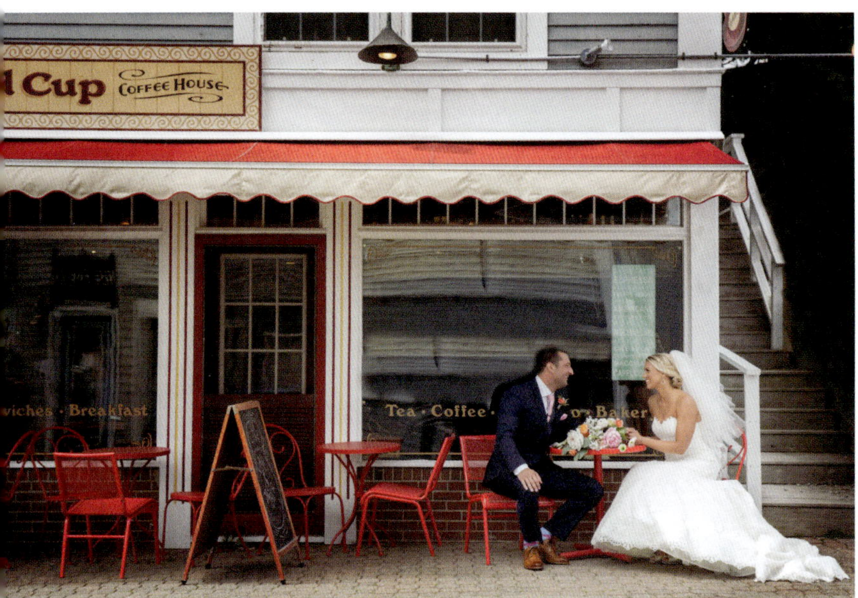

Don't include photos you are not proud of, or those with technical flaws. But, it's far more likely, especially for newer wedding photographers, to have a hard time keeping from delivering too many, rather than too few, images. Many seasoned photographers, us included, look back on the delivered sets of wedding images from years back and cringe at how many duplicate images they delivered. We're here to tell you to get this right far sooner than we did!

As we tab through using the Library module of Lightroom, we use the dedicated keys of the Loupedeck + keyboard *(see sidebar)* to assign the desired star rating. The keyboard also has navigation arrows that allow us to work quickly when we're in the flow.

This leaves us with somewhere around 500 images that we haven't previously

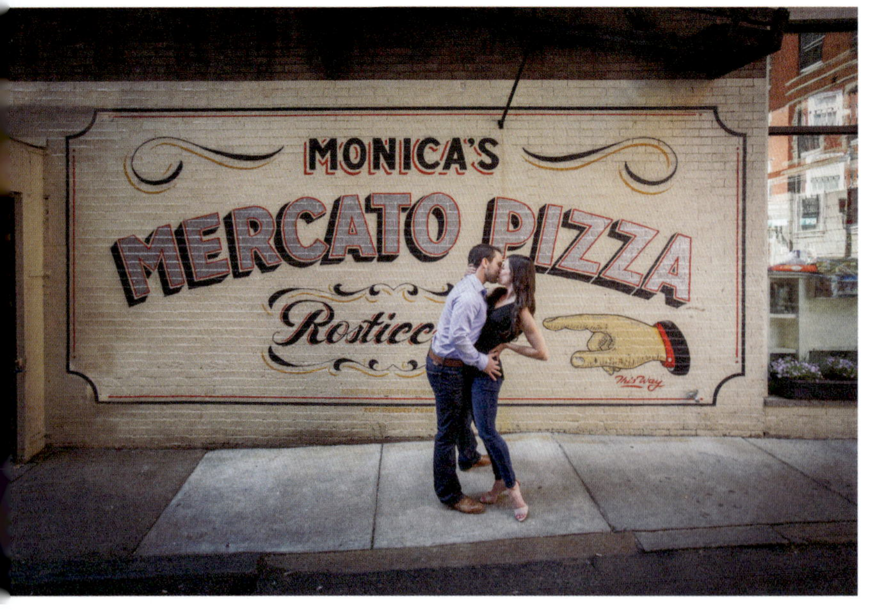

edited. We can now set the Lightroom filter to 2. This will make visible only the images requiring basic editing. Recall that only the 3-star images necessarily get our *full* editing at this point, but don't hold yourself back from doing further edits on 2-star images to improve the product you're giving to your clients.

The Loupedeck + keyboard also has all manner of physical knobs and buttons for the settings you'll most often use in the Develop module in Lightroom. It is fully customizable to suit your needs. We get lots of use out of it because we like to shoot at +0.3 exposure compensation to generate Raw files with the most data content to maximize highlight control. We also fine-tune the overall exposure and then the shadows. Using the external physical keyboard saves lots of wrist movement and helps us use our non-dominant hand to share the workload, thereby reducing the development or worsening of repetitive motion injuries caused by lots of mouse activity.

With a high amount of focus and lack of distraction, the editing process for these ~500 images to be "basically" edited can be as little just two to three hours. This comes after many years of experience. With less experience and perhaps some distractions and interruptions, this process could take up to a day and a half. Being that time is money, it's prudent to work diligently on refining the editing process, without making sacrifices in quality, to the point of reducing your workflow time.

Publishing the Web Gallery

When the editing is done and the 2-star or higher filter is applied in Lightroom, we have our finished set of images. Now, how do we get these to the client?

The first thing we do is publish the photos to our client's web gallery. This is done in the Web module of Lightroom. It's a great feature, and one we rarely see used. We have a dedicated website for image hosting. Once posted to our web host, we send the URL to the client via email to allow them to view their gallery.

Setting up a dedicated image hosting website is as easy as having your website company provide log-in credentials. If you're not ready to venture into publishing your galleries on your own site, you can turn to one of the many photo publishing and hosting sites available. Do a search for "photo hosting sites for photographers."

In our email to our clients, we include offers for prints and canvas gallery wraps.

Special Offers

In our email to our clients, we include offers for prints and canvas gallery wraps. Having a call to action with a ten-day expiration helps clients to not procrastinate.

Using White House Custom Color for prints and Canvas On Demand Pro for canvas wraps has proven very advantageous to us. Their pricing allows for a reasonable profit margin, even when offering half-price specials, as with our ten-day offer mentioned above.

File Sizing and Archiving

File sizing and archiving are aces in your pocket if you are looking for ways to build on your income from each wedding you photograph. Let me share our process.

File Sizing

In our contracts, we specify that our clients will receive the digital image file set on a USB drive. We capture our photos in Raw, but when we write (export) them to the USB drive, they are in the JPEG format. In the contract, we're clear that the file size will be 3000 pixels on the long edge. For many clients, this is just fine. Files of this size will make perfect 8x10-inch prints at 300dpi (10x300dpi=3000 pixels) without extrapolating or up-sizing. Additionally, we always include a duplicate set of watermarked images at about 1000 pixels/72dpi to make it easy for the client to share their photos on social network sites.

For anyone who wants full-size JPEG files, we offer that option via the archiving form we send out before making the USB drive. More on that follows.

Archiving

It's more than a good idea to keep a permanent copy of the set of wedding images from each contract for future use. Client copies are sometimes lost in fires and floods; other times, clients will tell you they have misplaced them.

Photographers don't *have* to do this. In the Image Delivery section of this book *(page 37),* we noted that our contract clearly states that if archiving options aren't purchased by the client, the delivery of the USB drive constitutes transfer of the master files from the photographer to the client and, retrieval of images, if needed, cannot be guaranteed, unless the client purchases an archiving option.

We send our clients a form that gives them three options for their digital image file set.

So, we send our clients a form that gives them three options for their digital image file set. Option 1 does not guarantee archiving by the photographer. In this case, the client understands it's their responsibility to carefully maintain the files, as they are considered the master set. There's no cost to the client for this option. We tell the couple that we may or may not choose to keep a set. We also explain that if a replacement is ever required, if it's even possible to provide one, there will be a substantial cost. The reality is that we *do* keep at least the original set and perhaps a backup, but not more.

Option 2 provides that we, the photographers, keep the original set, plus another copy

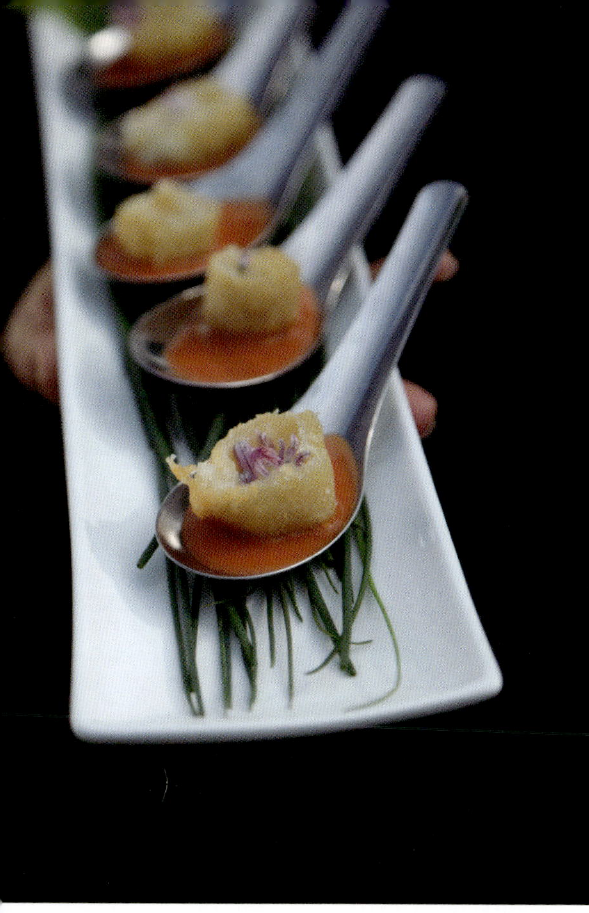

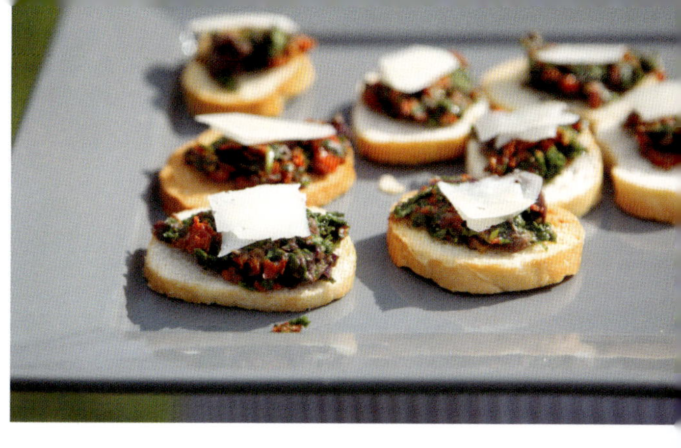

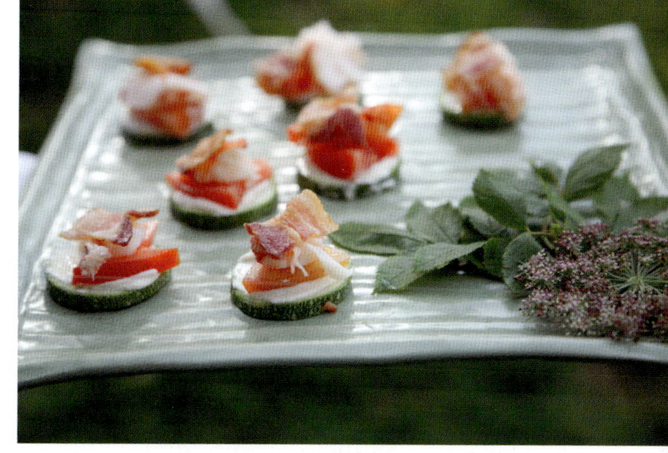

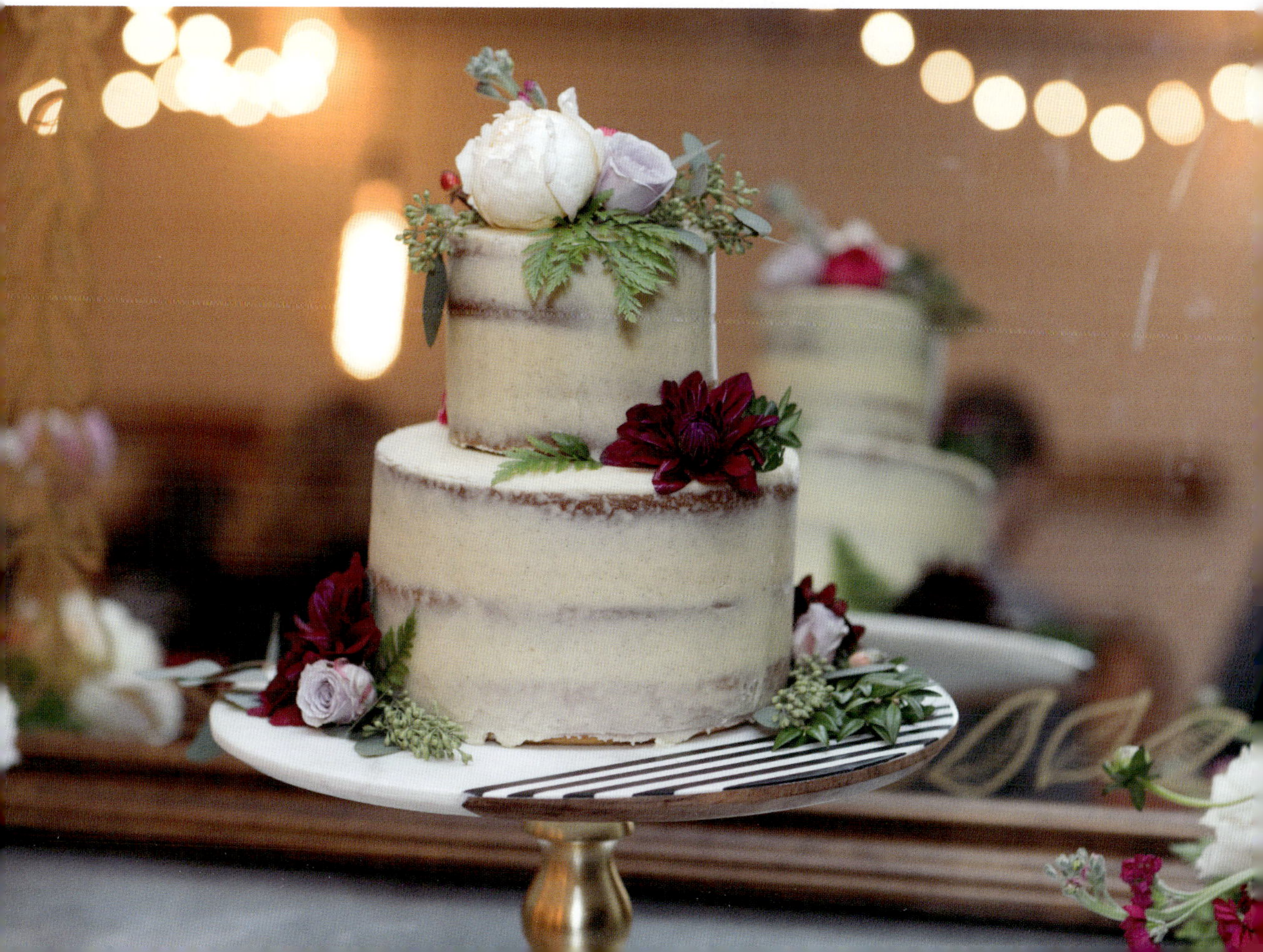

on a portable hard drive in a safe, and another copy on a portable hard drive stored off-site. The client will pay a reduced price should we ever need to create another set. This option sells well, at a price point of about $100.

Option 3 is like option 2 but adds Cloud storage. We store a full set of finished JPEGs on Dropbox. The price to re-create another set of images, should it be needed, is even lower with this option, which we price at about $199.

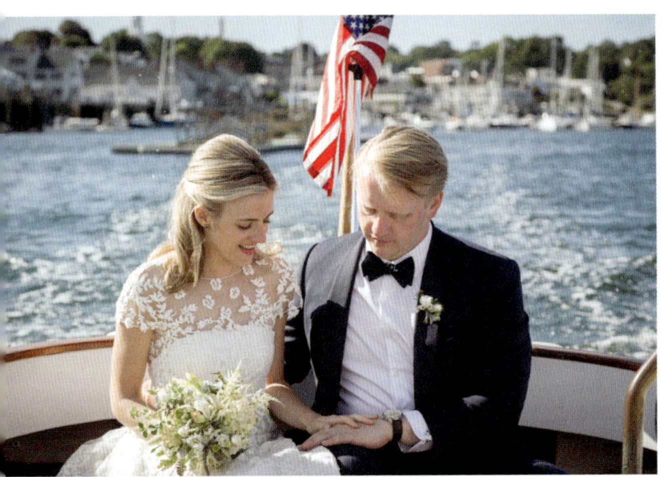

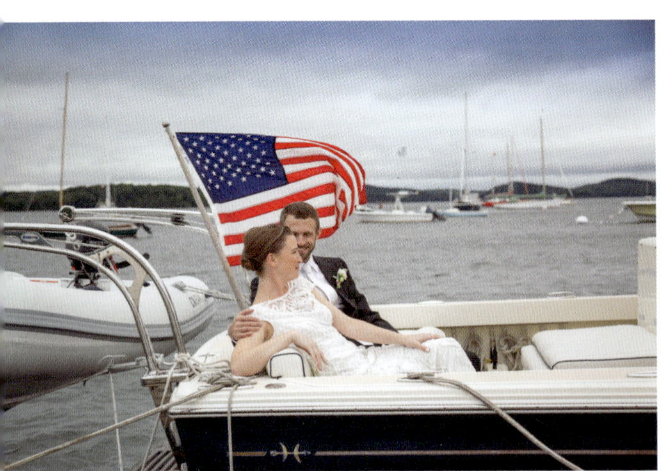

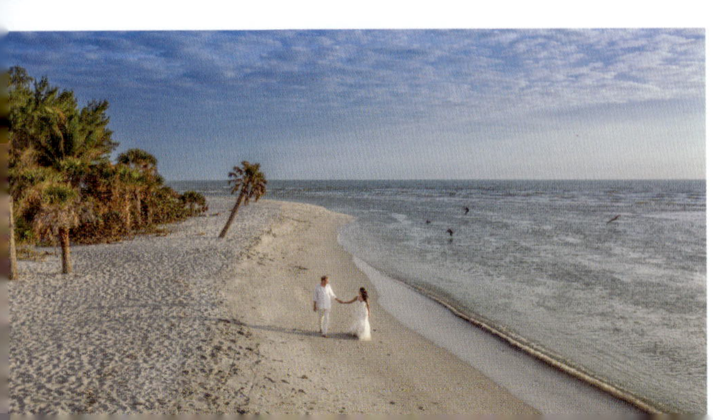

On this form, we also offers clients the option to purchase full-size (not limited to 3,000 dpi) JPEG files. Most, though not all, select this option, at around $89.

Copyright License

In virtually all situations, photographers working for themselves own the rights to the images they take. This is imperative. Photographers need to be able to use their images for marketing, websites, and to share with preferred wedding partners and vendors.

However, to grant our clients the ability to use the images, we provide a "personal-use license." This allows them to legally make prints, enlargements, wall art, canvas wraps, etc., for their personal use. It does not allow the use of the images for any commercial gain or profit. In 99.8 percent of the cases, this isn't an issue and suits the uses the client had in mind. Say, though, that the client wanted to use their wedding images to promote a business that they own. Use of this type requires a commercial-use license, and that's not in the scope of the contract for their wedding photography. A commercial-use license costs more.

The copyright license specifically names the couple as the licensees.

We allow the client to make copies of their digital files; however, these copies are explicitly for their own use and backup purposes. Clients aren't allowed to give the images to anyone else, nor can they share them with their wedding vendors. We ask them to have anyone who wants access to the images to contact us so we can properly address the issue of the copyright licensing.

Sharing Images with Venues and Vendor Partners

We openly share the "best of" images with the venues where we love to work. Makes sense, right? We do have the venue agree that any use will be credited back to us. This applies to both print and online applications. In the event a venue or vendor wants an image without a watermark and without a photo credit, they're required to purchase from us a commercial-use license for that image.

Similarly, let's say that a set of parents wants access to their daughter or son's wedding images. While there isn't any way (nor would we ever seek a way) to prevent a copy from being given to them, they will not be able to get prints made from legitimate places without a copyright license in their name. Therefore, we offer an option to make a full duplicate set of images with a new copyright license to a separate party, for a modest fee.

When the client returns the archive form, we make their deliverable USB drive per their instructions and per what they paid for in terms of file size and archiving option upgrades. We use a high-grade, name-brand USB 3 drive in 16GB size. USBs that are custom-printed with your logo are fine and attractive, but they may not be USB 3 speed, often much more expensive, and honestly, we don't feel we've ever lost a referral or a job for the lack thereof. The USBs we use are often available at great prices. We package the USB in a nice little box with a shredded paper lining. Enclosed on the USB are the large (either full-sized or 3000-pixel width) images, the smaller image set for social media use, and a PDF copy of the personalized copyright release. We also include (see page 125) a letter describing what our clients can and cannot legally do with their images. We hand-write a sincere thank-you note, provide an offer for a free canvas wrap for referring us to anyone they know who will be getting married, and include two of our business cards. We protect everything in bubble wrap. All of this fits nicely in a USPS small flat-rate box, the label for which we prepare using the Click It and Ship It option on the USPS website. It makes for a very professional presentation.

You're Done! Or Are You?

In cases where the client did not include a wedding album in the contract, you can mark this job closed. (There are follow-up and marketing tasks that will need to be done, however, and we'll get to those shortly.) At every step along this process, we maintain a record of what's been sent, returned, completed, etc., in our master database. If you're managing more than a handful of weddings per year, there's no way to commit all of the details to memory. You've got to write down everything along the way. One year, we had two weddings in a row in which each of the couple's first names were the same. Just imagine trying to keep things straight in that scenario without copious notes.

Part 4

Follow-Up Work

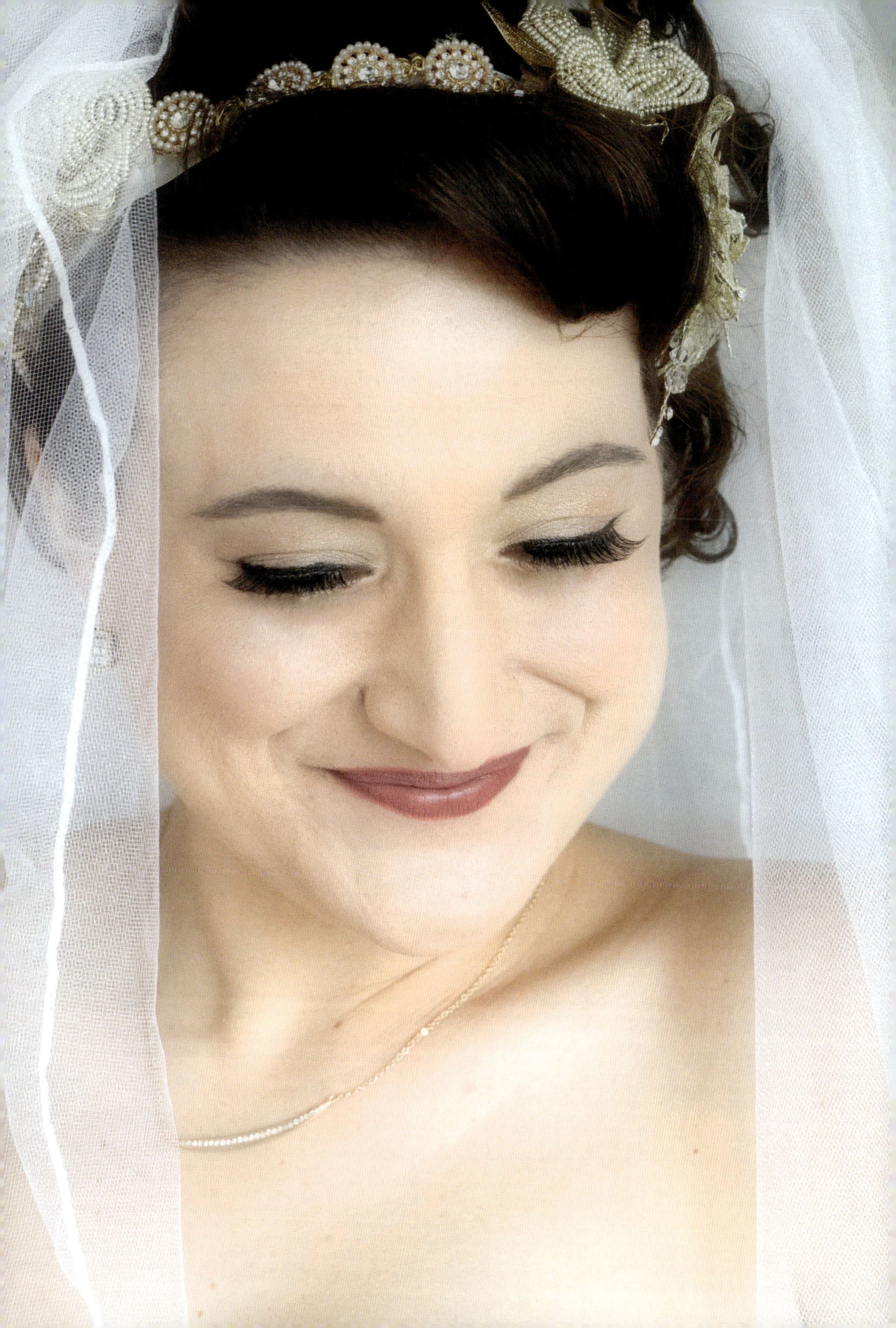

Album Sales

When a couple does not purchase a physical album, money is being left on the table. So, maybe you're not quite through, after all.

Not too long ago, most couples would want a printed wedding album, and would purchase one for themselves, plus a set of replica albums for the parents. Times have changed. Today's millennial client is much more highly focused on the wedding day experience than on physical goods. If you are able to show your millenial clients that you will make the day low-stress and all about having fun, you should be able to close more sales. Because they live in a world where their photos live on their smartphones and are rarely printed, though, making an album sale can be a challenge.

The Album Pre-Buy Discount

We've set what we feel to be realistic "list prices" for our albums and provide these in our catalog. There's a reasonable level of profit built into these prices, yet for an heirloom, the cost is not out of line.

Offering a deal toward the cost of the album, the balance of which would not be paid until it's ordered, has worked well for us. For $250 with the wedding contract, we offer (in addition to their $250 applied to the net cost) a 25 percent discount and a guarantee that, within a year after the wedding, the prices in the catalog in effect at the time of the contract will be locked in and will not increase. What we like about this sales model is that it brings in money to purchase the album from your publishing company just when you'll need it, not earlier, when there's a chance you will forget to set aside enough money to complete the printing.

Some clients do want an "everything" bundle. So, our top package includes a 10x10-inch, 50-page album, plus two 6x6-inch replicas.

When determining pricing, factor in how long the design will take.

Album Design Software

When determining pricing, factor in how long the design will take. Like everything else in this process, you'll get better at as time goes on. We use an app by P'xellu, SmartAlbums2, to design and edit our albums. It couldn't be any more intuitive. You should be able to fully design an album, once your images have been pulled, in under an hour at first, working down to ~20 minutes or even less with experience.

Once the album is designed, we use the SmartAlbums Cloud Proofing option. This sends a digital mockup to the client, and they're able to comment, describe desired revisions, and approve the design during the viewing. Ultimately, for pricing, a good rule of thumb is to take the raw cost for the album size you'd most like to sell, add the cost of the cover you want to feature (such as full leather) plus any embossing, boxing, custom features (such as double-thick pages), and multiply that number by at least 4 or 5x. This covers the costs associated with completing the design and maintaining the SmartAlbums and Cloud Proofing apps.

Setting a Limit on Album Revisions

We touched upon this in the section on contracts, earlier in the book, but it bears repeating: ensure that your contract specifies a limit, in either number of revisions or hours, that's included for no-cost album redesign. You cannot leave this as an unlimited number! While rare, you could end up with "that" client who can literally drain every single cent of profit you made from their wedding with countless infuriating revisions. You'll also want to state a time limit in which a reply to the provided album revision is required. Clients are busy and can neglect to get back to you.

Sometimes the number of pages included in the album the client purchased isn't enough to do the story justice. Don't be afraid to suggest adding spreads! Clients like to know that you're giving them a price break on this, but this doesn't mean you cannot make an excellent profit. We like to show a usual price for added spreads that we can discount by 50 percent when we, the photographers, have suggested add-ons. Even at that discounted price, we can maintain a 4 to 5x profit margin.

Album Vendor Recommendation

For albums, we've used Zookbinders since the start, and have nothing but positive things to say about the quality of their workmanship, their customer service, client satisfaction with their products, and fair pricing. A true testimony to how comfortable we are using Zookbinders is that we routinely just have the albums drop-shipped directly to the client. There have been zero issues for us in doing so.

Confirm the details before going to print. Do not hit the Publish button for a client album until you've double-checked with them that the design is approved, including the spelling of their names, the wedding date, etc., whenever you've included text in the design. Also, be sure the page order uploaded correctly. The SmartAlbums Cloud Proofing app we use shows only the interior pages, so we ensure that our clients understand that the covers aren't shown. The album proofing app at Zookbinders does, however, show the covers, so we can use that link for final confirmations.

It's A Wrap!

This wedding is done, now on to the next! That's a lot of steps for one wedding, isn't it? This isn't meant to scare anyone off, but a key point that I have tried to make in this book is just how much time a single wedding can take. You need to be sure you're charging accordingly and are actually making money. After all, this *is* a business.

Keep Your Head in the Game

In most areas, weddings are seasonal, and this provides an opportunity to sharpen your skills during the off-season. There are so many educational opportunities available. Seek out training not only in wedding photography, but in business. It's often recommended that photographers do 75 percent of their training in non-photography topics to sharpen their skills

Weddings in most areas are seasonal, and this provides an opportunity to sharpen your skills in the off-season.

in profitability, social media, search engine optimization, branding, and the like.

Professional Organizations

Organizations like the Professional Photographers of America (PPA) and Wedding and Portrait Photographers International (WPPI) are fantastic resources, and becoming active within one or both of these groups can do nothing but help keep you at the top of your game. PPA has local chapters in every state, and this is an excellent way to meet other photographers in your area.

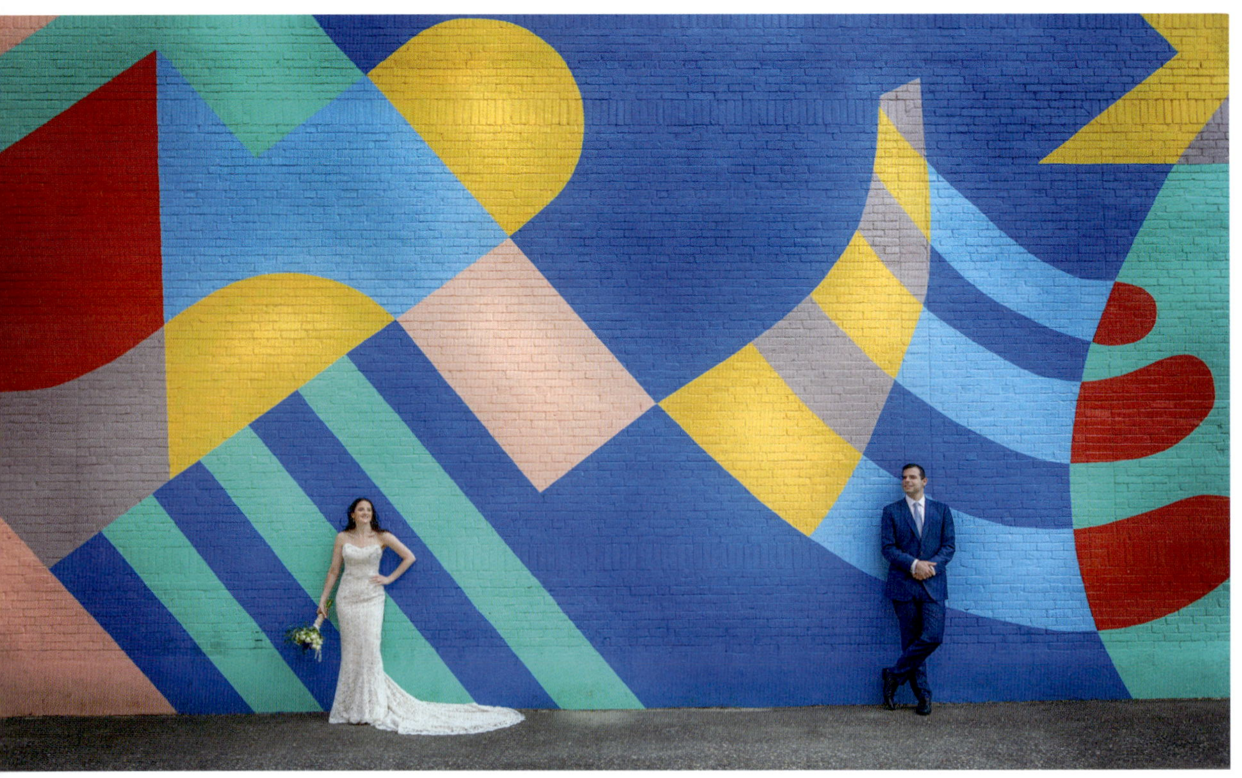

Image Competitions

Being active in professional image competition is one of the best ways to keep yourself challenged—and it takes only one award to legitimately call yourself an award-winning photographer, right?

Wedding Industry Groups

In many locales, there are groups dedicated to the wedding industry. This is a great way to get to know others in your industry and build a solid referral network from like-minded peers.

Personal Projects

Personal, non-wedding photography projects are very valuable to us. We love doing the "365 challenge." In participating in it, we commit to taking, processing, and posting to social media a new photograph every day, all year long. It sounds much easier than it is due to our busy schedules, but it's fun and allows us to come up with fresh, new photo ideas.

Most of the groups mentioned in this chapter have a bigger presence in the off-season, so there's no reason to not take part. The more you're out and about with the wedding pros in your region, the more likely you'll become a household name and be referred often.

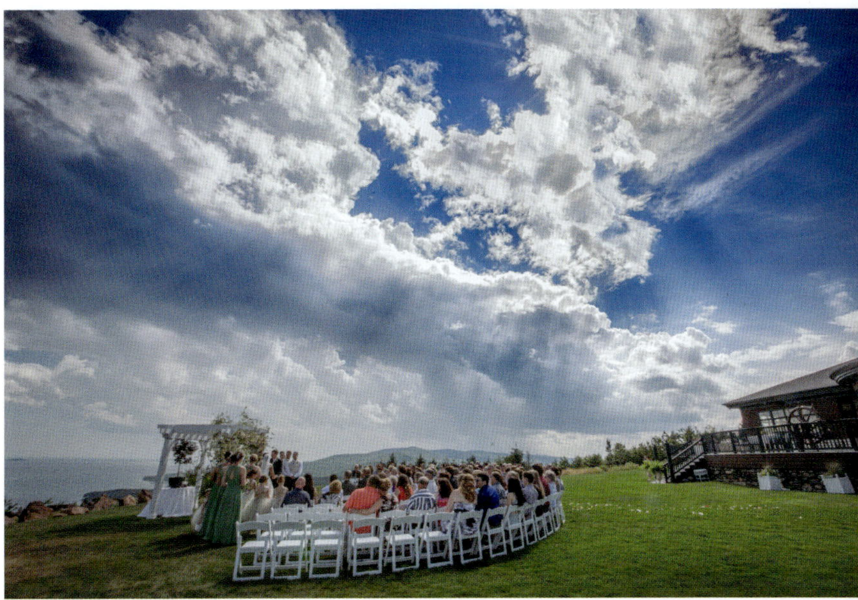

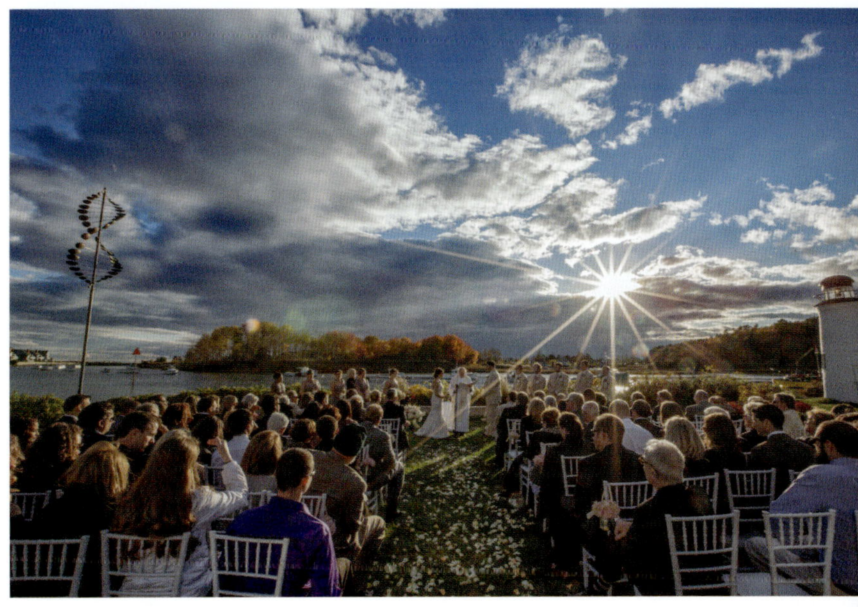

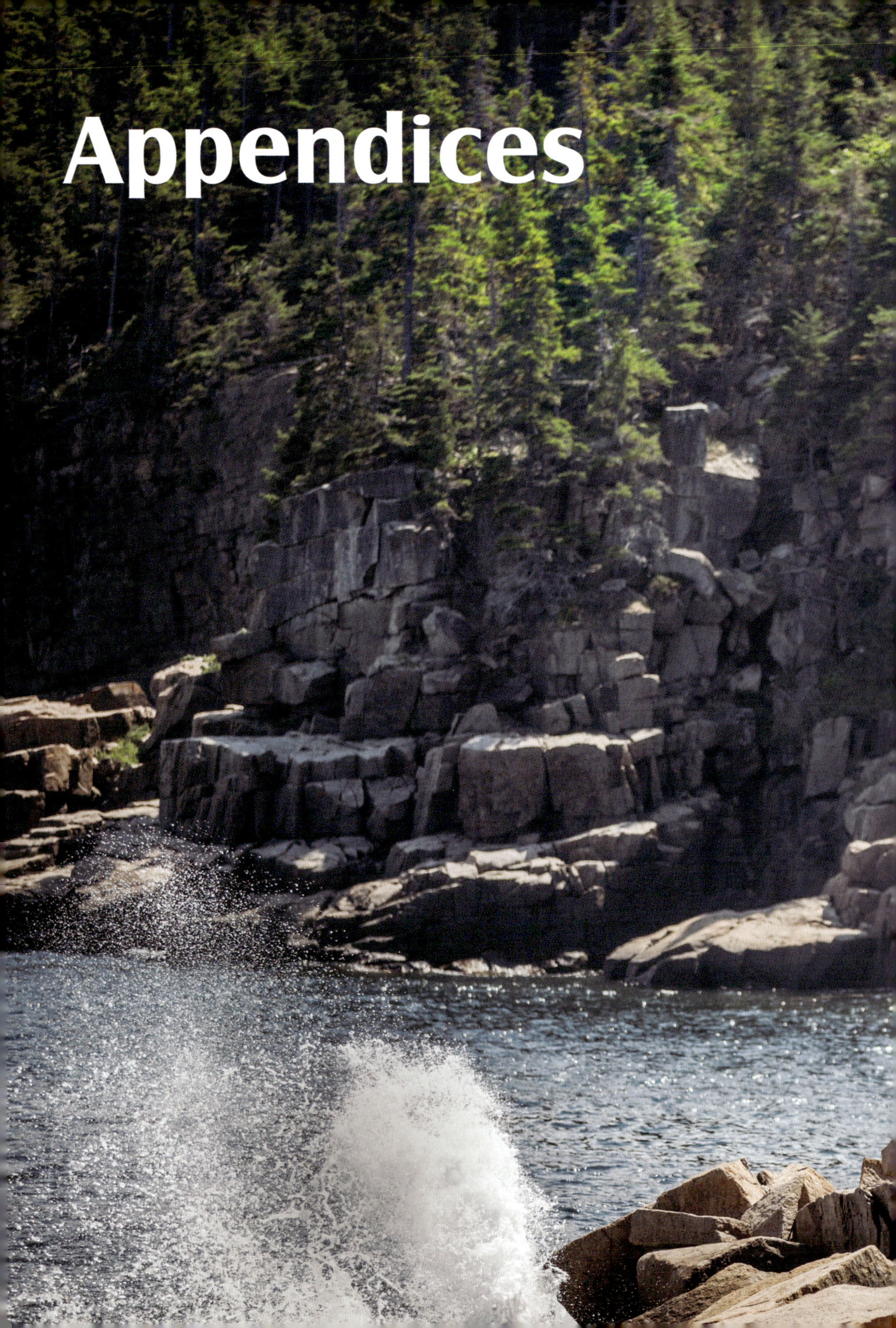
Appendices

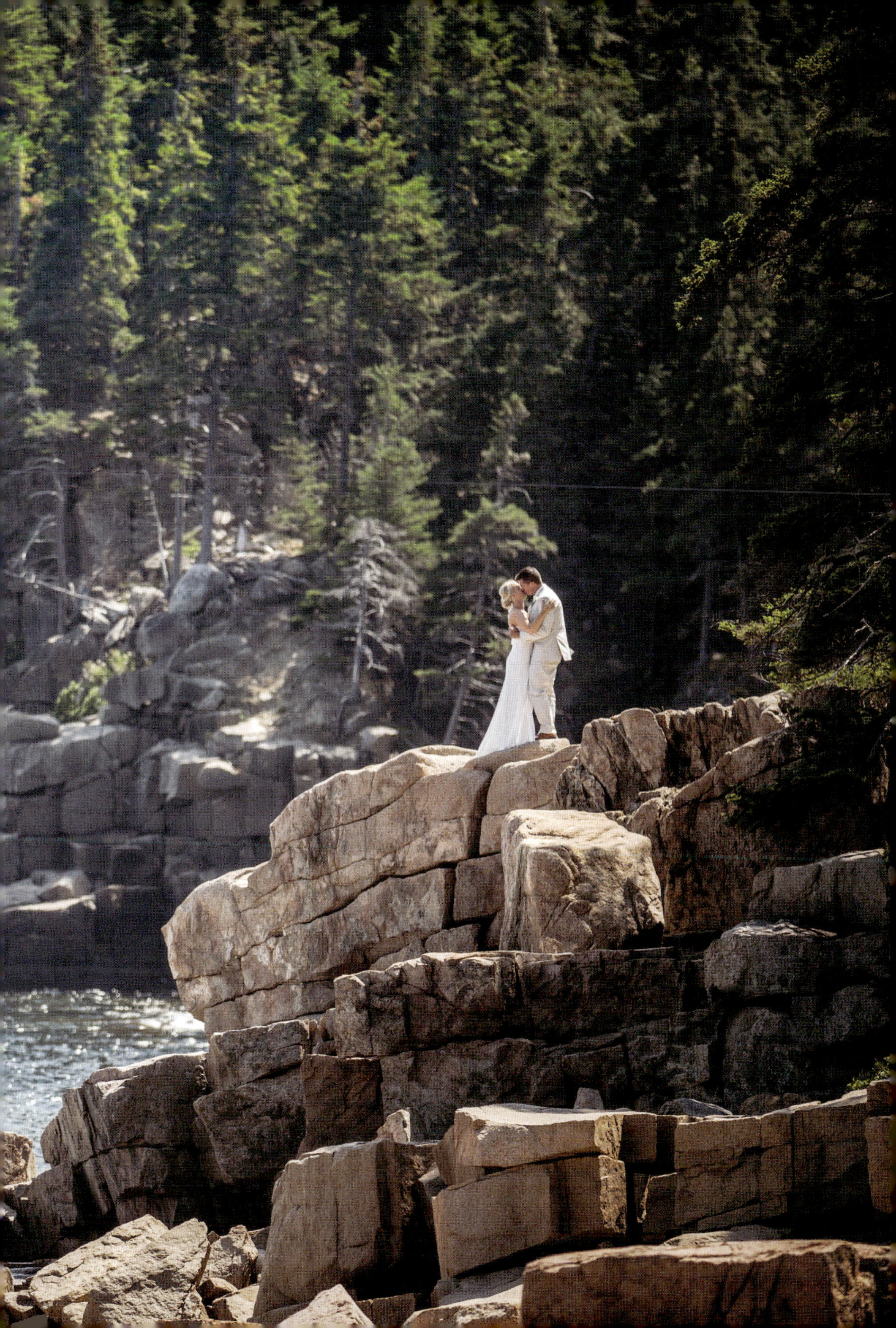

Appendix A

The Pre-Wedding Interview

This document includes everything you (and we) need to know to plan for your wedding photography and an awesome wedding day.

Dear soon-to-be bride and groom,

Your wedding is just a few months away, and there are a few details to go over. It won't take too much of your time, and it'll help your wedding day run as smoothly as possible.

The wedding day is just that—your wedding day. It's not a photo shoot, but of course it will be exquisitely photographed by us without our being intrusive or obtrusive. A little bit of time together that's carefully planned will yield huge dividends in terms of the artistry we can create with you.

Here are some things to think about and, where applicable, the reasons we hold that opinion. Do rest assured, however, that every decision you make is totally yours and will be honored and respected.

Discussion topics include:

- choosing to do a first look
- why an unplugged wedding is important to you and your guests
- when there will be a videographer
- family photos
- the bride's hairstyle
- the day's timeline

There's a form to fill out at the end of the email so you can share your thoughts.

Let's get started!

Will You Do a First Look?

What is a First Look? A first look, as the name implies, is when the bride and groom see each other in an orchestrated time and place, generally in complete privacy, with only their photographers present.

Here are reasons why couples choose to do a first look:

- A substantially improved timeline for the wedding day. Committing to a first look allows for most of the posed photos to be completed prior to the ceremony. These photos would otherwise have to be squeezed in during the short period after the ceremony and before the introductions at the reception.
- We have control over the location and the light when photographing this vitally important moment.
- The photographers can stand well back of the couple, thus maintaining their privacy.
- The first look provides unlimited freedom of emotion.
- There's a second, and often different, "first look" at the ceremony.
- The family is more relaxed, knowing their photos are finished early on.

- The bride and groom share some alone time they otherwise wouldn't have for many hours.
- The couple can be present for the entire cocktail hour and visit with their guests. This allows more party and dance time for the bride and groom—a win-win!
- We're not aware of a single couple that has regretted doing a first look.

Here are reasons why some couples may choose to not do a first look:

- They want to share the emotion of the moment with everyone present.
- The bride or groom wants to uphold the tradition of not seeing one another until the bride approaches the aisle at the ceremony.

Rest assured that no matter your choice, we'll be happy with your decision.

Will you do a first look? We'll collect your responses when you use the reply link at the end of the email.

What Is an Unplugged Wedding?

We'd love for you to consider having an unplugged wedding. An unplugged wedding is when the couple has requested that guests refrain from using their smartphones, tablets, cameras, video recorders, iPads, and electronic devices during at least the ceremony portion of the wedding day.

Why Should This Matter? The honest answer is that when people attending a wedding are using their electronic devices, they're not present in the moment and aren't participating in the witnessing of your ceremony, which is likely why they were invited.

An interesting and related study of concert-goers who weren't allowed to bring their electronics into the event reported an unexpected sense of relief, were more relaxed, and reported a more enjoyable experience.

As professional photographers, we've encountered all manner of interference from well-meaning guests trying to capture "the moment" or to be the first to post wedding images on social media. In no way are we suggesting that your guests would do this, but at other weddings, guests have used selfie sticks and stood, jumped into the main aisle, and gotten between us and the bride and her dad walking up the aisle. They've blocked access to aisles, caused us to have to ask them to move, and have been a disruption. We've even lost precious photos of emotional parents because a guest had a phone covering their faces. It's understandable, as your guests are super excited about your wedding. They just need to be more aware.

Your professional photographers will use long lenses and largely won't be seen by your guests. To that end, we don't use flash photography in most cases. Guests' cameras and phones, on the other hand, do use flash and can violate the rules of some houses of worship and ruin the shots the professionals are trying to take without flash. Device-using guests don't realize how distracting they're being, even when they feel they're being discreet, and often don't realizing they are negatively affecting your photos.

A priest we know described the view from the pulpit as a circus, and has, at times, had to stop a wedding ceremony as it was becoming as out of control as a media event. We really don't want this to happen at your wedding. Unchecked, this issue is truly at epidemic levels. We know you can appreciate that if it wasn't very important, we wouldn't ask you to consider this.

Here's how to gently and tactfully ask for an unplugged wedding:

• Include some wording in the invitation. There are many ideas out there. Here's one: "We're honored to have you as witnesses to our vows and the beginning of our marriage. We invite you to be truly present at our ceremony, and respectfully request that all cameras, phones, and electronic devices be turned off. We look forward to sharing our professional photos with you soon!" If it's too late to include this in the invitation, no worries. These following methods work well, too.

• Have your officiant make an announcement once all of the guests have been seated for the ceremony. Something like this usually works well: "The bride and groom respectfully ask that you refrain from use of phones, iPads, and cameras during the ceremony so that you may be fully present with them as they marry. They'll be sharing their professional photographs with you."

• Place a nice sign outside the ceremony location to remind guests that yours is an unplugged wedding. There are countless examples of such signs on Pinterest.

Remember that the more of these options you incorporate, the better the results.

Guests are more than happy to heed your request, and we usually see 100 percent compliance. Even when it isn't 100 percent, it makes a huge and positive difference to have asked for an unplugged wedding. Thanks for considering it.

We want to note that if you decide not to have an unplugged wedding, we're *still* going to rock your photos.

Will you have an unplugged wedding? Please respond using the link in the email.

Other Important Things

Family Photos. To ensure that the family photography runs smoothly and quickly, each side should prepare a list of the names of the people to be included in the family formals. This list isn't for us; it's to be provided to a designated "photo captain" or "helper" from each family. This person is in charge of speaking to those included and ensuring that they know to go to the appointed location at the predetermined time for the photos.

Tip: The people to include should be limited to parents, grandparents, and siblings. In most cases, we can do these groupings, with proper pre-planning and assuming everyone is present, in 15 minutes or less. When additional groupings are added, figuring conservatively on three minutes with each added group, it can be seen that adding just ten groups would cost everyone a half hour.

Bride's Hairstyle. If you have a hair and makeup trial before the wedding day (and we strongly encourage you to do so), decide on an alternate style in case the weather is uncooperative. That way, there are no surprises, and you know you'll be happy with your look on the wedding day.

We've seen it all, and we've had brides spend a lot of time and money on their hair, done by the best of the best stylists (well lacquered with hairspray!) only to have it ruined as soon as they stepped outside.

replies, we'll be in touch soon with a proposed timeline. We really appreciate your time in answering these questions.

Thank You!

All that's left is to follow the link in this email to record your preferences. Based upon your

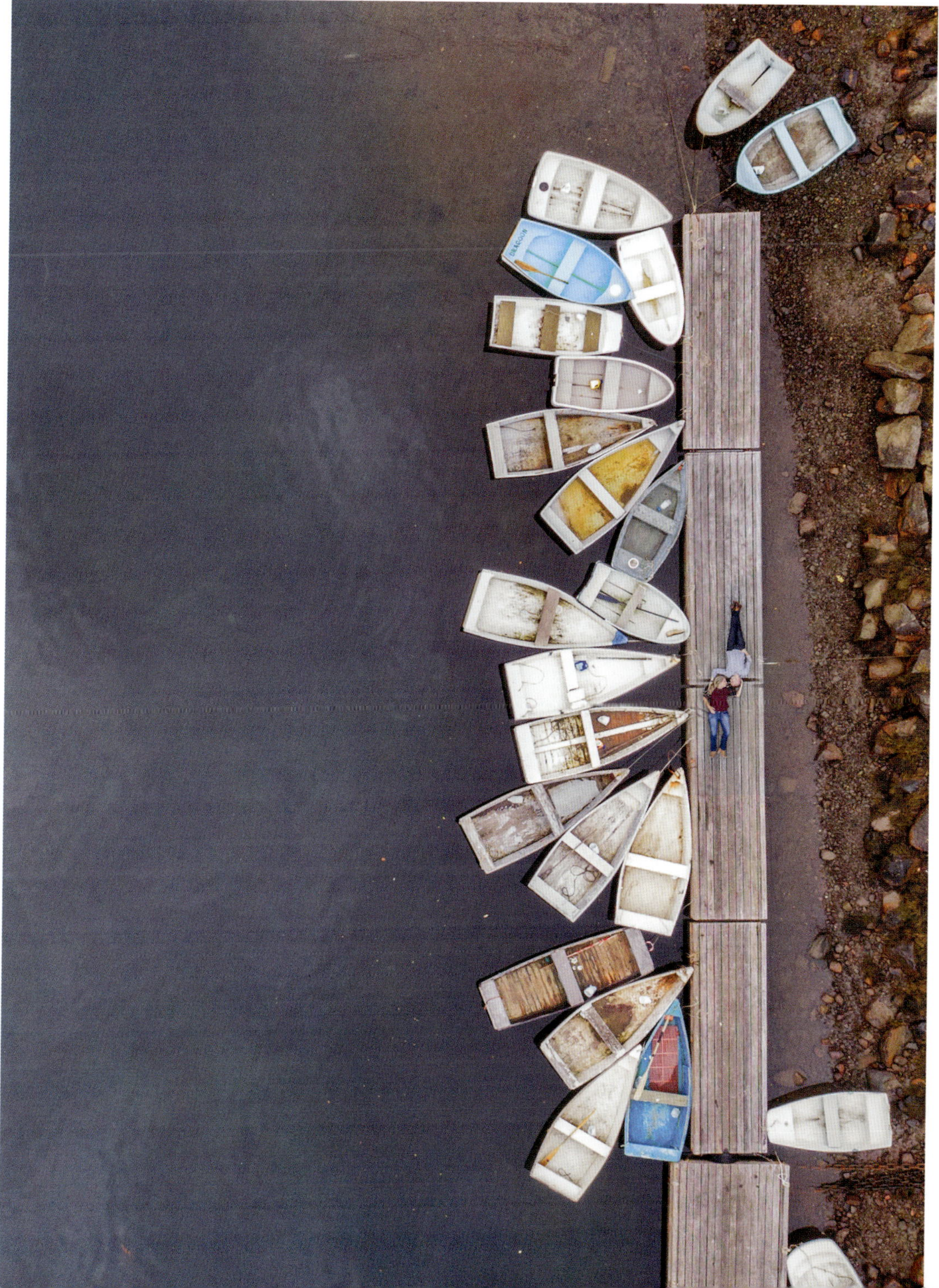

Last-Minute Tips

This list comes from all the things we see that work well and, frankly, from things that don't work so well. Thanks for considering them!

Toasts

Toasts should be just that, *toasts,* not speeches. Keep them under three minutes; under two is even better. Your guests, and especially the kitchen staff, will thank you.

Bring a glass for yourself to toast with. At the end of the toast, be sure to have everyone raise a glass. You'd be surprised how often this is forgotten.

Boutonnières

Know ahead of time who will be pinning on the boutonnières. This can be anyone who has done it before—a mom, aunt, sister, or groomsman. Too often, we have lost photo time we had with the men because no one knew how to pin on the boutonnières and they were still sitting in their boxes when we arrived.

Pocket Squares

The same holds true for the pocket squares. They need to be folded and placed in the jacket pocket in a uniform manner.

Bow Ties

The wedding day isn't the time to Google how to tie a bow tie. Practice well ahead of time.

Phones in Pockets

The bulge that phones can leave is unsightly, to say the least. If you must have your phone with you, please use a back pocket.

The Bride's Diamond

The week before the wedding is a great time to have your diamond cleaned at a jewelry store.

Gather the Details

Prepare a box or bag that contains your shoes, jewelry, and a new, flat, clean set of your paper suite (invitation, save-the-date card, reply card, meal choice card, envelope, directions, and other attachments). This saves a lot of scurrying around gathering things we'll need to photograph shortly after we arrive.

Unplugged Weddings

If you've having an unplugged wedding, be sure to have the officiant announce, immediately before the service begins, something like: "The bride has requested that all cameras, cell phones, tablets, and electronic devices not be used during the ceremony. They couple will be sure to share the professional photographer's photos in just a few days. After the ceremony, you may take all the photos you please."

We've found this approach works best, and even with announcements made in invitations, programs, and on signs, a verbal reminder can ensure that the rampant use of electronic devices during the ceremony is kept in check.

Flowers/Florist

We need the bridal bouquet when we arrive. Please ensure your florist's delivery time matches our start time. We won't keep the flowers out of water for long. The bridesmaid's florals will be needed shortly after we arrive, too, so they should be delivered at the same time. The men's flowers should be delivered to them. If needed, and if the timing works favorably, someone from the florist's delivery team should be available to help the men pin them on.

First Look

If you've chosen to do a first look, please have everyone know that, for the genuine emotion of the moment, no distractions will be allowed. For us to capture all the emotion of this special time, we ask that it's totally private—just the two of you and your photographers doing their thing! Thanks so much for understanding.

Assign a Family Photo Captain

This "ringleader" will speak to everyone who is to be included in the family photos (keep in mind, this is generally limited to parents, grandparents, and siblings) and let them know where they need to be and when. Time is tight during the family photo segment, and anyone who is not there won't be in the photos. Call or email us at any time if the timeline we provided is unclear. We'll be happy to help.

Planning on Sparklers?

We strongly urge you to hold a staged exit in the middle of the evening, for the following reasons: The lighting may be better; more guests will be there; and, assuming alcohol is being served at the reception, doing this earlier than later is generally a really good idea. We'll be happy to help you schedule a time that works.

Oh, two more things: Be sure to have *lots* of lighters (the push-button kind!) on hand, and purchase the longest sparklers available. Short ones just don't work.

At the Rehearsal

Remind the girls to walk slowly, but not the "graduation march"—just slowly.

Be sure the maid of honor returns the bouquet to the bride before the recessional. Surprisingly, almost half of all brides recess without their bouquets. If this happens, it isn't a big deal, but it's worth mentioning.

If your officiant isn't a clergy person or a professional, have them write in their script to announce, "Everyone, please be seated" after the bride and groom have met at the top of the aisle to avoid the awkwardness of everyone remaining standing because the officiant forgot to tell them to sit.

Who's on Which Side?

Unless you have a specific or religious reason to do otherwise, we recommend that, from the guest's perspective, the bride and bridesmaids are to the *left,* and the groom and groomsmen are to the *right.*

Hair and Makeup Timeline

We cannot stress how important it is that your hair and makeup be done no later than the time on the schedule we provided you.

Running even five to ten minutes behind can wreak havoc on the schedule for the rest of the day. We work hard to keep your day as low-stress as possible, and this is a huge help. If you're done early, all the better! For this reason, some brides "pad" the end time by a half hour or so from the time we've specified.

The Gown

Ensure that the maid or matron of honor unpacks the wedding gown, takes it off the delivery hanger, and—if possible—replaces the basic hanger with a wood, white padded, or customized hanger. Remove all stuffing, packing, and cardboard forms, and clip off any unneeded hanging straps. If there's a perfect place to hang the gown where nothing will happen to it, please hang it there. Otherwise, it's fine to hang it in a closet once it's unpacked. We'll ask your maid or matron of honor to help us move it to a suitable photo location if or when we need to.

The Wedding Bands

The bride should have the wedding rings/bands with her; we'll need them for the photos. Once we're done with them, someone can get the rings back to the best man.

Lunches and Water

Have a plan to ensure the bridal party is fed and drinks plenty of water during the preparation phase. Most venues will have a great handle on this for you, but in the absence of a venue coordinator, this is something to think about and to have your maid of honor help with.

Parent Dances

The guests' interest in watching the father–daughter and mother–son dances tends to fade at around two minutes. At this time, people stop watching and background commotion increases. If your song lasts more than three minutes, we recommend that you have your music professional "fade out" of the song at about two-and-a-half minutes. Some, though not all, find that a shorter dance is more comfortable. Additionally, keeping the dances brief keeps things rolling along, which means more party time.

Where to Look

Should everyone look at the camera, or not? This one's easy. Look directly at the camera only when we tell you to. Otherwise, just do what you're doing. For example, photos taken during the bride and groom's first dance and parent dances look more natural when the subjects are not turning their attention to the camera. All of the images taken on the wedding day will look better if you follow this simple rule.

The Copyright License

Important Information About Your Copyright License

The following are frequently asked questions about the digital files on the enclosed flash drive:

What Can I Do with My Digital Image Files? The person named on the copyright release may use the photos as desired for personal use. This includes unlimited printing and posting online per the guidelines below. The spouse of the person named on the copyright release, along with future children of this couple, are granted, by default, an extension of the named person's license.

This personal-use license expressly prohibits the sharing of these files with anyone, including family members, your wedding vendors and venue, magazines, newspapers, etc. Any party other than you must obtain a license for use of these images from Russell Caron Wedding Photography. Sharing means making or sending a copy of any images which are on your USB drive or on our online gallery.

If you plan to print the digital images on your USB drive, keep a copy of the included copyright release. It'll be required when you purchase prints from reputable photo finishers.

This release also allows you to sign that you have the legal right to print the photographs, something some facilities will ask you without having to show the actual document.

Please use high-quality printing facilities, avoiding the low-priced department store printing facilities. Your professionally made images deserve top-quality prints, which don't cost much more. Try neighborhood photo and camera stores. Alternatively, you can use reputable online printing sources such as Mpix, Shutterfly, Kodak Gallery, Snapfish, and Adorama Pix.

The printing rights include the making of canvas wraps, wall-size prints, and photo books. We hope you'll contact us, however, when you want a professionally designed heirloom bridal album.

Can I Post My Photos Online? Yes. However, photographic credit to us must always be indicated. Only the watermarked images provided on your USB drive should be used on social media. Do not crop out the watermark.

Can I Back Up My Files? The person(s) named on the copyright release may make unlimited backups of these files on computer systems that they own and/or software applications that they license, for personal use and backup only.

What Can I *Not* Legally Do with My Photos? This is critical, so that's why we wrote it twice: The most important, and frequently misunderstood aspect relative to file handling is that *you cannot provide them to anyone else.* Your personal-use license does not allow distribution to any other party. Any distribution to any other party must be requested through the photographer. "Any other party" includes all family members, vendors, and publications.

The full-size, non-watermarked files are not to be uploaded to any public or private sites where anyone other than the person named on the copyright license can access the files.

It's not legal for any person, other than the individual named on the copyright release, to make or have made any prints. Please do not give your disk to anyone to copy or use.

The unlimited personal-use copyright license does not cover any image being used to make a profit of any type by any person, including the person named on the license.

The files cannot be submitted for consideration for publishing in wedding or other magazines or on websites without consent from the photographer.

What If I Would Like or Need Another Set of Files Licensed to Someone Else? We can provide an identical full set on USB media with copyright release license documentation to another named party. Please contact us for details.

Final Thoughts

Please Don't Alter Your Images. We ask that you do not alter your images in any way. The copyright license, as granted, assumes you'll use the images as presented. In the event that you open your files in an image-editing software application, or in mobile applications such as Instagram, please do not post these altered images in any public locations.

Any Questions? If you would like clarification on anything here, please ask us, and we'll do what we can to help.

Congratulations on this very exciting and busy time of your life. We hope you'll refer us to your friends and family who may need an awesome wedding photography team.

COPYRIGHT LICENSE RELEASE

Here is the text used in our copyright release.

Dated March 28, 2019 with no expiration

to: Client name

The person(s) named, by this document, is authorized to reproduce unlimited copies for personal use of any images in their possession with our copyright metadata indicating copyright owned by Russell Caron Photography Inc.

Image use is limited to the above-named person(s) and may not be shared, given, or otherwise provided to any other person or entity.

Others requesting the images must contact the photographer.

Please direct questions to the undersigned.

Signed,
Russell Caron

Take this release with you when having prints made, and please use high-quality printing facilities.

Index

AmherstMedia.com

- New books every month
- Books on all photography subjects and specialties
- Learn from leading experts in every field
- Buy with Amazon (amazon.com), Barnes & Noble (barnesandnoble.com), and Indiebound (indiebound.com)
- Follow us on social media at: facebook.com/AmherstMediaInc, twitter.com/AmherstMedia, or www.instagram.com/amherstmediaphotobooks

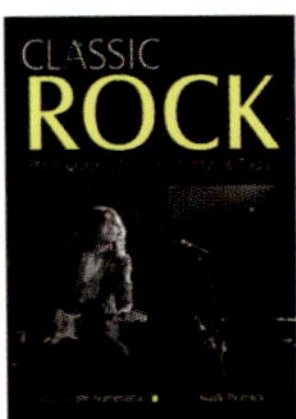

Classic Rock
PHOTOGRAPHS FROM YESTERDAY & TODAY

Mark Plotnick and Jim Summaria present photos and text about rock and roll's legendary musicians. *$24.95 list, 7x10, 128p, 235 color images, index, order no. 2205.*

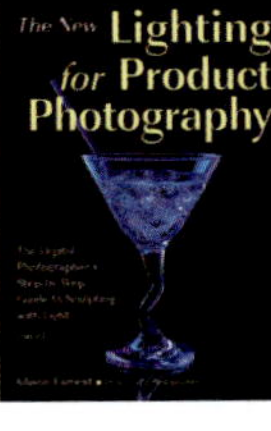

The New Lighting for Product Photography, 2ND ED.

Allison Earnest reveals the secrets of creating product photography that engages viewers and results in sales! *$34.95 list, 7x10, 128p, 225 color images, index, order no. 2210.*

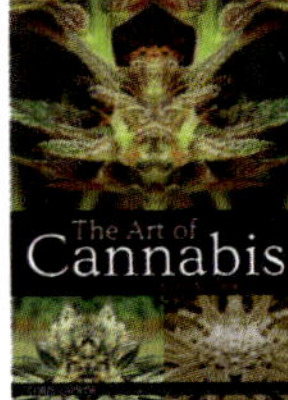

The Art of Cannabis
A VISUAL TOUR

Chris LaPrise presents imaginative, artistic interpretations of cannabis that will alter your mind and mood. *$24.95 list, 7x10, 128p, 150 color images, index, order no. 2206.*

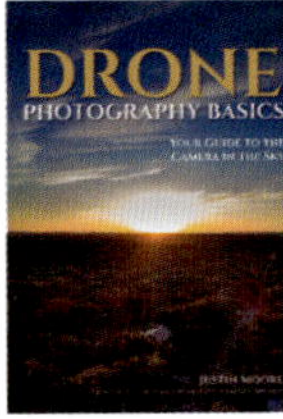

Drone Photography Basics

Justin Moore teaches you the fundamentals of using a drone and creating top-notch aerial photographs. *$34.95 list, 7x10, 128p, 130 color images, index, order no. 2211.*

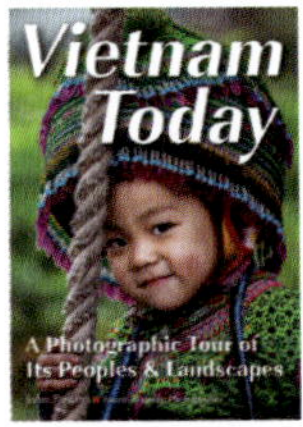

Vietnam Today

Vietnam veteran and acclaimed travel photographer John Powers explores both the rural and urban sides of Vietnam today. *$29.95 list, 7x10, 128p, 180 color images, index, order no. 2207.*

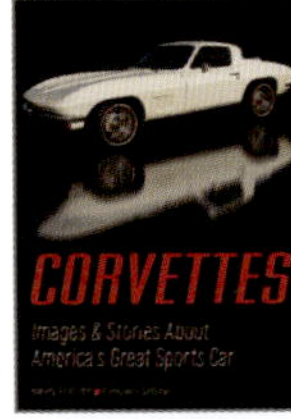

Corvettes IMAGES & STORIES ABOUT AMERICA'S GREATEST SPORTS CAR

Harvey Goldstein talks with owners from around the country about their love affair with these iconic cars. *$24.95 list, 7x10, 128p, 300 color images, index, order no. 2212.*

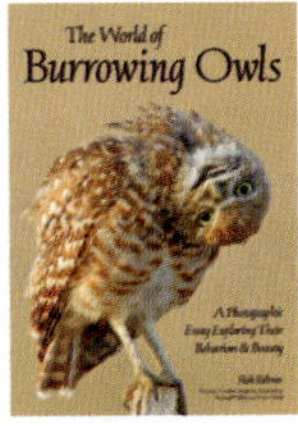

The World of Burrowing Owls

Rob Palmer takes you inside the lives and antics of one of the most endearing owl species. *$34.95 list, 7x10, 128p, 160 color images, index, order no. 2208.*

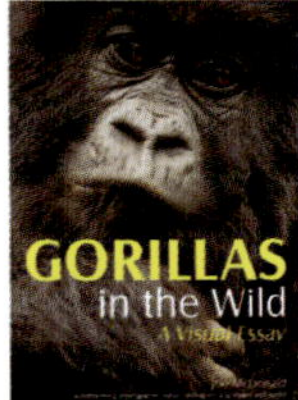

Gorillas in the Wild
A VISUAL ESSAY

Joe McDonald provides a captivating look at the behaviors and characteristics of these beloved great apes. *$29.95 list, 7x10, 128p, 175 color images, index, order no. 2213.*

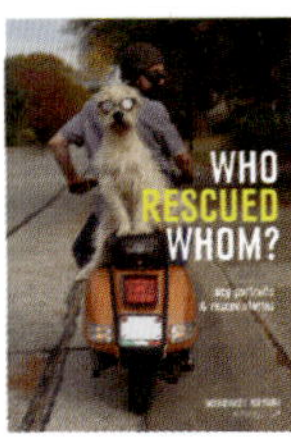

Who Rescued Whom?
PORTRAITS & RESCUE STORIES

Photographer Margaret Bryant shares unforgettable images and stories that celebrate the unbreakable human–canine bond. *$24.95 list, 7x10, 128p, 200 images, index, order no. 2209.*

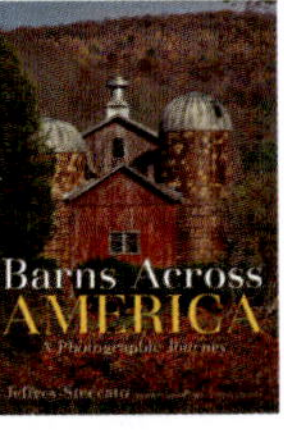

Barns Across America
A PHOTOGRAPHIC JOURNEY

Take a nostalgic look at America's great barns—some dilapidated, and others gloriously restored. *$34.95 list, 7x10, 128p, 200 color images, index, order no. 2214.*